THAT
UNTRAVEL'D
WORLD

To all those who welcomed me
along the way.

THAT UNTRAVEL'D WORLD

SEVEN JOURNEYS THROUGH TURKEY

NICHOLAS DYLAN RAY

Interlink Books

An imprint of Interlink Publishing Group, Inc.
Northampton, Massachusetts

First published in 2019 by

Interlink Books
An imprint of Interlink Publishing Group, Inc.
46 Crosby Street, Northampton, MA 01060
www.interlinkbooks.com

Copyright © Nicholas Dylan Ray, 2019

Published simultaneously in the UK by Signal Books Limited

Library of Congress Cataloging-in-Publication data available
ISBN-13: 978-1-62371-930-2

Front cover image: Frantisek Staud/photostaud.com
Typesetting, pre-press production and cover design: Baseline Arts Ltd, Oxford
Image on page vi: Dave Allen Photography/Shutterstock.com
Photographs: Nicholas Dylan Ray
Map illustration: Sebastian Ballard

Printed and bound in the United States of America

CONTENTS

CHILDHOOD ADVENTURES

As a child, I lived next to an immense tract of forested mountain land, a national park, through which passed the Appalachian Trail. Jumping out of the second-story window of my room, I would escape my troubled home by exploring the forest and hills, seeking out the sources of unnamed and inchoate streams, lost lanes leading to the foundations of forgotten buildings, demolished when the land became a park. This was the sylvan playground of my boyhood, a realm of solitude and beauty, whose exploration formed me as a man and was never complete until I was lost, unsure of my bearings, not knowing which path or stream could lead me home by dark. When I grew up I continued to explore foreign countries and cultures. My mission was not complete until I was lost in the semiotic forest of foreign symbols, cultural practices, and meanings.

In the summer of 1977, when I was twelve years old, I went on a trip to the Grand Canyon with a group of backpackers. We were traveling cross-country from Pennsylvania, so the land passed by for days on end. I was the youngest in the group, the others being high school students. Thinking of it now, much of my life having passed and a lot of it traveling, perhaps this trip was what ignited in my young spirit the wish to see the world's far reaches. For me, 1977 was a time of great duress. My family had recently broken up in a bitter and hateful way, shaking the moral foundations of my world. At the same time, I was game for adventure, looking to extend the domain of my explorations beyond the mountainside above our house. I remember vaguely the preparations for the trip, the exceedingly heavy and primitive equipment, and my departure for the three-week journey.

We traveled in a van, around ten of us, ignoring seatbelts and lounging in all manner of postures on the floor and seats while Jon, the leader of the group, and another driver, took turns at the wheel. We drove straight through, watching the landscape slip by like a movie punctuated by the diurnal rhythm. Arriving in the West, we visited a number of places, from Four Corners, a spot where four state boundaries touch, to Mesa Verde, where the Pueblo Indians lived in dwellings hollowed from cliff faces, to the Painted Desert wilderness area. We made camp in this Painted Desert, earth sculpted by millennial flows of water into hills and valleys devoid of life, only to realize with the premonition of an oncoming storm that our camp was in a dry riverbed, a *wadi* or *seyl*, as Arabian desert explorers might say—terms I learned much later. I remember hurriedly moving our camp to higher ground as the wind increased in intensity.

I still vividly recall one image from this place. One of our group, I think his name was Phil, a troubled young man always aloof from the rest of us, wandered off from the new camp into the storm. Surveying the surrounding hilltops, I saw him on top of the highest, an earthen pyramid perhaps forty meters above the desert floor, his plastic rain poncho billowing out behind him like a spinnaker sail. He was facing into the storm like Job facing God when He speaks from the whirlwind, as if to say, "I exist. I am here" in the face of immense power. It was an act of self-affirmation and defiance that marked me. I wanted to be that man, alone to face the elements, bearing full responsibility for himself before the world, before life. At the time there was no way I could have followed Phil—the howling storm would have blown me off the promontory like a leaf. But this image has stayed with me for my entire life, and I have striven to emulate it.

After this journey came many others. My first exposure to the wider world was a year studying abroad in Paris in 1984, aged nineteen. Before that I had not left North America, my spirit anchored in and emboldened by its wilderness. During that year I learned French and traveled. Christmas Day in an Amsterdam bar drinking shots of genever with an ancient mariner, listening to his stories of the world. A month-long trip through Italy, Greece, and Yugoslavia, alone. Then another, hitchhiking to the North Cape of Norway in the midnight sun, camping all the way, again alone. Back in the US, I completed my university degrees in mathematics and French literature. Later I returned to France on a teaching fellowship in 1986 for another year, and met Hélène, who would become my wife. I also conceived a yet greater journey, this time to Central Asia, that of Henry Rider Haggard's imagination and Sven Hedin's reality. I made that one also, in 1987–88, from France across Eastern Europe to Turkey, all the way to the Iranian border, then to Pakistan, over the Karakoram to north-western China, Tibet, Nepal, and India. The voyage lasted six months, culminating, topologically and spiritually, at the Dolma La on the pilgrimage route around Mount Kailash in Tibet.

Then twenty-five years passed, half a life gone by, filled with studies, work, and family. This book is a voyage that is homeward bound, back to the inner life I had as a child and a young man. When I travel I am still alone. I am still the same boy as I was then, lost in the wilderness. I have followed Ariadne's thread, scouted the faded blaze marks on the ancient trees to find my way back. I know that I am on the way. I can see the tracks and will follow them back to whence I came.

The travels described in the coming pages took place, for the initial chapter, in 1987, at the beginning of my journey to Central Asia. The subsequent chapters are based on trips undertaken from 2014 to 2016, covering much of Turkey, from central Anatolia, Istanbul, to the southern Mediterranean coast and the region near Syria, to the north and the Black Sea coast, and finally to the western Mediterranean.

A note on the choice of Turkey as the destination and subject of this book is perhaps necessary. Given my knowledge of Arabic and experience of the Arab world, it would have been more natural for me to select the countries of the Fertile Crescent, especially Syria and Iraq. But the enormous upheaval and destruction of millions of lives which have occurred in these countries also caused one tiny additional casualty—the abandonment of my project. Turkey provided a second home for my travels, as it has hospitably done for millions of Syrian, Iraqi, and other refugees.

I

1987
A FIRST JOURNEY

Rosalind: *A traveller. By my faith, you have great reason to be sad: I fear you have sold your own lands to see other men's; then, to have seen much and to have nothing, is to have rich eyes and poor hands.*

Jacques: *Yes, I have gained my experience.*

Shakespeare, *As You Like It* (Act 4, Scene 1)

LOOKING BACK TO 1987 FROM THE PRESENT, the words in my old diary and the letters from my youth take on premonitory meaning, looking to a future which was unknowable but much of which subsequently happened. I was alone then, recording my young life based on feeling, not knowledge. I am far from there now. Some of the places and cultures I crossed, as an ignorant but thoughtful and open young man, I have now studied and know well. But knowledge and experience are poor compensation for what I had then. I want it back again, the thirst for knowledge, the belief in transcendent experience, the hope for transformation.

The journey would start with a long train ride. After a year in France, I wanted to cleanse myself of everything familiar. A train rumbling away from the woman I love, who would later become my wife, the mother of my children. Rennes, Paris, Geneva, Milan, Venice, Trieste...Burdened with an overloaded backpack weighing nearly forty kilograms. Now, in middle age, I carry my burden in my soul, but materially I travel very light.

AUGUST 1, 1987

In the railway station in Rennes, the woman across from me in the train compartment gave me a dirty look as I raised the wine bottle to my lips. I knew it was a good wine, a Saint-Émilion from the early 1980s, perhaps even 1982. Hélène and I drank it on our last night together to celebrate my impending departure and for some reason didn't finish it. So, finally, after two years of planning, my voyage is underway. Blessings upon it!

I thought of stopping in Geneva, but I had no youth hostel card and the cheapest hotel was too expensive, so I stayed on the train. Also, Geneva is francophone, and I wanted something foreign, new, distant. Milan was next, but the train arrived there at 4:00 AM. As I was deciding whether or not to get off, the train pulled out, continuing its journey and deciding for me. In the back of the train where I was sitting, I couldn't see the platform anyway, just tracks. Now I was *en route* for Trieste. On the train, I met a girl from Rennes, who studied in the university where I had just spent a year teaching, in the same department (English), and had recently become a teacher. She had a shaved head and spoke good English, but I detected her French accent and spoke French with her. I also met a group of Yugoslavs. They asked if I was married, and I said I was not but that I had a "girlfriend." This was not understood, so after several iterations of various words I settled on "fiancée," which they understood.

AUGUST 2, 1987

Through Trieste and on to Zagreb. Finally I got off the train in the afternoon of August 2, thirty hours after leaving Rennes. I walked around the town and took some photos. I was starting to get into the swing, but I missed Hélène. Wandering in Zagreb, watching, thinking, I realized that *I am not here*. As a traveler, I am but a phantom through whom other people look as if I were invisible. I have no place in their lives, am only an observer, an absent presence. I ate in a working-class restaurant full of manual laborers. Good simple food: steak, potatoes, and beer. A young man needs nourishment to lug a heavy backpack around town all day. I will take the night train south through the Serbian part of Yugoslavia to Belgrade.

AUGUST 3, 1987

I spent the night in a train compartment with five other men, one of whom would not shut up. I wanted to sleep, but the seats were hard, the man was speaking incessantly, and I could not lie down. The overhead luggage racks, deluxe couchettes for savvy backpackers, were full. The night was long, reminding me of another spent around this same place but traveling in the opposite direction, north, in 1985. I was nineteen, returning to France from a month-long backpacking trip through Italy and Greece. I was in a train compartment for eight, with two Finnish girls my age. We talked for several hours and then dozed off until we were woken in the middle of the night by four Serbian peasants, drunk and raucous, who barged into the compartment and took up residence, continuing to drink spirits from a bottle. Only the most basic linguistic communication was possible. The girls and I adjusted our positions so that one of them was next to me near the window, and the other opposite me, also near the window, putting me between them and the drunken men. The Serbs, one of whom was very large and clearly uncommonly strong, started eyeing the girls lasciviously. I gazed back at him sternly, giving no ground. After a while, the big man got up and moved to sit in the only empty seat, directly across from me and next to the Finnish girl, and began to move closer to her. Then he lifted up the armrest separating the two of them and put his massive hand on her thigh. She was terrified. I slipped my hand inside my travel bag and took hold of the hilt of my fixed-blade knife, reached across the compartment with my leg, looking straight in the man's eyes, and firmly but slowly used my foot to lower the armrest onto his arm, forcing him to remove his hand from the girl's thigh. In that moment I was ready to fight the four of them. After this confrontation he moved back to his original seat. I remained awake and alert for the rest of the night, and the Serbs got off at dawn at a village along the line. Not knowing it then, I had acted according to a Prophetic *hadith*,[1] which I learned later: "Whosoever of you sees an abomination, he must change it with his hand. If he

---

1. A *hadith* is a story about, or saying of, the Prophet Muhammad.

cannot, then [he must change it] with his tongue. If he cannot, then with his heart, and this is the weakest degree of faith."[2] I changed this abomination with my foot.

After this long night, I finally arrived at 7:00 AM. At such an hour, after a night in a train and no proper sleep for two days, I was not in possession of my full faculties. A conductor on the platform shouted, "Belgrade," and I duly got off, despite the evident industrial wasteland around me. I queried the conductor, and as he entered into a detailed explanation of the situation the train pulled away. There were two Belgrade stops, one the "old city" and the other this wilderness of warehouses and housing projects. The next train was not for a long time, so I took a tram to the old city. The enormity of my backpack was the marvel of the morning commuters. I wandered the streets of Belgrade looking for a place to stay. Despite the early hour I was sweating profusely due to the weight of my load, and I resolved to lighten it as soon as possible by mailing some of my unnecessary equipment back to France, starting with my heavy Himalayan mountaineering boots. The Himalayas are far away from Belgrade, though I did end up reaching them and buying a poor-quality used pair of boots that were also too small, causing, along with the cold, several of my toenails to fall out. I found a room for $17, which was more than I wanted to pay, but I took it anyway. After a shower and rest I went out to walk around and find the Bulgarian Embassy, where I needed to get a transit visa, but it was closed. I also bought two boxes at the post office to make a first attempt at disburthening myself. I ate, called Hélène quickly from the post office, and returned to my room.

AUGUST 4, 1987

I got up at 7:30 AM. The packages had been prepared. One Himalayan mountaineering boot in each, a large Puma knife, contact lenses, my cool Vuarnet sunglasses, which I couldn't wear without contact lenses, and some other belongings. I mailed them from the post office, a process

---

2. Al-Nawawi (Arabic text with translation by Ezzedin Ibrahim and Denys Johnson-Davies), *Forty Hadith*. Beirut: Dar al-Manar, 1976. Hadith 34, pp. 110-11.

which took an hour and a half. This was the first of an irregular series of reverse care-packages, one of the last of which, sent from northern Pakistan, included the backpack itself, too big for what I had kept with me at the end. I also mailed several letters, to Hélène and to friends. I got my Bulgarian transit visa in two minutes. Who said communism spawns inefficient bureaucracy? I wasn't, however, able to reserve a seat on the night train to Sofia. A final administrative task: by chance I passed in front of the US Consulate and had extra pages added to my passport to be filled with future destinations.

I walked through Belgrade for most of the day. Sitting in a churchyard, I saw an old gentleman, or so he seemed, escorting a woman, somewhat less aged but more fatigued by her years, whom I took to be his wife. I was touched by the courtesy, even worship, manifested in his manner towards her. She seemed so tired, almost broken, her step unsure, yet she would surely make the next one—more enfeebled yet infinitely stronger than her companion.

The night train to Sofia. Always night trains. Cheaper that way. I sat with an Iranian couple, Reza and Sima, and they told me about Iran. I have a feeling there is something there for me. They told me some phrases in Persian, which I wrote in my diary. Unfortunately, my new Iranian friends were detained at the Bulgarian border by the police, lacking proper travel documents. We may all have been created equal, but we are not all equal.

AUGUST 5, 1987

I arrived in the morning and checked my bag at the station. Bulgaria. First hole-in-the-ground toilet of the trip. Passed with flying colors. I thought, "You've got a future in this, dude!" Gray, squat, and ugly communist architecture, specializing in grayness, squatness, and ugliness. Someone should invent a special kind of film for places like this, black and white, grainy, low resolution, and low-contrast, to reduce the definition of the ugliness. But the people were pleasant, though Yugoslavia seemed less monotonous, more vibrant, more diverse than Bulgaria. Any traveler to these countries, as I was to the USSR in 1985, could see immediately that communism was a failure. Nothing was beautiful. Art reduced to propaganda, the crude muscular workers in the slap-up advertisements for the regime. Nothing was well made, not even hunting rifles. Everything was diminished, reduced to its basic representation. I knew it would not last and would collapse from the inside.

I walked around Sofia but was tired now and it was too hot. I was waiting in the station, lounging on the floor with my backpack, still above thirty kilograms after its disburdening. The train to Istanbul was to leave at 9:46 PM. Night train again. I wrote a letter to Hélène and considered my future route: Iran, Syria, or elsewhere. Looking back on it now, the path I took seems to have been the only path, the others dead branches in the quantum tree of choice.

AUGUST 6, 1987

Still another night train, rumbling into the rising sun, a journey east dreamed of since childhood. "We are ... going away again this time to Central Asia, where, if anywhere upon this earth, wisdom is to be found, and we anticipate that our sojourn there will be a long one. Possibly we shall not return."[3] Despite my scientific education, I left believing in mysteries, believing in wisdom, believing in miraculous occurrences.

Seeker
"Where do you live, traveler?"
"I live I cannot tell you where."
"Why wander you so? Have you no roots?"
"They were torn out long ago, and have never grown back."
"Have you no wife, no family?"
"None."
"Then what seek you in life?"
"I seek Truth, Beauty, and Wisdom."
"But you must know, you shall never find these. They are only visions."
"No, I will never find them. But I will search."

---

3. Rider Haggard, Henry, *She*. This quotation comes from the Introduction to the book.

And on my road I will discover many truths,
And I will see things of great beauty,
And at the end of my journey I will be wise.
And yet Truth, Beauty, and Wisdom will have eluded me.
But this matters not."[4]

Now, thirty years later, I believe in much less but know much more.

I arrived in Istanbul and walked from the train station with my heavy backpack. I found a hotel in Sultanahmet, or rather a place on the roof of an institution by that name. It cost $1.50 per night. It was my introduction to filth: intermittent running water, toilets full to overflowing with excrement, cockroaches. I left my pack there and explored, finding the Pudding Shop restaurant, famous among travelers from the great overland-to-India era of the 1960s and 1970s, before war and revolution blocked the route. I had a beer there and drank to the travelers of that era. I met a young Turkish man named Akin, and he took me around Istanbul. In return I bought him dinner, chicken and rice. He seemed genuinely interested and friendly and didn't try to scam me or take me to shops to get a commission. Due to the linguistic void, we were not able to communicate much and didn't meet again.

That night, on the hotel roof, a group of travelers convened. Some talked, some drank; one, an English guy named Jed, had a guitar. He played some songs and I played a few, including "Wish You Were Here" by Pink Floyd, inspired by Hélène, whom I already missed terribly. Sleep came easily bathed in the cool air, surely better than it would have inside one of the ill-ventilated rooms.

AUGUST 7, 1987

I awoke with the sun, with the other travelers sleeping around me, the *muezzin* calls from the mosques prefiguring the same calls in Cairo a few

---

4. I published this poem in the literary magazine of the University of Rochester, *Logos*, I think in the spring of 1986.

years later. In 1986, during my last year of university, in a haze of marijuana smoke with friends, someone had shown me a copy of *Newsweek*, I think, with a photo of a Lebanese militia fighter, saying, "Nick, it's you! This guy looks exactly like you!" At the time I had a full beard, and I remember holding the magazine and staring intently at its cover, looking at the man depicted there and indeed seeing myself looking back. I remember thinking that I must have something to do in the Arab world.

Jed and I wandered around Sultanahmet, visiting Hagia Sophia and the Blue Mosque, but not Topkapi due to the long queue of tourists. We had beers together in the Pudding Shop and engaged in the deep conversation of youth. I also located the Iranian Embassy, determined to attempt to enter that forbidden country until they definitively refused me. The second evening on the roof was not as memorable as the first. I looked at the moon and stars, imagining I could bounce my salutations off them and back to Hélène in Brittany, as she would be gazing at the same celestial bodies.

AUGUST 8, 1987

I was sick all day. Hardly went out. Trips from the roof to the toilet. I wrote letters and played Jed's guitar. The sight of my still-enormous backpack depressed me. Travel is about freedom, lightness of spirit. Paring down possessions to the bare necessities, of which some are surely unnecessary. It is salutary training to lighten one's baggage. I decided to send back my camping stove, tent, down parka, and mountaineering gloves. Those last two I ought to have kept. Several months later, I regretted them bitterly in the minus 22°F (-30°C) temperatures, sitting on the back of a loaded truck bouncing over the high passes of Tibet, leaving Mount Kailash.

I had now been traveling for over a week. It was not what I had imagined. Everything seemed flat and uninteresting. The trip from the roof to the toilet was far from scenic. I hoped things would improve. It would have been good to have a friend with me, but none of my friends could come. A traveler must accept solitude. Others often cannot make the necessary sacrifices, or do not have the means to leave their normal lives behind.

AUGUST 9, 1987

Today I woke up having soiled my pajamas. "It smells of mortality." I spent roughly a third of my days in Turkey on this 1987 trip in a state of gastric malaise due to the food, despite being relatively careful, especially after the initial week. To those who idealize the "village life" or other artificial Waldenesque visions of primitive happiness, I submit that economic development is largely for the good. In any case, despite today's inauspicious beginning, I felt better than yesterday. After washing my clothes and sleeping sack (placed inside the sleeping bag for just such an eventuality), I left the hotel and went to the Iranian Embassy, which was closed. I packed up the belongings mentioned above, and sent them from the Istanbul post office. Miraculously, everything I sent, from Belgrade, Istanbul, Islamabad, and Lhasa arrived safely. Some of the packages took months to arrive and seemed by the look of them to have taken a more circuitous route than I did.

AUGUST 10, 1987

Today I went to the Iranian Consulate. It was open. The staff informed me that they couldn't grant a visa to an American here, but that perhaps in Ankara they might. In retrospect, I should have recognized this for what it was: Middle Eastern politeness—the profound reluctance to answer any request in the negative. A greenhorn, I didn't understand and remained hopeful that I would be granted an Iranian visa. I was later definitively disabused, not in Ankara but in Erzurum, the fourth Iranian Consulate I attempted. The rest of the day I relaxed, having recovered from my gastric problem, thought about the next phase of my journey, and had a meal with Jed, Mark (an American), and a Danish girl whose name escapes me.

In the evening on the roof, I saw a new face among us, sitting, chatting, and listening to us taking turns playing the guitar. His name was Ali, and he was from Kuwait. By the time I met him he had most of a bottle of cheap whisky to his credit. He was obviously very distressed, and as the evening passed, I talked with him and he shared his angst with me. He had a girlfriend in Kuwait, who the week before had been forced by her family to marry a man she neither knew nor loved. Ali wanted to marry her, but was not from the appropriate social background for her family to accept him. He had spoken with her after her marriage and she had told him that her new husband had jumped on her "like a chicken," effectively raping her, and that she felt terrible. I asked whether he had been intimate with her and he said that he had, but not in the ordinary way. He explained to me that some young Muslims practice anal sex because the girls are expected to be virgins when they marry, and this status is sometimes even verified by a doctor before the wedding. Presumably it is not possible to verify anal virginity. A strange introduction to a culture I was to explore much more deeply later in my life.

AUGUST 11, 1987

I got up, ate, and went to the Topkapi Palace. I was impressed by the resources devoted to the Sultan's sexual enjoyment. An entire section of the palace, the Harem, was for housing his wives and slave concubines and protecting them from other males (the guards of the Harem were neutered men, eunuchs). At the time I did not understand, being a young and simple man. Of the artifacts I saw in the palace, the one which most caught my attention was the oblong metallic case for the Black Stone of Mecca, like a shimmering silver rugby ball ripped open to extract the prize. It is back in Mecca now, set into one of the cornerstones of the Ka'aba.[5] The Topkapi was embellished with beautiful tilework calligraphic medallions in Arabic script, illegible to me. Afterwards I walked through the bazaar, looking at carpet shops and having tea with their proprietors, engaging politely in the game of haggling and all the while learning about carpets, both silk and wool. They were polite and personable, even though I bought nothing. A beautiful and very fine hand-knotted silk carpet cost $20,000! After dinner I called Hélène, a frustrating experience, as she was out and I only spoke to her father. This cost me $9, six days of my accommodation budget, for just a few minutes. I will leave for Ankara in the next few days.

---

5. The Ka'aba is the building located at the center of the Grand Mosque in Mecca, which is circumambulated by the Muslims performing the *Hajj*, the annual pilgrimage.

AUGUST 12, 1987

I prepared this journey for more than two years by poring over maps and reading the accounts of those who had gone before me: Jean de Chardin, Gerard de Nerval, Marco Polo, Ibn Battuta (in translation initially), Aurel Stein, and above all Sven Hedin, great conqueror of blank white spaces on the maps of Central Asia. I also read several spiritual or mystical works, by P.D. Ouspensky and G.I. Gurdjieff, a philosopher, teacher, and founder of a method of self-development. From these readings, three quests were born. The first concerned Turkey, an attempt to posthumously honor the request of Gurdjieff to place an inscribed stela on his father's tomb. The second was to travel to Afghanistan (which at the time was a war zone, and still is) to see the Bamiyan Buddhas, an ambition as illusory now as would be a repetition of Philippe Petit's tightrope walk between the Twin Towers in New York.[6] And the third quest, the only one of the three which it was granted me to accomplish, was to make the pilgrimage to Mount Kailash in Tibet. After a long and arduous way, I circumambulated Kailash on November 6, 7, and 8, 1987. It was the greatest of the three quests and remains one of the high points of my life.

Today I began to consider how to accomplish the first quest. Gurdjieff—whose works I had read as an adolescent on the recommendation of my father, and which marked me—exhorted his sons (in blood or in spirit) in *Meetings with Remarkable Men* to locate the tomb of his father and to erect a stela there with a particular inscription. When Gurdjieff was young, he founded a group called the Seekers of Truth and undertook expeditions to search for ancient knowledge. I envied the Seekers of Truth for the very idea that Truth could be found via perilous journeys to remote and barren locales, that it could be learned there and then be brought back to those who remained behind. My trip was firmly grounded in this view of travel as sacred pilgrimage. It was only later in my life, when such hopes were disappointed and I saw that Truth is much too elusive

---

6. The excellent film *Man on Wire* recounts Petit's exploit. The Buddhas at Bamiyan were destroyed by the Taliban in 2001.

to be imprisoned in a monastery on some mountain in Tibet, that I matured as a traveler and as a man. Or perhaps I simply failed in my quest, selecting my own consolation prize of jaded defeat.

In 1987, and still to this day, the fastest way to learn something is to ask someone who knows it. The problem was finding people who knew, or at least people who were honest enough to admit that they did not know, when this was the case. I asked a number of Turks I came across about Gurdjieff's father, and where it might be possible to find the town, near the border of the Soviet Union, which used to be called Alexandropol. I knew it was further east than Kars, but did not know how much further. Gurdjieff had spent much of his childhood in Kars, so I would go there, find the Kars Military Cathedral to which he referred so often in *Meetings with Remarkable Men*, and hopefully from there find his father's tomb in Alexandropol. Gurdjieff's father was, it seems, caught up in the murderous wave of annihilation which swept over the decaying Ottoman Empire in the early twentieth century. It turned out that Ismael, one of the hotel staff, was from Kars. I explained my search to him, and he told me that Alexandropol was now called Aksay.

AUGUST 13, 1987

Today I packed in preparation for departure, read, and visited more of Istanbul's sights: again the Hagia Sophia and the museum. I bought a train ticket to Ankara, another night train, but this time with the luxury of a couchette instead of a seat or the luggage rack. It cost $5, equal to three nights of my rooftop accommodation. I got to the railway station without incident and found my place in the couchette car. As I read *Meetings with Remarkable Men*, I was surprised when a Turkish soldier rudely grabbed the book from me as he walked by. After I showed him my American passport, he returned it to me. I suppose that he took the name Gurdjieff, printed in large letters on the cover of the book, as being related to the Kurds with whom the Turks were then (and are still now) engaged in a simmering civil war. Strange how the Turks, a people who fought so hard for their own independence and right to self-determination, see absolutely no hypocrisy in denying by force these same rights to another ethnic group of similar regional importance.

AUGUST 14, 1987

I woke very early. The Anatolian plain scrolled by outside my window, pale in the dawn light. There were hills or nameless tumuli from civilizations yet unknown and unexcavated. Turkey gives an impression of great antiquity, not like Europe, more distant, more unknown. That ruin between two dry streambeds could be a hundred, a thousand, or five thousand years old. Nobody knows, and few care. There are Hittite cities referred to in extant texts, but not yet located. Even now, in 2019, there is a register of archaeological sites in Turkey, the vast majority of which have yet to be excavated.

I arrived in Ankara just after dawn, found a hotel, and rested. I took a few photos of the city, though this was not really warranted by its (lack of) beauty. The tourist crowds of Istanbul were absent here and I saw only two foreign travelers during my stay. I wandered around the city, went to the tourist office to gather information, and then sat in a café and wrote letters to Hélène. These are the main source of this present narrative, and in one of them I foresaw that I would later read them and use them as the basis for a travel journal. I continued further research on Alexandropol, the site of the tomb of Gurdjieff's father, and started to become convinced that it was in the USSR, in Soviet Armenia, a town named Gümrü. The inscription Gurdjieff asked to be put on the stela over his father's tomb was this:

I am Thou
Thou art I,
He is Ours
We are both His,
So may all be
For our neighbour.[7]

---

7. Gurdjieff, G.I., *Meetings with Remarkable Men*. New York: EP Dutton, 1974, p. 49.

AUGUST 15, 1987

Hope springs eternal, often contrary to reason. Stubbornly rising early, I went, again, to the Iranian Consulate, the third one (Belgrade, Istanbul, and now Ankara). I was informed that American citizens were not to be granted visas to Iran. I therefore (almost) abandoned the idea of going there and bought a plane ticket from Erzurum to Istanbul to Karachi, Pakistan, for September 6. I required a cholera vaccine to go to Pakistan, so I went to a public hospital in Ankara to obtain it. There were no vaccines available, but by the time I returned to my hotel room late in the morning, I was dizzy and had a rapidly rising fever. I had never become feverish so fast, and was scared. I wondered if I had caught some communicable disease at the hospital, fallen victim to sunstroke (it was very hot and I had been out without a hat), or was simply sick from another round of the ongoing conflict of foodborne germs vs. my body's immune system, in which my immune system was receiving quite a thrashing. I took a sulfa-based antibiotic as a preventive measure and by afternoon my fever had diminished.

I was not ready to eat anything and was exhausted, so I spent several hours sitting in bed. I could not sleep. Instead, I made trigonometric calculations, all by hand, and developed two interesting systems. One was for estimating the height of an object a known distance away, using the lines at the joints of my fingers to measure elevation angles. I later tested this system and found it accurate to roughly +/- 5%. The second system used eye parallax (the difference in position of an object when viewed with one eye and then the other) in order to estimate the distance to an object of known length, for instance a tractor-trailer truck. Believe it or not, these systems actually proved useful at various times in my life. And it was better than just day-dreaming in bed. Finally, I bored myself to sleep with my calculations.

AUGUST 16, 1987

I needed to move again. I do not know why. I hardly saw anything of Ankara except the inside of a hospital and the inside of my room.

I went to the bus station and took a bus to Ürgüp, in Cappadocia. The bus ride was irritating, ruined by Western travelers with no idea of and no respect for local mores. An Australian blonde in shorty-shorts and a tank-top was oblivious to the choked, tortured sexual violence in the stares of the Turks. Her boyfriend's equally oblivious presence probably saved her from harm or at least from insult. The sexual frustration among Turkish, and, I learned later, many Muslim men, is thick and ever-present, like the low and constant humming of a great subterranean machine. I knew enough to respect local dress codes, which are less strict concerning men, and I have never felt comfortable flouting local customs. Such customs, ours or theirs, are arbitrary, but they constitute a manner of organizing life and deserve outward respect.

Arriving in Ürgüp, I found a room, rested, and decided to stay the following day as well in order to go on a guided tour of the sights of Cappadocia. After booking the tour, I hiked up onto a cliff and sat looking over the land in the fading light. I was alone and sad, feeling the pointlessness of my journey, the closed quality of the world, the futility of exploring it. Where was the Truth I was seeking? The mystical experiences? I felt insignificant. Looking back now, thirty years later, I see that a journey which seemed pointless in one instant was in fact one of my most significant experiences. A traveler must learn to attenuate the present moment, to see it in its larger context, in order not to be unhorsed by the jarring blows along the way.

AUGUST 17, 1987

Flexibility is one of the keys to successful travel. Ordinarily I shun groups, but in the case of Cappadocia in 1987, the tourism infrastructure had not yet been developed, and joining a group was by far the easiest way of visiting the main sites of interest, the churches built inside rock formations in Göreme, other rock formations, and an ancient underground city. I joined a one-day guided tour of French travelers conducted by a French-speaking Turkish guide named Mehmet. His tour was well-organized and he explained to us the various sites and artifacts. The underground city of Kaymaklı was the most interesting. Dating from the first millennium BCE, it was used as shelter by various peoples, from the Phrygians, who built it, to the Byzantine Christians and the modern Greek Christians, seeking safety from myriad invasions and pogroms through history. This cave complex was a real metropolis capable of housing thousands of people, complete with stables, a metal-working shop, and religious facilities.

The tour participants, around eight people, had dinner together and invited Mehmet. After dinner, he in turn invited us to his home for coffee. I felt thinly veiled hostility from him when I told him I was American. I understood, as Turkey was at the time a military dictatorship supported by the United States, and Mehmet was a communist. While I do not believe in communism as a viable way of organizing society, or as a religion, I do believe that individuals should be free to choose their views without risk of imprisonment or torture. From what Mehmet said, such freedom absolutely did not exist in Turkey.

AUGUST 18, 1987

I had a leisurely breakfast and left Ürgüp at noon by bus. Turkish buses vary wildly in terms of comfort. This one was at the low end of the scale, with barely twenty-five centimeters of space for my legs. I spent six hours hunched over, looking at the floor, with my head supported on the seat in front of me, interspersed with moments of staring out the window. The mysterious hills, perhaps tombs of ancient kings, had lost their fascination for me by now and were just more dirt. Arriving in Malatya, I met a French traveler and decided to share a room with him.

St. Expeditus was martyred here in the fourth century CE. A Roman centurion and early Christian, he refused to worship the Emperor and went knowingly to his death for this affront. There is a small shrine to him in Montpellier (France), where I learned of his story.

AUGUST 19, 1987

I decided to rest for the day, and finished reading *Meetings with Remarkable Men*. I felt moved by the book and disappointed that I would be unable to fulfill Gurdjieff's wish to put a stela on his father's tomb, given that Gümrü is now located in Soviet territory. I went out and ate, and wandered into a Turkish "pornographic" theater. There were Turkish males of all ages, from adolescents to granddads, and it was packed full on a weekday, though the sex acts depicted would not have rated as pornography in the West. I had lunch, then returned to the hotel, sick again from the food, and wrote a letter to Hélène and another to my father. I also did some practical chores such as washing clothes. When traveling, I developed the philosophy of "enough." Are my clothes clean? Clean enough. Is the food good? Good enough. Is my room nice? Nice enough. And so on. I have decided that I will visit Nemrut Daği, in south-eastern Turkey north of Syria, and after that I will go directly to Kars to pursue Gurdjieff's past even if I cannot see his father's tomb. I will visit the Kars Military Cathedral and other places there, at least to experience the region of his childhood.

AUGUST 20, 1987

I took a bus to Nemrut Daği, a mountaintop strewn with the ruins of ancient statues. The landscape on the way was magnificent, valleys narrowing as we wound higher into the mountains. Amid this rugged land, I imagined that I would become a geologist. Strangely, I considered myself uniquely well-prepared for that career, my preparation consisting of my love of the outdoors and in having done much camping, hunting, and fishing. Why I believed this to be even remotely related to a career as a geologist, I cannot now fathom. In the end I chose a different path and was not a geologist. Along the way, the bus made several short rest stops, and at one of these, next to a stream, I saw two young girls with their donkey, filling jugs of water to bring home. I arrived near Nemrut Daği in early evening, watched the sunset, and made camp for the night in a mud hut. Planning to rise early and having a broken headlamp as my only source of (no) light, I had no choice but to try to sleep.

AUGUST 21, 1987

I woke myself at 3:45 AM. While traveling, I developed an ability to wake up close to a pre-determined time although I had no alarm clock. Part of this skill was an old trick taken from one of Gurdjieff's stories, where he would gauge the proper amount of water to drink before bed in order to create the urge to urinate at the time he needed to wake up. Eventually I was able to wake myself at a given early hour even without this subterfuge. The track up to the summit of Nemrut Daği was easy, taking around an hour in the dark, picking my way carefully without light. No one else was around so early, giving me time alone on the summit before a herd of loud and bovine tourists arrived. They defiled the moment of sunrise with their raucous behavior. When more than a few people of a given ethnicity travel abroad, they create a semblance of their own society and become unable to fully appreciate their surroundings. Traveling ought to be about the Other, one's relationship to this Other, and one's relationship to the world in general. Fundamental questions, reflection, striving to ingest beauty, and to create meaning. Traveling in an organized tour with one's countrymen vitiates the entire experience. It is not travel; it is tourism.

I calmed my inner tirade and let the sunrise shine through my mind, surveying the broken statuary thrown down in one of humanity's many spasms of apocalyptic destruction. The temple on the summit dates from the first century BCE, built by King Antiochus, twelve centuries the junior of Shelley's "Ozymandias"[8]:

I met a traveller from an antique land
Who said: Two vast and trunkless legs of stone
Stand in the desert. Near them, on the sand,
Half sunk, a shattered visage lies, whose frown,
And wrinkled lip, and sneer of cold command,
Tell that its sculptor well those passions read

8. An early nineteenth-century poem by Percy Bysshe Shelley. "Ozymandias" is a Greek name for the Egyptian Pharaoh Ramses II, who ruled in the thirteenth century BCE.

Which yet survive, stamped on these lifeless things,
The hand that mocked them and the heart that fed:
And on the pedestal these words appear:
"My name is Ozymandias, King of Kings:
Look on my works, ye Mighty, and despair!"
Nothing beside remains. Round the decay
Of that colossal wreck, boundless and bare
The lone and level sands stretch far away.

I walked down the mountain and took a minibus back to town, planning to go straight from here to Kars to pursue Gurdjieff's youth. Kars was a long way from here. I got a ticket on a train leaving at 5:00 PM from Malatya, which would intersect the Ankara-Kars train line at 2:00 AM, at which point I would have to change trains and spend another sixteen hours on the train to Kars. In the train station I wrote letters, to my parents, to Hélène, and to Fataneh, an Iranian girl I had met in France. The train was two hours late and during the six hours waiting at the station I met some interesting people: a young man named Ibrahim, innocent and devout; a French traveler who had been on the road for two years: Egypt, Iran, Turkey, India, Nepal; and a Dutch anthropologist at the end of a year-long stay in Turkey, who explained some aspects of Turkish mores to me.

AUGUST 22, 1987

I have been all day on the train going to Kars. The slow train. They are all slow here. Somnolent spells of dozing in the dark. The repetitive rhythmical rumblings act as nepenthe for my loneliness. At daybreak, the land passes by before me. Again the feeling of agelessness, historical infinity beyond anything in Europe, and totally foreign for an American. The ruins I see from the train window could be from any era, perhaps from cultures that have no chapter or paragraph in history as we have written it. Sites like those are visited by no one. Passed by shepherds and their flocks, gazed on or ignored by passengers in trains. At one point I saw the remains of a fortified citadel on an island between two forks in a river. But now the river was no more, mere dry traces in the valley floor, perhaps flooded in the spring. The citadel followed clearly the edge of the island, courses of stone and mud-bricks still standing against time. What stone or bronze or iron weapons did these walls repel? What battles were fought here, what acts of courage dared upon these ramparts? And there are so many like this here. Gurdjieff writes of cultures which existed and disappeared before we even recognize the beginning of "civilization." He traveled for twenty-five years in Central Asia and the Middle East and must have seen fantastic sights. There is a secret current of the past here that helps me see our own smallness facing the ages. We are but one stage, and all our culture will die and disappear, leaving no more traces than those who went before, with the exception of the larger tumuli our great cities will form and our enduring radioactive waste. We think we are all-powerful. But we are wrong.

Seest thou not how thy Lord dealt with the people of 'Aad, of the city of Iram, with lofty pillars, the like of which were not produced in all the land? And with the people of Thamud, who carved out huge rocks in the valley? And with Pharaoh, Lord of Stakes? All these transgressed beyond bounds in the lands. And heaped therein mischief on mischief. Therefore did thy Lord pour on them a scourge of diverse chastisements. (Qur'an 89: 6-13).[9]

The train ride continued, interminable. My fellow travelers were all Turkish and very friendly. We attempted communication and they shared their lunch with me, salad among other things. Luckily for them they left the train before the effects of their generosity appeared in my digestive system, resulting in half-hourly visits to the toilet. On the first of these, for some reason, the door was locked. A tool on my Swiss army knife spared me the humiliation of soiling my clothes. I met a young Turkish man who could speak basic English. I showed him a photo of

---

9. The Quranic quotations herein are generally either from the Abdullah Yusuf Ali or the Sahih International translations, or else directly translated by the author, and will henceforth be cited in the format "Q X:Y" where X is the number of the *surat*, or chapter, and Y is the number of the *ayat*, or verse.

Hélène and he said she was very beautiful, and asked if I would marry her. I reflected for a moment and replied, "Yes." Three years later, I did.

In the early evening I arrived in Kars after nearly thirty hours of non-stop travel. I wandered through the dusty streets, found a hotel room, and took a hot shower after three weeks of cold ones. This, I said to myself, was worth all of the discomfort of the trip.

AUGUST 23, 1987

I slept very well indeed, for almost eleven hours. I awoke, relaxed, and hand-washed my clothes (as I generally did for the entirety of this six-month trip). Clean enough. I then went to the Kars tourist office, but to my dismay, nobody knew anything about Alexandropol or the Kars Military Cathedral. I made what was intended to be a brief phone call to Hélène, but by some miracle the pay phone was broken and we spoke for half an hour on one token. Love works miracles. I wrote, walked around Kars, an ugly city, and returned to the hotel.

AUGUST 24, 1987

Today I decided to go to Ani, the ancient Armenian capital and City of 1,001 Churches. I went to the tourist office, where by chance I met Mark, the American with whom I had spent some time in Istanbul. Mark and I had met a Danish girl there that he really liked. At the time we agreed that he would write to me in care of American Express in Islamabad to tell me whether or not he had seduced her. When we met in the tourist office, he took out a postcard from his bag and handed it to me. It was addressed to me and bore the word "NO" in large letters. Mark was with a few other travelers and we all shared a taxi to Ani.

Ani is an ancient city, with myriad church ruins standing alone, deserted on the Central Asian plains. They are far from any present habitation, having been sacked by the Mongol hordes in 1236, then destroyed by an earthquake and progressively abandoned. We spent several hours there. Ani is situated very close to the border with the USSR, a tense military zone near a "secret" US nuclear missile base.

I explained to our driver Mehmet (the source of the information about the missile base) that I had wanted to see Alexandropol, and he confirmed that this was the city now called Gümrü, across the border in the Soviet Union. He offered to take me to within a stone's throw of the border itself, to a place called Akyaka (perhaps the same place mentioned by Ismael back at the hotel in Istanbul), even though this was forbidden. I concluded a deal with him to go there in two days' time, for a fee of $30. This was an excessive amount of money, "danger pay," since he could get into trouble for taking me there (this sum represented roughly fifteen tickets for a sixteen-hour train ride, or two weeks of a single hotel room in Ankara). On the way back to the town we stopped at Mehmet's family farm and met his family.

AUGUST 25, 1987

Kars was a blighted place. And to think that the Ottomans and Russians fought for centuries over it, passing it back and forth like a hot potato and destroying thousands of lives each time in the process. I saw the Kars Cathedral, a medieval Armenian church in the town, abandoned with weeds growing on the roof. I then wandered up to the Fortress of Kars, having assumed that it must be the location of the Kars Military Cathedral, of Gurdjieff's boyhood. Some of the stories in *Meetings with Remarkable Men* support this hypothesis. Unfortunately, it was closed today but will open on Thursday. I also strayed into a restricted military area, from which I was unceremoniously evicted by a guard. When young, I showed very little respect for walls or fences and I have not really changed. Luckily in thirty-five years of traveling I haven't yet been shot or even beaten, just yelled at.

AUGUST 26, 1987

Today I went to Akyaka with Mehmet, right up by the Soviet border. We drove on hidden dirt roads with embankments on both sides so we were not visible from afar, except perhaps by the plume of dust raised by our car. Mehmet stopped the car at the track's end and motioned to the nearby hillside, telling me to be careful, as we were very near the border. I crawled up the hill in the tall sere grass and recalled my childhood hunts for rabbits and groundhogs, crawling on my belly through the fields. Before the crest of the hill I stopped and listened. Nothing. Then a few more meters and I could see through the grass, an easy rifle shot from the Soviet border. Immobile, I watched the soldiers in their stilted huts across a ravine in which there must be a stream. I could see Gümrü, Alexandropol of old, in the distance. This was as close as I would get to it, closer than I did on my 1985 trip to Armenia, during which I visited Erevan and Echmiadzin, the seat of Armenian Christianity.

Back from Akyaka, I attended the wedding of Mehmet's sister, to which he had invited me and my fellow travelers two days before when we visited Ani. I was the only one of us who accepted his invitation. It was a celebration without alcohol (to me something of an oxymoron) but I was glad to be there. The Turkish men taught me to dance (men and women dance separately) and said I learned fast. I also chatted and flirted with two young women, school teachers, who were much more forthcoming towards me than I would have expected. The traditions at the wedding struck me as very materialistic, reminiscent of the legal origin of marriage as a contract of sale. The bride was literally covered with gold, and the guests made gifts in cash which were pinned to her bridal gown and to the groom's suit, with the amount and provenance of each gift announced to the audience. At the end, they looked like walking banks.

After the wedding, I returned to my room and slept. I awoke troubled by a dream in the night. I am in a boat floating towards a terrible waterfall. I am near the shore and watch and wait intently. At just the right moment, the only possible moment, I jump clear to the shore as the boat plunges over the waterfall to destruction, and survive. The dream was accompanied by a feeling of utter solitude, as if I were the last man on earth. After waking, I could not return to sleep immediately. I sang to myself, and then stopped. Silence resonated around me in the night. I am so alone here. I know no one. I make contacts and they pass. Sometimes I am "with" people, but never really. I am a ghost in their lives, who has no place, who watches and disappears.

After nearly a month of travel, I am now accustomed to the road, to my journey. I am alone but I am well, and as soon as someone or something infringes my solitude, I move on. The people I meet on trains, at sites, in hotels, I am content to share a moment with them, but no more. Alone, I feel that my guardian angel is there, watching me, guiding me on the Straight Path (a Quranic concept later subsumed as an idea by my mind, *Al-Sirat Al-Mustaqim*, from the *Fatiha*, the first *surat* of the Qur'an).[10]

After a few months more of traveling alone, bouncing over the high plains and mountains of Tibet in the back of a truck, this feeling of being watched over, as in Rockwell Kent's image *Godspeed*, became completely real to me. I began to construct an understanding of the relationship of feelings and mind, how to stay on the Straight Path. The mind must direct the feelings, creating positive ones when necessary and not allowing negative ones to sap energy. An outburst of uncontrolled negative feelings can cause the perceptible weakening of the entire being. This happened to me once on the road from Lhasa to Kathmandu. Chinese soldiers searched the bus full of Tibetans on which I was traveling. The soldiers deliberately insulted and humiliated the Tibetans, and I became so furious that I wanted to kill them. My anger weakened me so that during the ride afterwards along a treacherous road—iced over, and on the very edge of a precipice toward which we repeatedly slid—I was completely unable to master my fear. Usually in such situations I feel fear, but form a solidity in myself and realize with all of my elements that my life is in the hands of God and that I can do either nothing or very little. However, this time I was weakened by my anger, and could not achieve this solidity, this recognition of Life and, next to it, of the Abyss, and I was terrified. After this event, there was another branching moment, one at which I made the right choice, and thus regained the Straight Path. This understanding of the Path, deviations from it, and how to return, formed concretely during my journey.

---

10. The *Fatiha* contains the most oft-repeated verses of the Qur'an: "In the name of God, the Compassionate, the Merciful. Praise be to God, Lord of the Worlds, the Compassionate, the Merciful. Master of the Day of Judgment. Thee do we worship, and to Thee we turn for aid. Guide us on the Straight Path. The path of those on whom Thou hast bestowed Grace, not of those who have angered Thee or those who are lost. Amen." Q 1.

AUGUST 27, 1987

Today was a good day. After the troubled, dream-filled night I went out to do errands. First, I bought a bus ticket for tomorrow to Doğubayazit, near the Iranian border, but on closer inspection, I realized that the ticket was not for August 28, as I had asked, but for the following day. I returned to the desk and asked for a refund, since different bus companies operate on different days and this company operated no bus tomorrow. At first the clerk refused, but then I used a tactic that seems to be universally effective in military dictatorships. I spoke relatively quietly demanding my refund and then said, "... and if you do not give it to me then I will go to the POLICE!" I emphasized this last word and repeated it again louder so that those nearby, including the ubiquitous soldiers, could hear. The clerk's expression turned to anxiety and he hurriedly gave me my money back. I found the company with a bus leaving tomorrow and bought a ticket. I next went to the post office, signed and dated my copy of *Meetings with Remarkable Men*, marked it "Kars" and sent it home.

My errands completed, I went to the Kars Citadel in search of the Military Cathedral. Almost everything was in ruins, remnants of some not-so-distant war. At first I found a massively built stone structure with a vaulted roof and no windows, a strange cathedral. After inquiring of an employee, it turned out that it was the powder magazine. The actual cathedral was nearby, also in ruins. It appeared to have had a *mihrab*[11] added to it, having probably been converted to a mosque at some point when it was under Turkish control. The adjacent apartment, formerly occupied by Dean Borsh, one of the "remarkable men" and a close friend of Gurdjieff's father, was also in ruins. And so ended my first quest, far from its aim. Yet I felt some satisfaction at having seen Gümrü from afar, and having found the Military Cathedral and said a prayer there.[12]

---

11. A *mihrab* is a prayer niche in a mosque situated in the direction of Mecca.

12. Apparently, sometime in the 1980s the Canadian diplomat James George and Victor Kholodkov answered Gurdjieff's request and set a stela on his father's grave bearing the aforementioned inscription. http://gurdjieffclub.com/en/articles-essay-arkady-rovner-g-i-gurdjieffs-influence-in-russia-in-the-1960s1970

AUGUST 28, 1987

Last night I fell ill, as I had in Ankara. I think it was meat that was rotten and undercooked. I had had *köfte* (a sort of grilled meatball) both times. Hopefully, I will not be stupid enough to eat this again. I took a mélange of the various drugs I had with me, one of which, Flagyl, was actually designed to treat stomach bacteria. Why I took the others I am uncertain. Waking up, I still had a headache but my stomach problem had partially resolved itself. I skipped breakfast and got ready to depart. The bus to Doğubayazit was to leave at 2:00 PM. As I was traversing the city on the way to the bus station, I realized how awful a place Kars is. Dirty and ugly, with literally nothing to temper the ugliness. I wrote in my diary: "Kars: ugly, God-forsaken shithole of a town." As usual, I arrived early at the station and sat on the floor against the wall, waiting near a sleeping soldier. He woke himself up accidentally with a disgusting snorting noise, dropped his submachine gun clanging onto the floor, and stood up, disoriented. I started reading Marco Polo's *Le devisement du monde*, but most of the time was spent repelling the advances of conmen and salesmen. This type of hustling breeds distrust of others, which is unfortunate, as normal, non-predatory people live their lives and mind their own business, and it is hence difficult to make contact with them. How strange that the first person to approach me in Istanbul, the young man Akin, had no such malign intentions. Finally the bus was ready to leave. Though on the ticket was written "Doğubayazit," the bus only took me as far as Iğdır, and the people at the bus station said there was no bus to Doğubayazit. So I took a taxi with two others, found a room there, ate a copious meal, and slept.

AUGUST 29, 1987

I hardly went out today. A short trip is a whirlwind of activity but a longer trip requires periods of digesting experiences, resting, contemplating. I met people who had traveled too long, a year or more at a time, without reflection, and who could barely remember where they had been, much less what they had learnt there. So today I wrote, in my diary and letters home, to Hélène, friends, and family. And I thought about the future. First, the immediate future. Where will I go? I decided that my preferred route would be through Pakistan, over the Khunjerab Pass into north-western China, then Tibet, Nepal, and India, assuming I could obtain all the required visas and cross the high passes before snow closed them for the winter. As my thoughts looked further and further forward, other questions arose. Would Hélène and I marry? Where would we live? What would we do? I then focused on one particular question and spent most of the afternoon designing our future home. With no architectural training, the plans I drew bear a limited resemblance to where we live now, but the outside environment is exactly what I foresaw: a large piece of land in foothills surrounded by forest, with plenty of space between us and the outside world. Looking back on a life, it can be shocking how close one comes to one's imagined aims.

In late afternoon I walked outside, admiring the view of Mount Ararat, alone on the plain like a pyramid and snow-capped still in August. And on the way to the Iranian border, a few miles out of town, I noticed rugged cliffs, which for some reason caught my eye. I thought about Islam, a premonitory desire to learn about this religion. This journey through Turkey was my first exposure to a Muslim country.

AUGUST 30, 1987

Today I walked far out of town, on the road towards Iran. I went close to the border, with my urge to see that country still strong. I passed the steep cliffs I had seen from a distance yesterday, to the right of the road, sheltering a rubbish dump behind them. I clambered up as far as I could, over 100 meters above the ground, at the point where giant slabs of rock soared vertically upward like diving boards into the blue sky. A steady wind was rising against me, hot with the smell of decomposing rubbish, bearing small flies and seagulls feeding, shrieking their wild sea calls as they soared over me then returned to scavenge below. I was in the shadow of the cliffs, the limit of sunlight 500 meters toward the Iranian plain. Mount Ararat was majestic in the background, surveying this unnerving place. Sitting a few feet back from the cliff edge, I almost didn't trust myself. This was one of those places on our earth from which issues the clarion call of insanity, the call to destruction, the temptation to throw oneself down, off the cliff, over the waterfall, into the void.

If thou be the Son of God, cast thyself down: for it is written, He shall give his angels charge concerning thee: and in their hands they shall bear thee up...[13]

For some reason I didn't understand I sat there for a long time, over an hour. I gazed on Iran and Mount Ararat, felt the evil of this place, contemplated in silence. I wondered where so many seagulls had come from, as the sea was hundreds of kilometers away. I watched the truck traffic heading to and from Iran, and tested my eye parallax distance-estimating technique. I verified it and the calculated distance was close to the distance on the map between my location and the road. I then descended carefully, made my way back to the road, and hitchhiked back to town on a tractor.

I ate dinner, wrote in my diary, and attempted to make simple drawings. For some reason, probably because I wanted to be a perfect Renaissance man and achieve a basic level of skill in most things and advanced skill in some, I had decided that I should learn to draw. Of all the areas of human endeavor, drawing or figurative art in general (except photography) is the one where my own gifts are truly execrable and no better than those of a primary schoolchild. My efforts at drawing were cursed. The form of man's best friend, the dog, was my particular nemesis.

AUGUST 31, 1987

I got up early this morning. Or rather I got up twice, once very early and once some hours later. At around 4:00 AM, a group of Iranians prayed very loudly and then chatted at length in the corridor, and because my room had an open window into the corridor, they woke me up. I couldn't get back

---

13. *King James Bible*. Matthew 4:6.

to sleep until they left. When I re-awoke, I had breakfast and then set out walking, bound for the Ishak Pasha Palace, a seventeenth-century palace and caravanserai.[14] I saw a horse cart with a solitary rider overtaking me and decided to hitchhike. Riding on the back of the cart with a load of vegetables after a full month of traveling, for the first time I felt the jubilation of being on the road. The palace, an Ottoman monument, was built by the eponymous Pasha, a jewel of Islamic architecture in reddish stone carefully inserted into the mountainous desolation, with Ararat in the background. After exploring the palace interior, I noticed outside in the garden that there was an open window into the minaret, which was otherwise closed, around seven meters above the ground. The wall was vertical but the Ottoman masons had not been as careful as they could have been in fitting their stone blocks, leaving sufficient holds for me to climb. I mounted the minaret's spiral staircase rapidly and silently, earning a spectacular and illicit view of the landscape and buildings below. After a few minutes I came down, accepting the help of a German couple who caught my camera bag dropped to them so I didn't have to climb down wearing it. After a scolding from a guard who had seen me atop the minaret I walked around with the German couple and then they kindly drove me back to town.

In the afternoon I purchased a bus ticket to Erzurum for the next day. I also continued reading Marco Polo. He traveled here in the thirteenth century, during the dominion of the Mongols over all of Asia. This dominion made such a voyage possible, since if most of the land had not been controlled, at least nominally, by one political entity, it would have been much more difficult. It took Marco Polo roughly *three years* to travel from Venice to Peking.

SEPTEMBER 1, 1987

While waiting for the bus I met a young Iranian man, Ali, who was interested in going to the US. He was also heading for Erzurum. We

---

14. A caravanserai is a place for travelers to stay the night while on their way, a medieval inn or hotel. It is traditionally a walled rectangular structure with rooms along the inner walls and an open central courtyard.

exchanged addresses, and when I said that I would love to visit Iran, he told me that there was an Iranian Consulate in Erzurum and that I should request a visa there. During the bus ride, the two of us concocted a story about how my grandfather was from Isfahan and I wanted to return to see his native land. Ali helped me by translating this story into Farsi and transcribing it into Roman letters. I spent several hours memorizing this discourse, with Ali correcting my pronunciation on each repetition. By the end of the journey, which lasted four or five hours, I had mastered the pronunciation and presentation of my imagined family history. The whole presentation took around three minutes. Arriving in Erzurum I found somewhere to stay, and ate. My stomach had been continuously troubled for several days by a subterranean grumbling that would not stop, portent of a disgusting eruption yet to come.

SEPTEMBER 2, 1987

It came. I was sick again, spending the night shuttling back and forth from the toilet. Alimentary discipline admits no exception. Not drinking untreated water "most of the time" is useless. One must *never* drink such water, *never* eat unpeeled vegetables unless they are soaked in iodine water or boiled, and *never* violate any of the other rules of hygiene. When Hélène and I later lived for two years in the unsanitary conditions of Cairo, we learned these rules and obeyed them absolutely, managing to limit the time we spent ill, but in Turkey, as a neophyte, I was unsuccessful.

I rehearsed my presentation for the Iranian Consul in front of the mirror, emphasizing now its delivery, filling it with heartfelt longing and imploring looks. The longing was honest enough, though the story was fabricated. I went to the Consulate, a small informal office where a consular employee greeted me when I knocked, and beckoned me to enter. I then delivered my speech. A wry smile formed on his lips as he listened, and it was clear that he understood my words. After I had finished he asked me a short and simple question in Farsi. I understood nothing, and he laughed kindly, then changed to English. He admitted to being most impressed by my effort in memorizing my text but said that it was beyond

30

1987: A FIRST JOURNEY

his ability to issue a visa here in Erzurum. He invited me to fill out an application which would be sent to Teheran and then returned, probably with a refusal, in two months' time. I thanked him, declined, and told him I really hoped to be able to visit his country one day. He wished me luck.

Returning to the hotel after this disappointment, I decided to attack my stomach problem head-on. I stopped the Flagyl, which seemed not to work at all as I had been taking it for several days, and took Bactrim Forte, a sulfa-based antibiotic. Stomach problems are not among its indications, but it worked, and the next day I was better. Placebo effect, perhaps? Later I went out and bought some black stone Muslim prayer beads. They still comfort me today on my desk, and have done so for the past thirty years, though they need to be threaded onto a new string from time to time.

SEPTEMBER 3, 1987

I am preparing my imminent departure for Pakistan. My mind is no longer where I am. I have done all of my laundry and aired my sleeping bag. I have also sent home more unnecessary equipment, to the point that my backpack is now too big for what I have kept. Six weeks later, in Hunza (northern Pakistan), I ended up buying a canvas grain sack, and a new Canadian friend sewed two shoulder straps onto it and decorated it with a winged thumb, allowing me to send the backpack itself home with more unnecessary things. I also wrote many letters. I wrote to Hélène to request that she send me, *poste restante* in Islamabad, the second volume of Marco Polo's book, as I continued making rapid progress through the first. And I reconfirmed my airline ticket to Karachi at a travel agency.

SEPTEMBER 4-5, 1987

These days passed, leaving few memories. All was ready, and I had almost no more Turkish money. I decided not to change more, so I was eating little, resting, reading, and writing. I found Erzurum boring. I wandered but saw little. My mind has flown to Pakistan two days before my body. In the past seven days, I have only eaten nine meals, of which three were breakfasts. At least this way, I didn't get sick. Never in my life have I spent so much time waiting.

SEPTEMBER 6, 1987

I made my way to Erzurum's airport and flew to Istanbul. I change places so often now that it is blinding, but I am not blinded. I am accustomed now, and many deeper things do not change. I still love Hélène; I remain the same man, as the film of places I have seen plays on the screen of my mind. That is the miracle of the journey, that a person may go and live in a world in which all is strange, yet he is able to hold steady and represent to himself and in himself a whole other reality that is not his present reality, as it is so far away. This inner reality is stronger than the outer one. Odysseus finally returned home at the end of his journeys; he did not forget where he came from, though, for Tennyson, he had to go away again.

I am alone, called by my unfolding journey to Pakistan and then over the mountains to Xinjiang and Tibet. There is such a strange feeling in our international airports, as in train stations or ports, but stronger, more acute. Each person alone in the isolated bubble of his or her own life, drops of water in the human flow: refugee, tourist, businessman, homeward or outward bound traveler. People in transit from birth to death, through these places of transience. Joyce described their spirit best:

> The spell of arms and voices: the white arms of roads, their promise of close embraces and the black arms of tall ships that stand against the moon, their tale of distant nations. They are held out to say: We are alone. Come. And the voices say with them: We are your kinsmen. And the air is thick with their company as they call to me, their kinsman, making ready to go, shaking the wings of their exultant and terrible youth.[15]

---

15. Joyce, James, *A Portrait of the Artist as a Young Man*. London: Panther Books, 1977, p. 228.

INTERLUDE: HALF A LIFE GONE BY

After leaving Turkey I traveled for five more months. Pakistan, from south to north, into the Karakoram and over the Khunjerab Pass to Kashgar in late October, before the snows. I set out for Mount Kailash a few weeks after the Tibetan riots and Chinese reprisals in Lhasa. Tibet had been officially closed, its borders sealed and foreigners expelled, but having traveled so far and having failed in my two previous quests, I could not turn back. I skirted a Chinese Army checkpoint in the dark, then made the 5,000-km, six-week journey across the Kunlun Mountains along the eastern side of the Himalayas to Kailash and then on to Lhasa, sometimes at elevations above 6,000 meters, hitching rides on cargo trucks, walking and sleeping outside in temperatures as low as minus 22°F (-30°C). It was at this time that my interest in Islam became a fascination. I was riding outside on the back of a truck with a group of Turkic nomads. As the sun sank behind the high peaks of the Karakoram (we were quite near K-2), the driver stopped, and the nomads descended, rudimentarily established the direction to Mecca, and began to pray. We were a long way from Mecca, in one of the remotest places on earth. And yet they prayed. I could see the crescent moon of Islam rising above the distant mountains.

I arrived in Lhasa in December, exhausted and physically diminished, but euphoric. Another two months from there to Nepal, India, and home. By then home was no longer where I grew up in the United States; home was with Hélène. We traveled together to the United States and I began six years of intense study, pursuing knowledge with the same intensity with which I had pursued my travels. First a master's in linguistics, then a doctoral program in the history of science at Harvard, to study the transmission of ancient science and philosophy from the Greeks, through Arab thinkers to medieval Europeans. If I had been born wealthy, I would have devoted my life to self-directed study. I was not, so at first I planned an academic career. Advice from two of my mentors, themselves retiring academics, and my own natural reticence to focus solely on one field, led me to abandon this direction in favor of something more practical. Perhaps this was a mistake.

I withdrew from the program in the history of science, but continued studying the Arabic language and Islam. I won two successive Fulbright Scholarships to Egypt, from 1990 to 1992, improving my Arabic language abilities and doing doctoral research on Islamic law using original sources in Arabic. Hélène and I married, and we like to say we enjoyed a two-year honeymoon in Egypt. For my career, I considered and rejected diplomacy and concluded that I would work in the private sector, possibly in finance. While earning my undergraduate degree in mathematics, compared to the better students in my classes I was a mediocre mathematician, but finance was easy for me thanks to my mathematical background. So I transferred from Harvard to the Fletcher School at Tufts, where I studied finance, economics, international law, and Islamic civilization. I earned another Master's, first in my class, and then a PhD in 1994, and published my doctoral thesis as a book.[16] Our son Alexander was born.

Then I made a compromise. I ceded the choice of the subjects I would study and the problems I would solve to outside entities—clients, corporations or individuals—and in return they paid me, but I was still studying. At first I worked in the Paris office of The Boston Consulting Group, a global management consultancy, then in 1996, the year our daughter Marianne was born, I quit and started a small advisory firm with a Saudi classmate from Fletcher. For the next two decades, I lived between France and the Arabian Gulf, consulting for clients there. I managed investments and advised local companies in industries from fashion, to health spas, to newspapers, to aviation. My business prospered. I traveled widely in Saudi Arabia, even to the Empty Quarter desert, and continued to study Islam as well as other subjects which attracted my interest. Our children became young adults and went forth into life. And my dormant desire for adventure began to awaken again. My life thus far had been successful and satisfying in every respect, but the question kept coming back to me, as it does to many: "Is this all there is?" At first I took up rock climbing, trail running, and paragliding as hobbies, the first two of which I still practice. But this was not enough, so I went on two exploratory trips in 2012 and 2013, to travel again

---

16. Ray, Nicholas, *Arab Islamic Banking and the Renewal of Islamic Law*. London: Graham & Trotman (Kluwer), 1995.

as I had in my youth, and I began to write. This was what I needed. I reduced my professional responsibilities and conceived the project of this book.

I am the same person I was before. But between the previous and the subsequent chapters three decades have passed, and I have not wasted them. My knowledge and experience have increased in breadth and depth, especially concerning Islam and the Middle East. I have also grown older, with all that can bring: greater understanding, even wisdom or perhaps only the illusion of such; a recognition of the limits of human efforts or perhaps only disillusionment; a growing realization of my own mortality or perhaps only the fear of death. Age and experience have surely changed my vision of the world, and my voice when speaking of it. But the journey remains the same.

2

CENTRAL ANATOLIA

HALF A LIFE GONE BY. I am almost fifty years old now, a youth no more, and I am going away again. To be alone, to pass unnoticed. To take stock, not of what I have or what I do, but of what I am. To see the outside world pass by as a cinematographic marvel while only the observer in me remains unchanged. I first left home for foreign lands when I was nineteen. There are many in the long lineage of travelers before me, seeking freedom, truth, knowledge, fortune, adventure. Ibn Battuta, the great Arab traveler of the fourteenth century, was one of these.

My departure from Tanjah, the place of my birth, was on Thursday the second day of the month of God, Rajab, in the year 725 [1325 CE]. I intended to make the pilgrimage to the House of God [in Mecca], and to visit the tomb of the Prophet, the finest prayers and peace be upon him. I was alone, without a companion whose fellowship I might enjoy, nor a caravan whose journey I might join, but I was moved by overpowering resolution, and the wish to visit these illustrious sanctuaries, which lived within my heart. I thus decided to leave my friends, male and female, and abandoned my home as the birds abandon their nests. My mother and father were still living. I resigned myself sadly to part from them, and both they and I were afflicted by this separation. I was twenty-two years old.[1]

Ibn Battuta did not return to his home for twenty-four years. He had been trained as a jurist and scholar, and visited most of the Islamic world, from Andalusia to the Far East, as well as several non-Muslim countries, often acting as a judge or legal scholar. He was generally very well received by the local rulers due to his exceptional knowledge and, as the years went by, to his virtually unique experience of the world.

I am sitting in the connecting flight to Ankara, waiting to take off in Istanbul. I was next to two French people on the way here, a young man and an old man, perhaps grandson and grandfather. They were going together to Kathmandu. Looking around the plane, I couldn't tell where I was. The in-flight magazines on Turkish Airlines advertise the same brands with the same glossy images as American or European in-flight magazines. I read during the flight, and while taking inventory of the digital books I brought I realized that I had forgotten to transfer various pieces of information I had gathered in a document, intending to copy it to my tablet. I will do without it, or get it from the internet if needed. Ubiquitous connectivity changes the nature of travel. Maybe it creates the need to go further afield to escape it. I read the introduction of Coleman Barks' Rumi interpretation[2] and that of *Mystical Dimensions of Islam*[3] by the late Annemarie Schimmel, a professor at Harvard when I was studying there, and pre-eminent scholar of Sufism.

It was quite hot outside when we landed, around 82°F (28°C). I wonder whether I will feel the same fascination with foreign cultures in

---

1. Harb, Talal, *Rihla ibn Battuta*, Explanation and Commentary by Talal Harb. Beirut: Dar al-Kutub al-'Ilmiyya, 1971, p, 31. Translation from Arabic by the author.

2. Barks, Coleman (Translator), *The Essential Rumi*. San Francisco: Castle Books, 1997. Coleman Barks worked using existing academic translations, and does an excellent job of interpreting Rumi into a modern idiom, without having actually read the original Persian. This book was given to me by my father in the summer of 2014 and led to my choosing Turkey as the destination of my travels. I thank my father, with whom I have alternately an exceedingly difficult relationship or no relationship at all, for that gift.

3. Schimmel, Annemarie, *Mystical Dimensions of Islam*. Chapel Hill NC: University of North Carolina Press, 1975.

this era of homogeneity. I am not sure. This trip could tell me. In 1987, I did this trip, Istanbul to Ankara, by train. It was long and dusty, I remember, an overnight train ride.

OCTOBER 8, 2014

I just awoke from a nap, or rather a period of lazy drowsiness. Last night I had dinner in the restaurant of the Rahmi M. Koç Museum of Industry, attached to the hotel where I am staying. Both are magnificent older buildings, renovated sixteenth-century Ottoman caravanserais, thoughtfully restored with the previously open courtyards now covered by a glass ceiling supported by a metal structure. My table was next to an antique car, a Ford Model T, and there were blue faience medallions bearing inscriptions around the upper part of the arched walls, with Arabic calligraphy. I have difficulty reading calligraphy. At least here I have the excuse that some of the texts are in Ottoman Turkish, not Arabic, so I am not overly despondent at being unable to read some of them. My dinner was really excellent: slow-braised lamb shank with the "olive oil plate" as appetizer. And I didn't even get sick! When I was in Turkey in 1987, I slept and ate in the cheapest places, and spent nearly half the time ill. So economic development, both mine personally and that of the country, has at least one benefit: less time sick and more time for "non-expulsive" experiences. Turkey has developed immensely since then, and the food is much more hygienic regardless of the price paid for it. To those claiming to search for authenticity in the guise of poverty: filth and disease are not culturally authentic—they exist everywhere.

This morning, I was anxious to begin my explorations. After a good breakfast, I crossed the dirty street into the Citadel of Ankara. For Muslims anywhere in the world, the Arabic "*Al-Salam 'aleikum*" ("Peace be with you") as a formal greeting elicits the formal reply, "*Wa 'aleikum al-salam*"[4] ("And with you be peace"), so I prefer it to "*Merhaba*" (the basic Turkish greeting, though it comes from an

---

4. This greeting and the reply are formalisms practiced throughout the Islamic world, based upon the practices of the Prophet Mohammad himself.

Arabic word). So far, however, nobody here speaks Arabic. One of the walls of the Citadel is a true amalgam of multiculturalism, with blocks bearing Greek (Byzantine) inscriptions sideways, and others with Latin inscriptions (so probably older) sideways and upside-down. We all borrow from each other and from the past, though we often try to dissimulate it. In Cairo the top of the Great Pyramid was quarried to build other buildings millennia later. The columns in some medieval Cairene mosques are Roman, the capitals still intact.

The multicultural construction of the Citadel wall provides an opportunity for a back-of-the-envelope summary of Turkey's long history. The territory of modern Turkey, Asia Minor, was home to some of the very earliest forms of civilization. Göbekli Tepe, discussed in Chapter 5, the first known temple complex in human history and carbon-dated to 9500 BCE, is south of here, near the Syrian border, and apparently predates the Neolithic revolution.[5] DNA analysis has shown that the first variety of wild einkorn wheat to be domesticated for agriculture was probably from south-eastern Anatolia.[6] Asia Minor was the site of many Neolithic settlements (the Neolithic period encompasses roughly 8000 BCE to 3500 BCE), including Çatalhöyük, discussed subsequently in this chapter.[7] The Bronze Age (roughly 3500 BCE to 1200 BCE) history of the region is also exceedingly rich, as witnessed by Homer and related narratives of the Trojan War. During this period, myriad smaller civilizations controlled parts of Asia Minor: Hittites (from Central Anatolia all the way to parts of the western coast), Lycians (southern coast west of Antalya), Luwians (southern coast east of Antalya), Mysians (north-western Mediterranean coast), Phrygians (west-central Anatolia), Carians (south-western Mediterranean coast), and others. Many of these were specifically

---

5. "Neolithic revolution" is a term referring to the development of agriculture and animal husbandry in the Neolithic period, which enabled hunter-gatherer societies to become sedentary and develop complex social structures and specialization, leading to further technological development. Göbekli Tepe actually turns this dominant paradigm on its head, as it predates the generally accepted date of the Neolithic revolution but itself implies an already complex social structure.

6. During, Bleda, *The Prehistory of Asia Minor*. Cambridge: Cambridge University Press, 2011, p. 48.

7. Due to its having been studied more recently, the prehistory of Asia Minor is less well-known than that of the Fertile Crescent (Syria, Palestine, Iraq), but is contemporaneous and as rich.

mentioned in Homer's *Iliad* as having contributed troops to the defense of Troy in the Trojan War, which occurred most probably around the thirteenth century BCE. Subsequently, the ancient Persians and Greeks fought back and forth over Asia Minor, until Alexander the Great blazed through all the way to the Indus River (in present-day Pakistan), creating a momentary empire incorporating all of Greece and all of Persia and everything in between, as well as Egypt and the Fertile Crescent, but which then fragmented upon his death. After that, the Romans took control of Asia Minor,[8] and from them the Byzantines, in the fourth century CE. The Byzantines progressively lost territory over the centuries to a variety of Muslim principalities, including the Ilkhan Mongols and Seljuk Turks, until the fall of Constantinople to Mehmet the Conqueror in 1453 and the establishment of Ottoman dominion over much of the Mediterranean world. The Ottomans finally succumbed to history at the end of World War I. I wonder if the citizens of each of the polities to have successively controlled this land thought their dominion was permanent.

I wandered through the Citadel area, a poor neighborhood, then tried to find my way down towards the main part of the city. I spoke with a polite man at a bluff near the top of the Citadel overlooking the city, where a road dead-ends. He pointed out the Haji Bayram Mosque. I walked down to it, saw the ruins of the Temple of Augustus, and strolled around the mosque but did not enter it. Then I came across an excavation in the garden amidst government buildings. Two meters down were subterranean water pipes (Byzantine), then four meters down the flagstones of the Roman Road leading to the Temple of Augustus. Everything is covered up and lost. The mosque is a lesser monument than the temple must have been, and the city probably less beautiful than it was in ancient times. It reminded me of the filthy open sewers in the present-day town near ancient Mohenjo-Daro in Pakistan, 4,500 years older but better planned and executed (and with underground sewers), in sum more civilized. I walked further, went to change money in a bank, and bought a knife. Or rather, I bought two. I found the hunting and fishing market area, with around ten shops selling

---

8. The Battle of Magnesia, mentioned in Chapter 7, in 190 BCE marked the beginning of Roman dominion over all of Asia Minor.

knives, firearms, and other outdoor equipment. Having investigated the knives in nine of them, I settled on one which I did not particularly like but was passable, and bought it, but then stopped in the last shop, found a much better one, and bought it too. I left the first one in the hotel room, a gift for the housekeeper, and carried the second for the whole trip. I always carry a knife when I travel (but since I check in no baggage, I leave each as a gift upon my departure).

I have just visited the Museum of Anatolian Civilization. It was underwhelming as an experience, though an excellent museum. It is always amazing to me that no matter how far we look back and how rudimentary a civilization's level of technical mastery, the essentials of humanity remain. Women adorn themselves. Men fight. Material needs are addressed. If we modern people were transported back to the Neolithic era, we would understand the people's lives once we had internalized the extreme difficulty of their daily existence. Some contemporary people could enter the Neolithic without a hitch, as there are still those who effectively live in similar conditions now. Here, some of the most remarkable items were from the Hatti people, 2500–2250 BCE, before the Hittites: gold ornaments, ceramics, of equal beauty to what came later. Who were these people? They were not Indo-European, as is known from their names recorded in Hittite texts. The museum has left me with a melancholic feeling. When I was young, I imagined that with time I could survey the breadth of human history. Now it seems so vast, and I so small. I do not have enough time.

I am at dinner. Something funny. I consciously try to imitate Robert Byron's hilarious dialogues in *The Road to Oxiana*:

NDR: "I would like another glass of wine, but a different wine."
Waiter: "The same?"
NDR: "No, not the same. Different. Other, otro, différent, mukhtalif."
(Waiter brings wine)
NDR: (After tasting) "This is the same wine."
Waiter: "Yes, the same."
NDR: "I WANT NOT SAME WINE!"

OCTOBER 9, 2014

I am sitting in a pub in Kızılay, surrounded by young people. Last night, I was intending to write about a disappointing aspect of age and experience: the more I have seen, the more I know about the world, the harder it is to experience something new that impresses me. And yet today, I saw something which impressed me. I remember little of Ankara from my stay here in 1987. I did not visit the Museum of Anatolian Civilizations. I also did not visit Atatürk's mausoleum, the Anıt Kabir, nor, to my recollection, the Citadel. Mainly, I remember being sick in a plain hotel room. Regarding the Anıt Kabir, in 1987, I made a special point not to go there. Turkey was my first experience of a military dictatorship and the personality cult of an authoritarian ruler. At the time, I had no patience for autocrats. My view has not changed. All the same, I decided to make my way to the Anıt Kabir, and I am truly glad that I did.

Before describing it, I will complete the *précis* of Turkish history started above, through to the present. The Ottoman Empire collapsed under the weight of losing World War I due to the disastrous leadership of the Young Turk Pashas, who also perpetrated genocides against the Armenians and the Assyrians and large-scale ethnic cleansing against the indigenous Greek population, descendants of the ancient Greeks and Byzantines. After World War I, the victorious powers divided the carcass of the Ottoman Empire among themselves and their allies as spoils, leaving nearly nothing to the Turks. Mustafa Kemal, later known as Atatürk ("Father of the Turks"), opposed this unjust situation, fighting and winning the War of Independence to establish the Republic of Turkey, with himself as its first president. Large-scale population transfers were organized and conducted with Greece, resulting in a relatively homogeneous Turkish population (except for the Kurds). Atatürk then implemented drastic and controversial reforms seeking to modernize Turkey, discussed below. After his death in 1938, Atatürk's deputy, Ismet İnönü, became president. In 1939, Turkey annexed Hatay Province, up until then a part of French Syria. Turkey subsequently joined NATO and cycled between multi-party democracy and military dictatorship, remaining staunchly secular under both regimes until the rise of Recep Tayyip Erdoğan's AKP (Justice and Development Party) in

2002. AKP is an explicitly Islamist political party, similar to Egypt's Muslim Brotherhood, though it has up until recently largely preserved democratic rights and the rule of law. In the larger context of Turkey's history as an Islamic nation, the partial return of religion to the public sphere can be seen as a natural long-term reaction to Atatürk's secular reforms. The recent (from 2016 on) undermining of the rule of law and clear steps towards dictatorship taken by President Erdoğan, using the excuse of the recent coup attempt against him, are much more troubling, as it seems that Turkey is on a path from which it will not be able to easily return. As popular opposition to the coup demonstrated, AKP and President Erdoğan have the strong support of a large part of the Turkish population, but history is replete with cases in which a leader with popular support becomes an absolute autocrat, with disastrous consequences.[9]

Now back to the Anıt Kabir. On a purely architectural level, Atatürk's mausoleum is a powerful monument. To reach it, one must pass down a broad avenue guarded by statues of lions, Anatolian, Hittite lions. This avenue is also guarded by soldiers bearing beautiful M1 Garand rifles with chrome-plated actions. This rifle entered service in the late 1930s after Atatürk's War of Independence, so I wonder at its choice here. At the end of the avenue one arrives at the monument proper. Monolithic in its sobriety and geometrical purity, it cannot be mistaken for anything but a homage to a king, and in this it resembles funereal monuments from remotest antiquity. Of the modern monuments I have seen, it is one of the most moving (the Washington Monument, Lincoln Memorial, and Mount Rushmore come to mind, but I can think of nothing comparable in Europe). As I mentioned, having a negative bias towards the hero worship or quasi-deification of a man, I did not visit in 1987. Today, having studied Islamic history and lived for years in the Muslim world, the Anıt Kabir raised the question in my mind as to whether the monument might be a just measure of the man and his role in Turkey's history. When looking at modern Turkey, one cannot help but be impressed with what one sees. Compared to the murderous, corrupt, and incompetent dictatorships in several neighboring countries,

9. At the time of editing this manuscript, fall 2018, President Erdoğan is attempting to extend his dictatorial powers to the financial markets, providing a humorous spectacle for the world. Humorous except that it is tragic for the Turkish economy.

hell-bent on self-annihilation, unable even to keep themselves out of *fitna* (Arabic for civil war or general chaos), here is a country largely free in religion, where women's rights and education are respected as well as or better than in any other Middle Eastern country; where ethnic divisions exist but where respect for objective knowledge in the form of science and technology, and the power they confer, rules out primitive tribalism. And what is more, all of this was done by the Turks themselves. All that one need do to appreciate the extent of Turkey's development is to compare it with present-day Egypt and then to realize that Egypt and Turkey were on a comparable footing a few generations ago.

The neighborhoods through which I passed today on the way to Kızılay from the Anıt Kabir are a testament to Turkey's success. No such places exist in Cairo except as ruins of (colonial) times past, nor do they exist in the Arabian Gulf countries despite their GDP per capita being much higher than that of Turkey. These districts were clean, charming, organized by a sophisticated system of urban planning, a boon to their inhabitants and to passers-through like me, content to sit on a bench in a narrow verdant park with the sun on my face and watch the people go by. Perhaps such districts existed in Syria. It will be generations before many Arab countries could create, or re-create, such a neighborhood. Judging by the end result, perhaps Atatürk was right. He must have believed that to survive in the modern world, his society had to pass through violent social convulsions: abandoning its alphabet and creating a "new" language; eliminating religion from the public spheres of education and law; and imposing European practices and customs by force. In short, Atatürk saw Islam in Turkey as an impediment to modern public life which had to be—and was—relegated solely to the personal sphere in order to stop it from preventing the creation of an effective modern society. This experiment was undertaken at huge cost, and the results seem clear: Turkey has largely succeeded. The Arab world is largely failing, as is Afghanistan, and it is not unreasonable to posit that these countries are failing at least partially due to the difficulty of adapting Islam to modernity, complicating the development of modern education, modern legal systems, and modern scientific and technological inquiry, and now threatening the existence of several modern states and even the very idea of the modern state. Afghanistan, Iraq, Libya, Somalia, Sudan,

Syria, and Yemen no longer exist as states. In much of the Middle East, a murderous retrograde interpretation of Sunni Islam, an equally murderous secular order, and violent Shi'ite extremism are in a tripartite fight to the death, in which all sides must lose. Egypt is one small step away from a similar fate, its present regime less legitimate and more terribly repressive than the Mubarak regime in the 1990s when I lived there.[10] Some other Arab countries are also on a knife-edge, financial resources and an efficient security apparatus all that separate them too from *fitna*, and the same could be said of Iran. When looked at in such a light, Turkey is an unambiguous success story, the best example of a Muslim country in the Middle East adapting to modernity while at least partly retaining its inherent nature. It seems fair to attribute much of this success to the efforts of one man— Mustafa Kemal Atatürk. I think he actually deserves this monument.

OCTOBER 10, 2014

At breakfast, I noticed that the English-language newspaper here is totally different from its equivalent in many Arab countries, notably Egypt. Yesterday's paper had the Education Minister admitting failure in achieving important goals, while today's carries articles criticizing the government. So the press is relatively free here.[11] The bus station was also not what I had expected. I had seen a huge outdoor lot, choked with dust and diesel fumes. That must have been for city buses. The ASTI Otogar (*autogare* is a French word, borrowed into Turkish) is modern, quite clean, and very well organized. It has nothing to envy the NY Port Authority or other large city bus stations. I am on the bus now to Sungurlu. The highway is beautiful. Shame we're only going eighty kilometers an hour. Next phase, a taxi to Boğazkale. I felt the freedom of the road for the first time on this trip: the

---

10. I lived in Cairo from 1990 to 1992 as a Fulbright Scholar, studying Arabic language and civilization and doing research on Islamic law for my doctoral thesis. While there I witnessed large numbers of bearded men herded like cattle into prison trucks and driven out of the city.

11. This was written in 2014. Between then and now Turkey has drastically reduced press freedom, arbitrarily imprisoned journalists, and gone straight down the road to dictatorship. According to a recent article, President Erdoğan has arrested 40,000 people without due process, and dismissed or suspended from their jobs 120,000 others (Reuters, "Victims of Turkey Purges Fear Heavier Crackdown after Referendum," The New York Times, April 13, 2017.) He has also constructed the world's largest presidential palace for himself.

bright sun, an empty ribbon of road through the Anatolian steppe leading towards the ancient Hittite capital of Hattuşa. I want to live this way. I do not know if I will be able to write well about it, or if anyone will read what I write, but I will live it.

I became interested specifically in the Hittites in 1988–89, a few years after my initial trip to Turkey when I was studying historical Indo-European linguistics. Ferdinand de Saussure, one of the founders of historical linguistics in the late nineteenth century, developed a theory of phonetic changes which he observed over time in languages (for example, the phonetic correspondences between Latin and the various Romance languages descended from it are regular and obey certain fixed rules).[12] Extrapolating from these observable rules, Saussure attempted to reconstruct the past forms of a hypothetical Proto-Indo-European language from which the extant Indo-European languages would have descended.[13] In the course of these reconstructive studies Saussure hypothesized the existence of consonant sounds which were later termed "laryngeals,"[14] but which were not attested in any known Indo-European language at the time. Later, with the discovery and translation of the Hittite language (which was completely unknown at Saussure's time), these consonant sounds were positively identified.[15] The student of the physical sciences, or the layman, might not appreciate the utter rarity of such a phenomenon in the inexact sciences such as linguistics. When Einstein developed his General Theory of Relativity, which predicted the degree to which sunlight would be "bent" by gravity, experiments were done during the solar eclipse of 1919 which verified his predictions.

---

12. De Saussure, Ferdinand, *Cours de linguistique générale.* Paris: Payot, 1972. Chapter III of the section on Diachronic Linguistics.

13. Much work on this subject has been accomplished since Saussure's time, though scientific certainty is rare in this field. Cross-disciplinary studies with archaeology have also been undertaken, seeking the *Urheimat*, or Proto-Indo-European homeland. I studied this subject and made a small related contribution with my Master's thesis: Ray, Nicholas, *Indo-Aryans in the Ancient Near East: Linguistic, Archaeological, and Historical Considerations.* Rochester: University of Rochester, unpublished Master's thesis, 1989.

14. The term "laryngeal" refers to the hypothesis that the sounds in question were pronounced in the larynx.

15. Lehman, Winfred P., *Historical Linguistics: An Introduction.* New York: Holt, Rinehart, and Winston, 1973, pp. 97-9.

In historical linguistics, the discovery of Hittite and confirmation of Saussure's hypothesis is the only event of its kind ever to have occurred. I arrived at the simple hotel near Hattuşa, and arranged with the taxi driver to come back in two days to take me to Yozgat. I had a quick lunch, then left, walking for Yazılıkaya, an ancient Hittite temple contemporaneous with the nearby city of Hattuşa. I walked fast at a good sustainable pace, passing a female Japanese traveler from the hotel on the way up. The walk took twenty-five minutes for three kilometers of steady uphill. I found the stone carvings at Yazılıkaya unremarkable, images of deities in the gray stone worn down by time, though Chamber B had a sacred air about it, so I made a wish. I then wandered over the site behind the chambers and did a bit of bouldering[16] on the clean limestone before returning to the hotel where I had dinner with the Japanese woman, with whom I shared fewer than ten words in common. Enough communication nonetheless went on for me to understand that she was very weird, as if being alone in Hattuşa (as I was) was not enough to prove this!

Sitting in bed after dinner, I read the entirety of Professor Jürgen Seeher's excellent book, *Hattusha Guide: A Day in the Hittite Capital*.[17] For many years, Professor Seeher was the director of the excavations at Hattuşa, for the German Archaeological Institute. I subsequently engaged in a detailed email correspondence with his successor Professor Andreas Schachner, who was kind enough to answer my archaeological questions. In 1987, even though I had not yet studied Indo-European linguistics, I had developed an interest in visiting Hattuşa. It was the only site in Turkey I missed and regretted missing on that trip.

OCTOBER 11, 2014

After a light breakfast, I walked from town to the site, arriving just at 8:00 AM, when the ticket booth was supposed to open. Of course nobody was in the booth yet. Turkey is modern, but it is not Switzerland or the US.

16. Bouldering is a type of rock climbing involving short sequences of (difficult) moves done relatively close to the ground, without ropes or other equipment.

17. Seeher, Jürgen, *Hattusha Guide: A Day in the Hittite Capital*. Istanbul: Ege Yayınları, 2011 (4th revised edition).

I folded a banknote and stuck it in a crack in the sill of the ticket window, then proceeded to explore the nearby portions of the site. I looked at the section of defensive wall built by Professor Seeher's archaeology team based on a model found in the ruins and using only ancient building techniques. What an excellent idea, to build as the Hittites had built! He found that one kilometer of wall would take roughly 1,000 man-years of work. I then wandered slowly through the first temple area, keeping an eye out for the opening of the ticket booth. I went into the temple and said a prayer in the better-preserved of the two cult rooms. I have said prayers everywhere from the top of the Great Pyramid, to the Dolma La Pass on the pilgrimage route around Mount Kailash, to the Idaeon Cave in Crete where Olympian Zeus was raised—at each place a different type of prayer. Praying in this manner is a superstitious habit, but it centers my mind, reminding me of those who have gone before. I then walked through the granaries of the lower city, presently being excavated. The giant storage jars, up to 2000 liters in volume, had been left in place 3,500 years ago and had not been moved since. The ground had accreted around them and in them, and some have been fully reconstructed from their constituent pieces by the archaeologists. Others just left their outlines, jagged edges of pottery sticking up through the dry grass, broken pieces all around. I presume that they had at least been emptied of food when the Hittites left, though even this is not certain. What does one take when civilization itself collapses?

The ticket office employee arrived, so I went to greet him and get my ticket and my change. I then continued, climbing atop a giant boulder (clean, solid limestone, as at Yazılıkaya) to survey the temple complex from the south-west. Coming down, I met a young man carving imitations of Hittite statuettes and walked on through the temple area until I saw, from a distance, the famous "Green Stone." It was larger than I had imagined it, a roughly seventy to eighty centimeter cube, partially buried under the level of the temple complex floor. This would put it at roughly half a cubic meter, so it must weigh at least a thousand kilograms. It had been worn smooth, so smooth that the corners were rounded. The hands of archaeology enthusiasts could not have accomplished this in the past eighty years, so I assume it was polished smooth by the countless hands of Hittite and other devotees during the long centuries the temple was active. Or perhaps it predates the Hittites, as the first settlement in this lower city was apparently from before 2000 BCE, of the pre-Hittite Hatti people. Professor Schachner remarked that nobody has any idea what the role of this Green Stone was. I contemplated it silently before placing both hands upon it, trying to imagine others who had touched it in years past.

After the Green Stone, I began to walk uphill. I estimated that the altitude difference between the Yerkapı Rampart (Sphinx Gate), the culminating point of the city to the south, and the ticket booth entrance was around 250 meters. I hiked fast for the workout but also to avoid sharing Hattuşa's wonders with the busloads of tourists I suspected of being on their way to interrupt my private visit. I noted the postern wall and granary on the left, then descended a ravine and ascended the cereal store building. I next hiked quickly to the high West Gate across terrain covered with dried grass, without visible ruins and yet littered with potsherds. When cities fall and civilizations collapse, pottery gets broken and left everywhere. What a mess those invading hordes invariably make, breaking everyone's family dinner service outside on the lawn. I cannot but be fascinated by seeing these articles of everyday life from thousands of years ago scattered across the ground as numerous as pebbles. Using my hard-earned orienteering skills,[18] I took a compass bearing and followed it, roughly, on an iso-altitude curve to the road. Continuing 500 meters more, I arrived at the Lion Gate. Here I met the third person of the day after the man at the ticket booth and the boy making statuettes. He was a fat, old Turkish man, perhaps the boy's main distribution channel since he tried to hard-sell me statuettes I didn't want. I politely declined. I inspected the Lion Gate, twin lions guarding the entrance to the city, carved from giant blocks of stone, then set off for another temple with the salesman following me at a trot, huffing and puffing. He recovered while I looked at the temple ruins, at which point I climbed up onto the Yenicekale Citadel. To my dismay, he followed me there as well, so I traversed (grade four climbing

18. Both of my children competed at orienteering in high-school, my daughter reaching the French national competition several times, and I participated occasionally with them at a much lower level of competence.

moves above a ten meter drop) and then down-climbed the far side of the Citadel. Irritated that his sole potential customer had eluded him, he quickly came down the way he had gone up and positioned himself between me and the road, thinking I would return to it like a sheep to its flock. Instead I took another compass bearing and headed straight up a steep slope at my maximum sustainable heart rate to the upper reservoirs and the Yerkapı Rampart, definitively leaving the salesman to prey on other visitors.

Though far from the scale of the Pyramids, the Yerkapı Rampart is nevertheless monumental. I followed Professor Seeher's instructions, given both on the local information panels and in his book, and entered the postern tunnel. I took out my headlamp and illuminated the huge rough-hewn blocks of stone which form the tunnel. The tunnel structure was built first, and then covered with dirt to form the rampart around thirty meters high. Throughout my time here I tried to imagine how people once lived. How their children would have climbed on the rocks I climbed on, how they would have walked to the edges of the city to be alone. And here in the postern tunnel, around seventy meters long, as I played light over the stones I imagined a Hittite captain, entrusted with guarding the tunnel, a task crucial for the defense of the city. Being human and weak, he may have broken the rules and invited his favorite servant girl to see the tunnel under the city's great rampart. Emerging from the darkness of the tunnel with my prurient historical fantasy into the bright light of day, I thought about the military significance of the tunnel and concluded that the archaeologists were mistaken in assigning it a purely ceremonial role. After having discussed the issue at length with Professor Schachner, I remain convinced that the postern tunnel had at least a secondary military role, as a sally port.[19]

I climbed the stairs up the rampart and approached the Sphinx Gate, only to be confronted by the twin puckered orifices of the Sphinxes, tails raised. I thought this a very unusual way of greeting illustrious visitors to the city of Hattuşa. Perhaps nobody important actually entered

19. A sally port is a well-defended door, sometimes hidden, enabling besieged defenders to sally forth and attack a besieging force, by surprise.

from this gate? Or perhaps the Hittites did not care for their southerly neighbors?

I sat on the wall, wrote a brief diary entry, and contemplated the rest of the site from this glorious vantage point, its summit. It was almost noon. I had completed most of my exploration and not one tour bus had arrived yet. Soon I saw the first (and only) one coming up the road from the ticket booth far below. The bus' occupants hardly saw anything, there for only forty-five minutes and never straying from the inside of the bus for more than a few minutes. I went down through the upper temples, then to the King's Gate, remarkable, as was the Lion Gate, with a parabolic archway and beautiful sculptures. The cylindrical pinions of the doors were huge, fifteen centimeters in diameter, hewn from stone. No doors are left now. I continued downwards, leaving the road, crossing a steep valley then the lower reservoirs, much shallower and broader than the upper ones for unknown reasons. I then climbed the hill to Büyükkale, the King's Citadel, took compass bearings, and looked down on the ruins of the wall to the east. The terrain going down and then up to the south was so steep that I do not know how they could have built the wall there, but Professor Schachner assured me that they had, and that its ruins were still visible.

I examined Büyükkale, finding it incompletely excavated. There was a small pool or cistern around two and a half meters below the surrounding level, built with monumental stone blocks. It had lush vegetation and large snails living in it. I wonder where the humidity comes from. I then went down a very steep slope, passed the House on the Slope, bade farewell to the Green Stone and slowly passed out of the city. It is truly a remarkable site. Not in the same way as Mohenjo-Daro, where I felt that I was wandering in the ruins of a city designed by a twentieth-century CE urban planner but executed with materials and technology of the twenty-fifth century BCE, but in that Hattuşa is a huge, magnificent city, great within the limits of what could be built at its time. In my experience, it ranks above every archaeological site I have seen except Mohenjo-Daro and the greatest Pharaonic monuments. I drank a soda at a local café, noting the clear inferiority of the present-day architecture, construction, and general level of culture compared to those dating from 3,500 years earlier.

OCTOBER 12, 2014

I am feeling down today. My trip here (to Göreme) was fine. Leaving Hattuşa, I had a great view of the south of Büyükkaya, a fortified hilltop and the only major sector of Hattuşa which I didn't visit on foot. The ride south, through the empty Anatolian landscape, was glorious, and I imagined Hittite ruins on every ridge along the way. Many probably existed. Arriving in Yozgat, I was fortunate to get a bus leaving in fifteen minutes for Kayseri. A stop at an utterly disgusting toilet was followed by a tedious bus ride to Kayseri. On arrival, two buses to Göreme were full and the next one was in five hours and so I took a taxi. It is truly liberating not to have to worry about money, thus avoiding a half-day wait in a crowded and noisy bus station. I also employ local people more than I did on my last passage through here, and hope I help them economically. Some travelers see a strange sort of moral value in spending as little as possible wherever they go. I do not.

After arriving at the hotel I had reserved, I walked into town and was disappointed. An unrepentant tourist trap, truly the type of place I hate. I managed to get a walking map from the fourth travel agent I visited. He was strange and impolite, asking where I was from, and when I said, "France and the US," he said, "You're safe here. Nobody will kill you. Here you can even say you are Jewish." How welcoming! He then went on to state that both the Kurds and Islamic State are terrorist groups, equally the enemies of Turkey, and that Islamic State militants are not Muslims.

This is a typical modern Muslim denial, which is part of the problem. Islamic State's denizens are Muslims, with an ideology clearly and solidly grounded in Islamic law. They know the foundational texts of Islam (the Qur'an and the *Sunnah*,[20] traditions of the Prophet) much better than many modernists such as that travel agent. Muslims themselves are responsible for addressing, refuting, and rejecting extremist views such as those who support Islamic State—outsiders cannot do it. In this, Muslims have largely failed. What does it mean to be a Muslim? How can someone educated in a modern educational system, like that of Turkey, who has

---

20. The *Sunnah* is the aggregate of the *hadith*, the recorded sayings and doings of the Prophet Muhammad.

not seriously read the foundational texts of Islam, assert that other people, namely those from Islamic State, are not Muslims and thereby ignore them instead of refuting their views? The thinkers of Islamic State, for all their retrograde barbarity, have read the foundational texts of their religion and have seized upon certain aspects of these to justify their medieval practices such as enslaving the "infidels" they capture. These practices were indeed legal and accepted under medieval Islamic law, as they were under Roman law or Greek law in earlier times.[21] The fact that modernist Muslims cannot effectively oppose such religious arguments with arguments *in the same religious language* means that they abdicate their role in determining who speaks for Islam and what Islam says.

Atatürk knew that religion was clearly a sub-optimal system of thought for conducting scientific research, developing technology or running a modern economy or administration, all of which were required for a powerful modern state. Religion is based upon "revealed truth," the antithesis of inquiry. Religion holds to tradition without reason, the antithesis of innovation. Religion passes judgment upon people by virtue of their quality of adherence or non-adherence to the religion, the antithesis of modern equality necessary for the rule of law. Religion's only legitimate role in such a modern society is a private, personal one. In a number of Islamic societies, religion has seeped far beyond the limits of private life and has vitiated the rationality of the population, the economic and administrative capacities of society, and the education of the young. Atatürk managed, through his drastic and convulsive reforms, to limit the impact of religion, which has been materially successful, but has left the role of interpreting Islam to the most extremist elements within its society.

---

21. There are key differences between the "modern" interpretations of Islamic State and the interpretations of medieval fiqh (Islamic jurisprudence), the main one being that Islamic State's adherents arrogate to themselves the right to say that other Muslims are not in fact Muslims *(takfir)*, and that they therefore fall into the category of apostates *(murtadd)*, who deserve death, or polytheists, who effectively have no rights under Islamic law and who can be killed or taken as slaves by Muslims. In case Jewish or Christian readers feel tempted to criticize the barbarity of Islamic religious texts on this basis, I refer them to their own Deuteronomy 20:12-16, a divine instruction to commit murder and genocide, of which the Bible contains many, and, for Christians, to Matthew 5:17, in which Jesus states clearly that his message incorporates and does not annul the Old Testament scriptures.

There were times in Islamic history when religion and rational pursuits co-existed fruitfully, and when great scientific inquiries and developments were made, but sadly that time has passed. In the early centuries of Islam, the *Mu'tazila* believed in the primacy of reason to interpret and define religious obligations.[22] Later, Muslim scientists and philosophers played a vital role in the transmission of ancient Greek philosophy and science to the Latin West, still in the Dark Ages at the time. Several of these eminent minds were well-known in medieval Europe, such as Avicenna (Ibn Sina) and Averroes (Ibn Rushd), the former famous for his works on medicine and philosophy, the latter for his commentaries on Aristotle as well as works in virtually every domain of knowledge of his time. There is a legend about Ibn Rushd that when he died, his body was carried by a camel, and on the other side of the camel were carried his writings, equal in weight to his body and providing a counterweight to it.[23] In the twelfth century, Ibn Rushd and Al-Ghazzali, another great Muslim thinker, engaged in an indirect intellectual duel pitting rationalist philosophy (Ibn Rushd) against the revealed knowledge of religion (Al-Ghazzali). Rationalism lost.[24] For Islam to successfully adapt to modernity, it must return to some of these lost paths of the mind, revisit arguments by these figures from its own illustrious intellectual history, and follow them to the end, a different end than that which was reached before. Atatürk removed Islam from the public sphere by force. This was not a viable long-term strategy among a Muslim population. What needs to be done now is to reinterpret Islam in the light of its own past currents of thought, to eliminate the deep-rooted aspects of tribalism which remain in many Islamic societies, to render Islam compatible with scientific and technological development, and thus put Islamic societies on an equal footing with the West, so that they may provide good lives for their citizens.

In 1987, here in Cappadocia I wrote, "I am kind of sad ... and feel

---

22. On this subject see Martin, Richard, Woodward, Mark, and Atmaja, Dwi, *Defenders of Reason in Islam*. Oxford: One World Publications, 1997.

23. This legend was recounted to me by Professor A.I. Sabra of the History of Science Department of Harvard, where I studied in a doctoral program for one year.

24. This intellectual duel provides an interesting substrate to the plot of Salman Rushdie's recent book, *Two Years Eight Months and Twenty-Eight Nights*.

that what I am doing is pointless. The world is so closed now compared to how it was before (when other travelers lived, in centuries past)." Well, now the world is even more closed, in the sense that homogenous modernity has flattened its differences and rendered it more uniform. Now we are always in contact with home, or almost always. Not using modern communication technologies would be as fake and inauthentic as suffering infections without using antibiotics. Our (Western) customs and habits are known almost everywhere, if not accepted. This place, Göreme, for example, is hardly part of Turkey any more, as it was in 1987. It is part of that large, gray mass that is the "modern world," the result of the entropy-producing machine of human civilization, reducing all differences, leading from a state of greater order with more distinctions to a state of lesser order with fewer distinctions, from hot and cold to lukewarm, to a world where everything is the same.[25]

OCTOBER 14, 2014

I did not write yesterday. Though I was disappointed with Göreme when I arrived two days ago, I am already starting to see some of its advantages. The hotel is nice, the topology both strange and wonderful, with the rooms hollowed out of the "fairy chimney" rock formations. The higher plateaus surrounding the town are reminiscent of the Badlands of South Dakota or the Painted Desert in the American southwest. Yesterday morning I went to breakfast on the family farm of Ali, the hotel owner. It is unlike me to take part in a group excursion, but this was an excellent experience. Ali told many anecdotes from the history of Cappadocia in general and Göreme in particular. There was no tourism to speak of prior to the late 1980s, as I knew from my visit in 1987, and he started his hotel in 1992–93. Before then, everyone worked in agriculture. "If you were poor, you had a donkey. If you were rich, you had a horse. If you were super-rich, you had a donkey and a horse!" Things started to change in the 1960s and 1970s, when

---

25. Lévi-Strauss, Claude, *Tristes tropiques,* Paris: Plon, 1955, pp. 495-7. I read this book twenty-five years ago and his description of cultural exchange in thermodynamic terms, as an increase in entropy, marked me profoundly.

there was high unemployment here and most young men went to work in Europe, hoping to save money to buy a tractor. Except that most of them never returned. Ali stayed at home, as the youngest brother in his family, taking care of his parents and starting this hotel. He could never have imagined what would follow. From carrying sacks of apricots up the steep slope from the farm in the valley to be sold, to taking a group of tourists to breakfast on that same farm, there is a lifetime. I told Ali that I had passed through here in 1987 and that it was nothing like now, and he was surprised that I had been here so long ago.

Today, despite a poor night's sleep, I got up at 7:15 AM and left for the Göreme Open Air Museum just before 8:00 AM, without breakfast. I walked quickly and arrived before any of the tour buses, one of the first visitors of the day. I found the churches, carved by eleventh-century Christian crusaders from the rock of the fairy chimneys, worthwhile for their paintings and architectural originality, but unfortunately, the "Taliban" (meaning vandals) had been there before me. Virtually every single fresco had been damaged, some perhaps centuries ago, but others recently. Some of the desecrators were even so historically minded as to leave the date next to their Turkish names, scratched into the paint of the ancient artworks. Other atrocities committed against these artworks were even more recent, as witnessed by the overwhelming stench of urine in one of the churches and several of the other buildings. And some days, perhaps tens of thousands of tourists pass through and leave thinking, "This is how Turkey cares for its historical sites." I asked for the name of the site's director, but an employee refused to tell me. I cannot help but think that it is ethnic and religious animosity that motivates this behavior. In Crete, they sell trinkets in a former mosque, money-changers defiling the Temple. In Turkey, they piss in ancient churches.

Two sources of light shone through the general darkness of this experience. First, I climbed stairs to the Maltese Cross Church, whose frescoes were solely white and red geometric designs. It was pure in its beauty, but the ill-starred architect had chosen for his church a cavity split by a cleft in the limestone through which water could seep. This church showed the wrack and ruin of the centuries, the reddish tones overcome by blue and gold fluorescing as the rock crumbled to dust, the church soon to fall victim to this decay and collapse under the weight of the surrounding stone. It was curious that the assault of the elements could render this church more beautiful than the others, or than it would otherwise have been, whereas the assault of ignorant and malevolent hands against the other churches had brought about only ugliness. There is nobility in facing off against Time and losing.

The second ray of light was the visage of a boy in the Dark Church, eyes gouged out (perhaps the vandals feared being ratted out in the afterlife by the images having seen them) but still projecting an innocence and beauty like that of Modigliani's *Fillette en bleu*. Some nameless eleventh-century artist has left us with this gift. I looked long at it, tuning out the rank sweat odor of the sole guard, there, I imagine, to prevent further indignities being visited upon the artworks. Finally, across the road from the Open Air Museum, where I fled the thirty buses of tourists which arrived near the end of my visit, there were other structures, some of them churches and some with frescoes. These were in a state of utter ruin, the open roof of one, magnificently painted with a religious fresco, serving to shelter mopeds from the afternoon rain showers. This fresco was as bright and clear, though damaged, as those inside the standing churches.

Leaving the Open Air Museum and heading back towards Göreme, I turned south on a trail and walked slowly, being tired. I was in the Zemi Valley. Just after seeing a warning about robbers, asking travelers to notify the police of any suspicious characters they see, I spotted a suspicious character some distance in front of me. He was suspicious, but was also a pig, hocking snot out of his throat in a disgusting manner. Not afraid but not eager to make his acquaintance, I retraced my steps and changed valleys. In any event, the next valley to the west provided the challenge of climbing out of it and returning to the heights around Göreme, off trail. At first, I had a blessed rest under a shady walnut tree, almost dozing off. Then I examined the terrain for a way up onto the plateau above the valley. I saw a possible route, which looked passable in both directions, key for solo climbing. One grade five move got me onto a mudstone slope, then a few dead ends, and finally I topped out on the plateau, saw the Uçisar Citadel and knew, roughly, where I was. I made my way to "Sunset Point," a place popular with tourists to watch the sunset, then walked down to Göreme.

OCTOBER 15, 2014

At dinner I am feeling better now. Yesterday was already an improvement on Monday, but today was excellent. I managed to make the stay here positive, despite the overly touristic nature of the place. What's more, I did a relatively serious walk today. I had breakfast, handed over my laundry to be washed, and packed my belongings to be moved to a new room with a nicer view. I then left the hotel and bought a bus ticket to Konya for the day after tomorrow. I intended to walk for a few hours, not expecting it to be very interesting. Thankfully, I was wrong. I started close to Göreme, past the Zemi Valley trailhead, which I took yesterday on my way home. I turned north off the road, instead of south, shortly after a horse ranch. I then saw myriad dwellings hollowed into the fairy chimneys and stone cliffs, many for pigeons, but some for humans. Ali, the hotel owner, told me that in the old days (up to the 1960s, according to him) young men would not be granted a girl to wed if they did not have a "pigeon house." In pre-modern times one of the main economic activities here was gathering pigeon droppings to be used as fertilizer. Looking at the locations of some of these pigeon houses, I cannot but respect the physical courage of those who built and used them. They are high on cliffs, hollowed out of the stone by hand, with an entrance permitting the excavation of a cavity but later bricked up except for small holes for the pigeons and another door for the "owner," who could intrude into this pigeon paradise in order to collect the droppings. Some of the access routes to these pigeon houses involved, for example, climbing a rickety ladder and then free-soloing a grade five off-width[26] crack in rotten rock. All this danger for a pile of crap!

---

26. To "free solo" means to climb with no ropes or equipment to arrest a potential fall. Climbing routes or moves are categorized by number grades, the higher the more difficult. "Off-width" means of varying and irregular width, necessitating the employment of different climbing techniques rather than the repetition of one.

The valley in which I found myself contained many pigeon houses whose internal pigeon holes had sometimes been exposed by the entire façade of the cliff crashing to earth, leaving a mass of gigantic jumbled blocks. But as I looked, I saw similar hollow spaces in the cliffs, decorated with red geometric designs like the Maltese Cross. And I realized that the same Christian soldiers whose works had merited entry into the Göreme Open Air Museum had also been active here. I climbed a steep slope, did one tricky slab move, and found myself in front of a simple carved altar decorated with the same ochre tones as the churches a kilometer to the south. I felt more holiness here than there. Solitude is holy, as is the effort often required to attain it.

I continued to keep my eyes peeled for other such structures, and saw several. Not being one to follow trails, I tried to traverse from one valley to the next, heading east. The first one was quite easy. But once on the next high plateau, I faced a dilemma. I could follow the well-trodden path to the intersection of trails overrun by tourist-laden ponies in Cavuçin, or I could strike out on my own. I chose the latter. I headed south on a path, looking for a break in the cliffs falling off to the east. I could see Rose Valley, full of tourists, and south of it, empty of people but inaccessible, Red Valley. I picked my way down steep slopes, hoping to reach it and thinking of Pierrot, my climbing teacher and a professional mountain guide, selecting his path carefully, saying, "*ça passe*" or "*ça ne passe pas.*"[27] After a steep slope of rotten mudstone with another below, I cut myself a ruler-length spike of sapling and carved a point on it, an improvised ice axe like the ones I had fashioned for myself at the southern tip of the Lofoten Islands of Norway, thirty years earlier, hoping to see the Maelstrom. I continued, reaching a place where I was fairly sure that a slide down a mudstone tube would enable me to reach the valley floor. The problem was that I was fairly sure, not *sure*. And getting back up that mudstone tube if I could not reach the valley floor seemed quite unlikely, despite my improvised climbing tool. I turned back.

I walked a three or four kilometers back to the tourist road and crossed the path of a young couple heading in the opposite direction, Leire and

---

27. French for, more or less, "it is passable" and "it is impassable."

Davide. I warned them that the path they were on was uninteresting and that they would do better to enter the valley below directly from here. They took my advice and we set off together looking for the entrance to the valley. We actually missed a turnoff to the valley, went to a road further east and then headed cross country down a *seyl* (a stream bed formed by an intermittently flowing stream) to see if we could get down to the valley floor by our own path. After a few steep sections and tight spots, we reached a three-meter drop with a ledge and pigeon house behind and an unknowable drop behind that. If the rock had been good, I would have tried it, being certain that I could climb back up safely. But with this rotten mudstone I was far from certain, even with the help of my two new-found comrades. So again I turned back and we descended the Red Valley on a well-established path that included twenty meters of vertical metal ladders. At the head of this trail, we parted ways, they northwards towards Çavuçin and Rose Valley, and I southwards towards Göreme. After a slight uncertainty, I found my way and passed.

On the road back, I decided to hitch a ride. The walk was utterly tedious and it was drizzling, yet I had great trouble forcing myself to ask the few passing cars for a lift. I made myself do it, though, and the first six or seven drivers ignored me; no eye contact, no clear refusal, just avoidance. Then a Turkish man with an older couple, judging by his manner of dress and his full beard an Islamist, picked me up. We talked a bit and he told me he was with his mother and his father, with whom he had a difficult relationship. I replied that father-son relationships were, in my experience, always difficult. He took me to Göreme; I thanked him, and left him with the formal Arabic "[Go] with peace," to which he replied in kind "[Go] with the peace of God." Then I returned to the hotel and occupied my new room. After half an hour, I met Davide and Leire for a drink. I was glad they invited me.

OCTOBER 16, 2014

Drinking a cup of coffee at the bus station. Last night with Davide and Leire, we spoke about traveling, life, society, religion. I feel now the sadness of departure, a vague unease, of longing already for what I will have left behind, will not have seen. The new vistas of the journey will open, then fall into the past, another layer in the ruins, one day to be excavated and sifted in the final instants of my life. Not many of the travelers I have seen are alone, and when they are, they are almost always men. The solitary wayfarer is an archetype. Unburdened by other people or by an excess of possessions, he goes where the wind and his will take him, free from all, but fair and kind to all, looking for something he will never find. I feel kinship with these solitary figures when I see them.

Leaving the hotel, I told the receptionist about the disgraceful state of the Göreme Open Air Museum's desecrated churches. He said it was the responsibility of the mayor, and that Ali and other prominent businessmen had already repeatedly complained. Someone should write a news article and publish it to shame the Turkish authorities. I plan to read *Mystical Dimensions of Islam* during the bus ride to Konya.

I am now in a hotel room in Konya. It is raining. It would have been ugly here anyway, but now it looks like a gloomy, industrial backwater dump of a town. What am I looking for, anyway? On the bus was a tug of war between worldly and spiritual. Worldly won. It was two against one. First, there was Wi-Fi on the bus. A $200 first-class train ticket in France does not get you Wi-Fi, but a $10 bus ticket in Turkey does. So I bounced back and forth from reading Professor Schimmel's book to surfing the internet, only some of which was for spiritual understanding. The knockout punch by the worldly side was the girl sitting in front of me, emissary from the fair courts of life. A student of economics, around twenty-five, going to Antalya. She was beautiful, and when I told her I was going to Konya, she made a face, mentioned the Whirling Dervishes, and gave me a look as if to say, "How uncool!" Afterwards, she gave me a chocolate bar. Consolation prize. Right now, I wish I had been brave enough to change my ticket and go to Antalya with her instead of getting off at Konya. Her name was Sanem, which I looked up, and means "idol."

OCTOBER 17, 2014

Breakfast. Do I just feel nostalgia for the successive waypoints on my journey, or is each place I arrive at actually worse than the preceding one? At least in Göreme, I could have decent dinners in the restaurant of a nearby boutique hotel, with good enough wine. Here in Konya, due to the city's religious heritage, no restaurants serve wine or any alcohol at all. Last night for dinner, I ate a *pide* (a sort of dry pizza sprinkled with ground meat and a few spices) with mediocre buttermilk, and then an unknown dessert, and was still hungry afterwards. The restaurant refused to serve me anything else when I asked.

The owners of the hotel are very agreeable and the hotel is clean and well-appointed. They made some of the breakfast dishes themselves from their garden, notably blackberry preserves. I am the only foreign guest here for now, though there are a few Turkish guests. Last night, there was a young Turkish woman waiting to take her bus back to Istanbul. She was thirty, lived with her parents, had just finished her MBA, but hardly spoke more than primary-school English and neither French nor Arabic. I wonder in which countries she plans to do business—presumably only in Turkey. And this morning, a Turkish family joined me for breakfast. Today I will go to the Mevlana Museum, Rumi's tomb. Jalal al-Din Rumi (1207–73) was a Sufi mystic and Persian poet of the first order. He is revered as *Maulana* ("Our Lord," *Mevlana* in Turkish) and he lived and wrote his greatest works here in Konya. Rumi had a mystical meeting with Shams al-Tabrizi which completely changed his life and which led to the composition of his poetic masterpiece, the *Mathnawi*. Ibn Battuta recounts the story of this meeting as he heard it when he passed through Konya roughly sixty years after Rumi's death:

> In that city is the mausoleum of the Sheikh, the pious Imam, the Pole Jalal al-Din [Rumi], known as Maulana. His renown is great, and in the land of Rum [Byzantine Turkey] is a [Sufi] fraternity which owes its existence to him and bears his name … It is said that he began as a legal scholar and a professor, and students came to him in his school in Konya. One day a man entered the school selling sweets, and on his head was a plate of them, cut into pieces, each for a penny. When he came to the study room, the Sheikh [Rumi] said "Bring your platter." The seller took a piece, and gave it to the Sheikh, who took it with his hand and

63

ate it. Then the seller went out before anyone else could taste the sweets. The Sheikh went out to follow him, and left his teaching, neglecting his pupils, who waited long for him. Finally, they went out looking for him but could not find him. Several years later, the Sheikh returned to them, speaking only in rhymed Persian poetry which they did not understand. His pupils followed him, and wrote down the poetry he uttered, authoring thus a book which they called "Mathnawi."[28]

I went to Rumi's tomb. I have not seen this level of saint-worship in Islamdom[29] before. Almost all of the visitors here are Muslim, and they seem to consider this place to be holy and Rumi to be nearly a god, saying prayers before his tomb with the utmost devotion. I silenced my mind and vowed to read *Mystical Dimensions of Islam* (a vow which I have kept only partially), asking for guidance once I have absorbed this introduction to Sufi textual sources. But I do not pray to men, alive or dead, prophets or fornicators. I had no trouble addressing a barbarous prayer to Zeus in the Idaeon Cave in Crete where he was raised, but Zeus was a god. I will not pray to Jesus, Mohammad, or Rumi. I can understand, when seeing this place, how strong the tendency is to *shirk* (polytheistic idolatry, abhorred by strict Islamic doctrine) and why strict Sunni Muslims take such an absolute stance against it. A rational religious person (is this an oxymoron?) must separate respect for history from idol-worship.

On a separate topic, it is interesting here to note a significant negative effect of Atatürk's reforms. The Turkish visitors here are totally cut off from their own past history and high culture, and are unable to read Arabic or Ottoman Turkish at all, even simply for pronunciation. In Europe, the loss of Latin literacy was slow and progressive, whereas here the loss of Arabic and Ottoman Turkish literacy happened within one generation. Modern Turks cannot read texts written before 1930 in their own language. My opinion of the reforms is still positive overall,

---

28. Harb, pp. 309-10. Author's translation.

29. The term "Islamdom," meaning "the domain of Islam," analogous to Christendom, was coined by Marshall G.S. Hodgson in his great sweeping historical work, *The Venture of Islam.*

but it is troubling to see an entire culture separated from its past.

As I was about to leave, years of study granted me an unexpected moment of intellectual joy. Arabic calligraphy has always been difficult for me to read, and here, with the added complexity of not being certain whether it is Arabic, Persian, or Ottoman Turkish, it is even harder. My pleasure was therefore great when I started to understand the text engraved in stone on the tomb of Hurrem Pasha Turkesi (the consort of a Turkish Pasha)—it was the *Ayat al-Kursi*, the "Throne Verse" from the Qur'an, and I was able to follow it through to the end although the crypt room was dark and the letters carved in a flowery manner.

I am now at the Hilton Hotel in Konya. I have successfully infiltrated the Small Ruminants Congress, and I scored an illicit mind-altering substance as well. After leaving the Mevlana Museum, I decided to walk to the Culture Center, where the *Sema*[30] (Whirling Dervish ceremony, from the Arabic word for "to listen") will be held tomorrow night. Adam, from the hotel where I am staying, said there was a Hilton near the Culture Center, so I hoped to find an oasis there from the Prohibition conditions prevailing in the rest of Konya. After confirming the location of the *Sema* and heading toward the Hilton, I saw a bizarre sign, "Small Ruminants Congress," featuring a picture of a kid holding a baby goat (pun intended). I did not realize that congresses on ruminants were divided into large and small. I suppose the Large Ruminants Congress might show the boy riding a cow? I walked through the metal detector guarding the entrance to the Congress with my bag and my knife without setting it off. Perhaps it was calibrated to detect only pipe bombs or assault rifles. I then proceeded to infiltrate the Congress, reading the abstracts of the talks being delivered, mingling and chatting with the participants. They had come from all over the world, France, the US, Egypt, here to Konya. Presumably someone in the event organizing department of some far-away university will be fired for this choice of location when the boss gets home. I hope they will not all be at the *Sema* tomorrow night, but they probably will be. (It turned

---

30. *Sema* is a particular expression of *dhikr*, remembrance of God, of the Mevlevi Sufis, the Sufi order founded by Rumi's immediate successors in the thirteenth century, which involves whirling to chanting and music. Sufism itself is Islamic mysticism. There has historically been tension between traditional Islamic legal doctrine and the actions and words of Sufi mystics, which in some cases has led to the latter being accused of heresy or even put to death.

out that they were better informed than I was, and did not attend.) I thought to gatecrash their lunch as well, but the sight of a well-stocked bar diverted my attention, and here I sit drinking an Efes (Turkish beer) while waiting for my lunch to arrive.

After leaving the Congress I read then went out for dinner. This restaurant is vaunted as being one of Konya's best, partly due to the wonderful terrace with a view of the Mevlana Museum. The terrace was closed, and instead I am in a room with fluorescent lights that looks like a bathroom. It has a strong smell of a cleaning product one would associate with a bathroom as well. They bring my appetizer and main course at the same time. Both are passable, but Konya really hasn't developed culinary culture the way Göreme has. There is something, after all, to the development of tourism. Konya offers only cheap food, nothing fine. Tomorrow I will have dinner at the Hilton, with alcohol. The food will probably not be any better but the alcohol should prevent my noticing it. Then I will go to the *Sema* ceremony. And then on Sunday night, Sifa, the "Turkish McDonalds," which is looking pretty good right now. Most of the world is so utterly boring. I do not know how I traveled so long through it before. To make matters worse, a group of tourists has just entered this Toilet Dining Room.

OCTOBER 18, 2014

Last night after dinner I took a walk. Slowly circling a wide radius due to the wall around the Mevlana Museum with its magnificent turquoise phallic dome, struggling to read the *thulth*-style Arabic calligraphy around it. And there it was. Again. The *Ayat al-Kursi*! It is one of the simplest and most beautiful verses of the Qur'an, which even an atheist, if he or she appreciates poetry, cannot be unmoved by:

God! There is no god but Him: the Living, the Eternal. Neither slumber nor sleep can seize him. To Him belongs all that is in the Heavens and all that is in the Earth. Who may intercede with Him except as He permitteth? He knoweth that which is between their hands, and that which is behind them. Nor shall they compass aught of his knowledge, except as He willeth. His throne doth extend over the heavens and the earth, and the preservation of them both tireth him not. He is the Exalted, the Supreme. Q 2:255.

Translations of Arabic scripture never do justice to the original, seemingly even less so than other translations. I loitered in the plaza in front of the museum and watched people enter and exit the mosque, which did not exist in Rumi's time. I imagine all the rest of the surrounding noise was not here either, as the dervishes lived in their simple cells in the structure around the mausoleum. These cells are better in almost every respect than the rooms I stayed in during my 1987 trip.

I finally returned to the hotel to read and write. I read *Mystical Dimensions of Islam*, read about Professor Schimmel, its author, and then slept. She really does seem to have been a "saint," as one of her students at Harvard, whom I knew when I was there, described her. She knew from a very young age that she wanted to study oriental languages and Sufism, and she devoted her entire life to these subjects, becoming a worldwide authority. I was interested in descriptions of the mystical experience of *fana'*,[31] annihilation, and looked for them in the book. One of the quotations I found was so stunning that I had to repeat it to myself several times before I could fit it into my mind. It draws a distinction between two types of advanced Sufis:

...the distinction made in speaking of the two types of advanced Sufis: some are those to whom the Primordial Grace and Lovingkindness has granted salvation after their being submerged in complete union and in the wave of tauhid (unification with God), taking them out of the belly of the fish "Annihilation" on the shore of separation and in the arena of permanent subsistence, so that they might lead the people towards salvation. The others are those who are completely submerged in the ocean of Unity

---

31. *Fana'* is an Arabic word with the technical Sufi meaning of "cessation of being" or "passing away."

and have been so completely naughted in the belly of the fish
"Annihilation" that never a news or trace comes to the shore of
separation and the direction of subsistence ... and the sanctity of
perfecting others is not entrusted to them.[32]

Professor Schimmel took this citation from *Nafahat al-Uns* by Maulana
Abdulrahman Jami, from the fifteenth century. I find it of almost unique
weirdness and purity, with a clear debt to the Buddhist concept of
Boddhisatva, similar to these enlightened Sufis who return to lead the
people towards salvation.

Today at 9:30 AM, Hallil came to take me to Çatalhöyük. Hallil is an
English teacher recommended by the hotel who sometimes guides travelers
around Konya. Çatalhöyük is a Neolithic archaeological site, one of the
most important in the world, inhabited from around 8500 BCE to 5600
BCE. It is twenty meters high and comprises eighteen levels of structures,
a huge mound on the Anatolian plain, perhaps ten percent excavated.
The settlement pattern is unusual, with successive levels being filled in,
ancestors buried in the rubble under the living room floor, and a new level
constructed over them. There were apparently few streets, access to the
structures being from the rooftops, which formed a large platform area
with ladders down into the houses. The earlier periods of settlement were
from the Aceramic (prior to the development of pottery) Neolithic. The
settlement was seemingly organized into coherent "neighborhoods," and
many wall paintings were discovered, as well as the intra-structure burials.
Çatalhöyük was discovered in 1958 by James Mellaart, but since 1993
has been the subject of extremely detailed archaeological research led by
Professor Ian Hodder of Stanford. This research effort integrates a variety
of sophisticated analytical methods in order to establish an understanding
of the context of life at the site that would never have been possible in earlier
archaeological research. It concerns subjects such as the precise diet of the
inhabitants, the species of plants cultivated and of animals domesticated,
the climate, chipped stone industries and the sources of their raw materials,
the development of pottery, and attempts to deduce social structures from

32. Schimmel, pp. 6-7.

physical ones.[33] To me, as remarkable as Çatalhöyük itself was that, on the way there, around eight kilometers north/north-east, I had seen another mound, similarly huge in size. On the way back, I asked Hallil to stop so we could look at it, and we hiked up to the top. The ground was strewn with innumerable pottery shards. There were even some human finger bones, phalanges, lying open to the air. This site, which I learned later was named Boncuklu Höyük, seemed not to have been excavated at all, except by a local farmer, who, according to Hallil's guess, wanted to try out his new tractor plough and made two shallow furrows around eighty meters long through the surface of the ground.[34] So much work still to be done to understand! For a North American, and to a lesser extent for a European, this is unbelievable, this ubiquity of ancient civilizations and artifacts. If I had been a child here, I would have conducted my own illicit excavations and would surely have ended up with a collection of grave-robbed human skulls and other contraband.

It is after *Sema*, the ceremony of the Whirling Dervishes. I feel lost. I don't know what I am. I am not a scholar. Not a businessman. Not an adventurer. Nor seemingly a traveler any more. I despised the *Sema*, absolutely hated it. A canned muzak soundtrack with a bunch of bozos pretending to play instruments while other bozos danced. Each "dervish" whirled in his own manner, out of synch with the others. I do not imagine Rumi would have been very happy—nothing ecstatic here, no Divine Love, no *fana'*, nothing. Not even real music. I felt the urge to end the suffering of boredom through self-euthanasia. A man I woke up when arriving, who then moved past me on the same row of seats during the performance, woke me in turn as he was leaving halfway through it. I had chosen sleep rather than death as a way out of the *Sema* purgatory. It was even worse than long business meetings. The audience was almost all Turkish tourists, I imagine the same ones who prayed to Rumi at the mausoleum. I didn't

33. During, pp. 84-121. I conducted a brief email correspondence with Professor Hodder about Çatalhöyük and about Göbekli Tepe.

34. *Ibid*, pp. 76-7. During mentions excavations at Boncuklu Höyük but absolutely none were visible to me. Perhaps they were back-filled after being completed. During also states that Boncuklu Höyük was contemporaneous with the earlier stages of settlement at Çatalhöyük, roughly 8500 BCE to 7500 BCE.

ascertain whether or not they were moved by the ceremony. Perhaps *fana'* is relative and they attained it while I slumbered.

The horrid ceremony initiated a cycle of self-doubt and anxiety in my consciousness. I miss music. I miss wine. I miss home. I feel like the organization of my trip was poor. I gathered some wonderful moments, the longest at Hattuşa, but in between were long periods of boredom. I do not know where this leaves me for the next trip, if there is one. Archaeology? Travel? Where? I feel like I would have done just as well to have stayed at home. The only unequivocal benefit is that I had decided to try to travel and write, and I have tried, keeping my word to myself. And Hattuşa. Aside from that, this feels pretty much like failure to me. Perhaps my view will be revised later if the key moments grow in importance as time passes.

OCTOBER 19, 2014

Before recounting the past twenty-four hours, a word on mood swings while traveling. During my six-month trip in 1987–88 I learned how to manage my own psychological states, as I believed and saw demonstrated to me that positive states of mind attract positive experiences and vice-versa. I can no longer do this with regularity in my daily life at home. During this trip, I have seen an outline of the cycles of my inner state, with last night's disgusting dinner and the awful *Sema* tourist ceremony as the lowest point of the trip. Today, I started out feeling sad, but came out of the trough and feel better now. I went out with the aim of exploring the main monuments of Konya other than the Mevlana Museum. I succeeded in this aim, and in riding the energy of the experience back up the sine curve of the cyclicality of inner life. I walked down Mevlana Street, first to the Karatay Madrasa, built in the mid-thirteenth century by a high-ranking person of that name. It also serves now as a museum for the magnificent Ottoman art of tile-making. I find it remarkable how humanity is able to latch onto something simple then develop and refine it to an extreme level. The actual thing being developed and refined is almost totally arbitrary. What makes civilization is the refinement itself, the creation and recognition of differing degrees of attainment in a defined art, like tilework, calligraphy, or fine wine. The Ottoman Turks refined tilework to an extremely high degree, perhaps one of its apogees in history. The only other tilework I have seen which attains the same expressive power as that here was in Istanbul, so also Ottoman, and in the cemetery at Makli Hill in the Sind province of Pakistan. I know that Iran also has magnificent examples of this art as well, and I hope one day to see them.

These beautiful tiles are an illustration of the value of travel. Even in this day of immediate and ubiquitous information, there is no substitute for direct experience. While I could surely find out more facts about the Karatay Madrasa online than at the madrasa itself, I could not see the depth of hue and subtlety of tone of the tiles except in person with my own eyes, not mediated by a printing press or a computer screen. And in certain places, fired bricks form the background with a few glazed bricks interspersed, probably on grounds of economy, the burnt red background rendering the turquoise glazing all the more resplendent. I was again pleased to read the *Ayat al-Kursi* around the archway of the main vaulted chamber in the Karatay Madrasa. I went out and continued around Ala'eddin Hill, to the Ince Minare Madrasa. This building seems of poorer construction, employing notably more simple kiln-fired bricks and fewer tiles, but with beautiful stone calligraphy at the doorway. Inside were many examples of masonry, mainly tombs, but also carved wooden panels from the thirteenth century. The calligraphic tile inscriptions from the Qur'an were in *kufi* style, utterly impossible for me to read. *Thulth* calligraphy is hard enough, but *kufi* might as well be Chinese.

My third destination was the Ala'eddin Mosque on the top of the hill of the same name. Apparently, in Seljuk times (eleventh to thirteenth centuries) there was a wall around this hill. For all I know, the hill might be a tumulus full of the ruins of that city, or prior ones. As I approached the mosque, around one of its cupolas was once more the *Ayat al-Kursi*. When I entered, I was surprised not to sense any religious feeling. Young men were messing with their phones and even horsing around. This mosque is a utilitarian structure. Arches of burnt brick sitting on marble pillars borrowed from former civilizations, probably Byzantine, though perhaps some Roman. But the *mihrab*, the niche in the direction of Mecca towards which prayer is directed, was different: beautiful blue and turquoise tiles, flowery *thulth* script of, again, those beautiful verses. I have been accompanied on this journey by the *Ayat al-Kursi*, as the wayfarer in the desert is accompanied by the unchanging moon. I see it on graves, on lost turquoise moonshine domes, inscribed on walls and on archways facing Mecca. From the first time I read these lines, I found them so essential, so simple in their expression of the adoration of God and His Creation, and the smallness of man. I know no other words that are so pure and so beautiful in this expression. They could almost convince a modernist sceptic like me of the primal uncreated nature of the Qur'an.

Before leaving the mosque, I strolled through its grounds. At a small decagonal tower, all locked up, I peered through and saw the tombs of one...two...three...four...five Sultans...just like that. There were around ten of them, a couple of centuries' worth of Seljuk Sultans lined up next to each other in regal sarcophagi meant to reign alone, now like sardines in a tin. After leaving the mosque, I sat on a tree stump in the sun. It was a cold day, and windy, the first such day of this trip, and I had not dressed warmly enough. So these moments in the warm sun were heaven's benediction. Tired of Turkish food and having spied a different type of arch earlier in the day, I returned towards the Ince Minare Madrasa and had lunch at McDonald's. No calligraphy on the Golden Arches.

I took a taxi back to the hotel, and on my way saw a sign for the tomb of Shams of Tabriz, realizing that I had forgotten it. I rested, had an excellent meditation, read, and then went out again before dinner. I located the tomb, which is in a very small and simple mosque. While approaching it I saw another, yet smaller, tomb. It was that of Ishak Pasha. I paid my respects, as in 1987, I had visited his remarkable palace in Doğubayazit. Given the pomp accorded to Rumi and his son, it seems odd that Shams is neglected in this manner. But those who built the monuments may have been the same who are suspected of assassinating Shams, which would explain the slight. Coleman Barks, poetic interpreter of Rumi, wrote that one was supposed to visit Shams' tomb before that of Rumi, which I had not done. I set off at a brisk pace to get to Mevlana before closing time, and succeeded. I walked through it again, and again was struck by the literal idolatry of the pilgrims. I left the mausoleum and looked long at the fluted turquoise dome. It is unique and beautiful, and the dark blue tiles with white *thulth* calligraphy, curved to follow the fluting, are magnificent. On it, the *Ayat al-Kursi* is preceded by the *Bismillah*[35] and followed by *Sadaq Allah al-ʿathim*, which does not seem so common, as the *Ayat al-Kursi* is usually quoted alone. Tomorrow I leave for Ankara, and the next day for home. I feel a traveler even when at home now. I look around me at the ebb and flow of the daily lives of others, and feel a stranger.

---

35. The first line of the *Fatiha*, the first *surat* of the Qur'an, is "In the name of God, the Compassionate, the Merciful." This line is referred to as the *Bismillah*. *Sadaq Allah al-ʿathim*, traditionally spoken after reading the Qur'an, means "Thus certifies God Almighty."

3

ISTANBUL

I LEFT HOME HAVING PREPARED THE HOUSE for a spell of emptiness, went to the airport, had a sandwich, and boarded my flight uneventfully. Now I am at a hotel in Istanbul, right on Taksim Square. Each time I have come to Turkey so far, I have been impressed by what I see as an economic phenomenon which plays to the advantage of developing countries. The fact that these countries have invested in their capital stock very recently means that it is all new. The Turkish Airlines plane coming here was a Boeing 737-800, the most recent generation of 737. The hotel is new, with modern design, high-quality workmanship, a beautiful view. The fact that such economies have been rapidly growing means that there are jobs, and the fact that they were recently poor means that the people really want to work, and that there are no rigid and growth-destroying laws such as there are in France. In several respects, it seems possible for a country like Turkey to catch up with and surpass a country like France. This hotel, in the center of the capital, is very reasonably priced. My luggage was in the room before I was. The staff paid attention. In France, you might expect this service at the top end of the hotel market, but not in the middle.

FEBRUARY 1, 2015

Cities are more beautiful at night. The darkness hides the squalor. This morning is hazy and windy, my east-facing room illuminated by the grey sun, the ropes of a window-washing apparatus suspended from the roof whipping against the side of the building in the wind. An arm of sea, one of several around Istanbul, separates the land where I am from another. It is traversed by numerous boats whose passengers must either be old hands or seasick with the wind and waves today.

I have just occupied a small apartment which will be my home for the next two weeks. Its Spartan simplicity gave me a strange feeling of euphoria. A new life. Empty cupboards. Space to colonize, but not too much. In the center of a living city I do not know. Strangers. I am no one. The young man who works here, Anas, came to pick me up at the hotel and we walked here in around ten minutes. I was speaking English with him when he said he was from Syria, so we spoke Arabic. I spoke with him almost fluently, which felt strange. Sometimes he spoke too fast, treating me as a native speaker, and I had to slow him down, nonetheless a tacit compliment. This small apartment gives me a similar feeling to a "Small White Room," from a prior journey, about which I wrote the following poem:

> I want to live in a small white room
> Decorated with silence and emptiness.
> Stick-figure furniture:
>> A bookshelf with room for ideas yet to be thought,
>> A corner kitchen for preparing simple meals,
>> A bed for pleasure, and for rest,
>> And a wall of windows to admit joy.
> Nothing here is mine, nor can cause unrest.
> Pure uncluttered space,
> To be filled with the life I choose.
> This is youth.

I just returned from a reconnaissance mission to the Turkish language school I will start attending tomorrow. Or rather a mission to the place where I thought the school was supposed to be. I couldn't find it, and now I have a headache, a taste of exhaust fumes and street dust in my mouth, and a dull warm feeling on my face as if it had been sandblasted at low intensity. The weather is awful. Strong wind, with rain soon to come. At least when it rains, the dust will fall back to the ground. Yesterday, I was impressed at the economic dynamism of Turkey and thought that such a country could catch up with and overtake more developed countries with socialistic economic rigidities. Today, I think it will take a few more generations. There is still a very large cultural gap, starting with cleaning the streets and abolishing the throwing of rubbish out of windows and onto the roofs of neighboring structures (an old Egyptian favorite I noticed while living in Cairo). I still have to go out again to eat dinner, and I so little relish the thought that I may just eat one of the prefabricated soups I bought. I should have bought some wine but didn't, nor did I buy an umbrella. A stupid oversight.

After dinner I descended from euphoria to disappointment and doubt. Why did I come here? I could have gone anywhere at all. The city is so crowded, mostly with men doing nothing, sitting around in public spaces, talking, smoking. Many of them have an excuse. They are Syrian refugees who moved here to escape the devastation in their country. More than half of the store employees here are Arabic-speakers, Syrians or Iraqis, while the stores' owners are Turks. At least using Arabic, I can buy food more easily than if there were only Turks. I made my own "dinner" after the fashion of Afghan refugees with whom I stayed in 1987 during their own cataclysmic war: I made soup and then filled it with broken pieces of pita bread. Except for the fact that I misunderstood the Turkish instructions on the soup and ended up eating crunchy rather than soft meatballs (confusing "seconds" with "minutes"), it was passably good. I washed it down with an Efes beer and now am sated. Now I will begin reading the Turkish grammar I bought some months ago, and which sat as a reddish decoration on my desk for all that time. I do not feel motivated and again question why I am doing this, creating a duty where none existed. Time will tell if it was a valid choice.

FEBRUARY 3, 2015

I wake up here in this wilderness of humanity more alone than on the high plains of Tibet or the empty mountains of Jotunheimen. My solitude is reinforced by the togetherness of others. Not that I know that they are "together"; they are just here, in their thousands, milling about aimlessly, having lost what cannot be found, cut off from their past and perhaps not wanting the future allotted to them, in a kind of transition which may last their entire lives. They are refugees and I feel like one too, though clearly I have no idea of what it must be to be uprooted as they have been. This neighborhood is depressing, its tourist apartments, one of which I am renting, having been transformed into the Syrian refugee quarter. When war forces people to flee, it also depletes or completely destroys the value of their main capital asset, their home. So these people must be living off whatever mobile capital they managed to carry or transfer, spending it to survive over the coming days and months. Much of the Arab world is like this now. There are Arabs here from Syria, from Iraq, from Libya, from Egypt. No place is home.

Yesterday, I had my first Turkish class. I enjoyed it but felt sad afterwards. It is a pleasure to learn a new language. Languages are arbitrary but systematic structures, and there is no best place to start when you learn one. I started learning about "home," buildings, floors, possessives, locative case endings, and the like. My knowledge should expand from there like a drop of oil on the surface of water, covering, if I spend the necessary time and effort, the entirety of the language. Yet in this case, it won't, as I do not have sufficient time. My teacher, Meriç, is nice but a bit disorganized. There is one other student, Sanaa, a refugee from Libya who is living here and so decided to learn the language of her host country. After class, I had lunch in Saray, a decent restaurant on Istiklal (an Arabic word meaning "independence") street. I had a *döner kebap*, an excellent dish made of fine slices of meat, then Turkish coffee, and a Turkish sweet for dessert, half of which I brought home as it was too much. Then I returned to my apartment in the rain and worked. I felt a certain relief at having a duty to perform since I do not really know what to do with myself here. The invented duty of reading my Turkish grammar did not compete well with the one which puts bread on the table.

Last night, I took a taxi, for an hour stuck in traffic, to meet a Saudi friend and colleague here on business. We smoked *shisha* and I had a whisky to relax my nerves after the horrible mental machinations brought on by sitting in a taxi breathing exhaust fumes. Then we went to a restaurant for a fine Turkish dinner, got caught in an enormous hailstorm that turned the roads to rivers, and went to his hotel to continue our discussion. I came home around 10:30 PM, slept, and just got up now. I feel alienated and sad, and wonder if I should have come here at all. The "milk" I bought turned out to be buttermilk. I have nothing against buttermilk, but it is quite a shock to eat your morning cereal with buttermilk. I do not understand myself. I live in a beautiful house on the French Riviera, with a large piece of land around it. Nature, sun, and pleasant solitude, interspersed with the visits of friends or family. My wife and I appreciate fine food and eat very well, and have a superb wine collection. Why then, malcontent at home, do I feel impelled to leave, to live in an ugly, dilapidated, filthy neighborhood with Syrian refugees, eat lousy food and breathe exhaust fumes? It would be better if at least I were happy doing this, which I was when I arrived, but am no longer.

After class, I came back to my apartment, did some work, then meditated and became annoyed with the perennial smell of cigarette smoke in my apartment. I wandered the streets, aware of many Syrians. I looked for a place to have an aperitif. Finding the hotel bars empty, I settled on an Irish pub. An Irish pub in Turkey. I ordered a Jameson and struck up a conversation with the owner whose name was Mehmet. He was a Kurd. I told him that I had been in eastern Turkey in October at the time of the siege of Kobani, and that I was happy his people had retaken their city from Islamic State. He said that they did not even deserve the name of "animals" and that the Kurds would crush them. I hope he is right. He was a civil engineer, traveling for work in many countries, and chose a calmer life by opening this pub. His wife is Irish, which must have helped in the decision. His employees are also Kurds, all polite and conscientious. It is reassuring that despite Turkey's discrimination against Kurds, this is not so serious as to prevent a person from running an apparently successful business in the capital. I will return to this pub while I am here.

I walked through the streets with the Jameson and a Talisker warming my stomach. Several times, I passed a young refugee mother and her baby sitting on the pavement in the cold. She looked at me plaintively but asked for nothing, humble and gentle. After calling my family, I went and gave her some money. She thanked and blessed me in Arabic (she was from Syria), and I felt I had done something good. Then, some distance further, another mother, this time *muhajaba* (wearing the Muslim headscarf) and carrying her baby, blocked my way. I couldn't, in fairness, ignore her, so I gave her the same amount as I had given to the first woman, but not only did she not express gratitude, she followed me and continued to demand more, saying that she had two children. I asked where she was from and she answered Syria. Then I said, "I have given you *sadaqa*. You should not demand more. Peace be with you." In Islam, charity is a multi-faceted religious duty, from *zakat*, which is the formal giving of (financial) alms to the poor and one of the "five pillars" of Islam[1] to *sadaqa*, voluntary and supererogatory charity which can take many forms: financial assistance, material help with a task, even the imparting of knowledge. Throughout the Qur'an are interwoven exhortations to charity, such as that in *Surat al-Doha*, one of the most beautiful:

Did He not find thee an orphan, and care for thee? And He found thee lost, and guided thee. And He found thee needy and enriched thee. So for the orphan, do not scorn him. And for the petitioner, do not repulse him ... Q 93:5-9.

---

1. Traditionally, Islam is said to have "five pillars": the profession of faith affirming the one God and Mohammad as his prophet *(shahada)*; the five daily prayers *(salat)*; giving charity to the poor *(zakat)*; fasting during the holy month of Ramadan *(sawm)*; and making the pilgrimage to Mecca, for all those who are able *(hajj)*. The primary source for the five pillars is the *Hadith Jibril*, or *hadith* of the Angel Gabriel, who takes human form and descends to teach the early Muslims their religion in a discussion with the Prophet. Interestingly, this *hadith* also gives two portents of the coming of the "Hour," the Day of Judgment. One of these signs is the most remarkable, indeed the only, occurrence I have ever seen of a detailed and specific prediction from an ancient text which has actually come to pass, namely, "... and you will see the barefoot, naked, destitute shepherds compete in erecting tall buildings." The Bedouin tribes of Eastern Arabia are exactly the people meant here, and the highest building in the world was recently constructed in Dubai. See Al-Nawawi (Arabic text with translation by Ezzedin Ibrahim and Denys Johnson-Davies), *Forty Hadith*. Beirut: Dar al-Manar, 1976. Hadith 2, pp. 31-2.

In the *hadith*[2] likewise are such exhortations, such as this, a *hadith qudsi* selected by Ibn Arabi,[3] also of exceptional beauty:

God, ever exalted is He, says: "I accept the prayer of one who is humble before My grandeur, who does not seek to subjugate My creation, who does not spend the night persisting in disobedience, who passes his days in My remembrance, who is merciful to the poor, to the son of the road, to the widow, and to all those who suffer misfortune. The light of such a one is as the light of the sun. I shall preserve him by My might, and shall protect him with My angels. I shall give him light where there is darkness, and forbearance where there is ignorance. His likeness amidst My creation resembles the highest of all the gardens in Paradise."[4]

I had dinner in a restaurant which proclaimed itself one of the best restaurants in Turkey, citing various "objective" sources. The food was mediocre. Information asymmetries abound, and are very hard to eliminate. After dinner I walked home and bought a bottle of Chivas whisky in a well-stocked liquor shop I had spotted earlier. I managed to trick the shopkeeper into thinking I spoke Turkish, greeting him with *"Al-Salam 'aleikum,"* then *"Ne kadar Chivas?"* ("How much for the Chivas?"). He replied with an incomprehensible stream of phonemes, which made me proud (as it meant he had understood me and presumed I would understand him), then I laughed and changed to Arabic.

---

2. As previously mentioned, a *hadith* is a story about or saying of the Prophet Muhammad. A *hadith qudsi* is a *hadith* which is considered to be the actual word of God, like the Qur'an. Early Islamic scholars developed the collection and analysis of *hadith* into a "science," and compiled very large volumes of them. The *hadith* literature, collectively known as the *Sunnah*, came to constitute the second primary source of Islamic law after the Qur'an itself.

3. Ibn Arabi is known as *Al-Sheikh Al-Akbar, "the Greatest Master."* Born in twelfth-century Andalusia, he was one of Islam's greatest mystics and is revered as a saint by Sufis. He was also one of Islam's most prolific intellectuals, writing on classical philosophy and theology in addition to mysticism. There is a story that, as a child, Ibn Arabi met Ibn Rushd, who was a generation his senior and represents the current of rational philosophy in Islam, whereas Ibn Arabi came to represent directly revealed knowledge, as did Al-Ghazzali, Ibn Rushd's main intellectual adversary.

4. Ibn Arabi, Muhi al-Din (Arabic text and translation by Stephen Hirtenstein and Martin Notcutt), *Divine Sayings, 101 Hadith Qudsi.* Oxford: Anqa Publishing, 2004, p. 40. Arabic text. Translation by the author.

I did not write yesterday. My Turkish classes are progressing well. So far I have had four days of lessons, have an idea of the nominal system, a decent command of the present tense, and an overview of the rest of the verbal system. Languages are interesting to me. They all seem to share certain primordial characteristics: they are arbitrary, mapping a well-defined world of objects and experiences into a less well-defined world of ideas and concepts by literally any path at all; they are redundant, with grammatical structures very rarely being limited to those necessary to communicate information (for example, in some languages using noun declensions, such as Turkish, word order can still be important and imposed, yielding significant redundancy); and they are human, with all of the irregularities, nonsensical qualities and capacity for beauty which humanity can muster. I learn languages very fast, perhaps faster than systems organized in a more linear manner, for reasons I do not understand.

I don't like the district in which I am living. The rubbish on the street, uninhabited shells of buildings and awful smells wafting over the air bring back bad memories of Cairo. The Syrian refugees here probably notice most the absence of gunfire, pockmarks on walls, or rotting corpses. To them it is a haven. To me a dump. The population here is transient. Only the shopkeepers seem to belong here. The stories of those who pass through are uncountable. Some, like me, are travelers who landed here by a combination of chance and economy. Others are injured men from the civil wars raging in Iraq and Syria, and yet others uninjured but harboring a dazed look in their eyes, and a hardness which evokes experiences I have thankfully been spared. Some are young families, shipwrecked on this coast with their babies whose future is unknown. A neighborhood like this is a metaphor for the transience of life, and I take it as a lesson. Realizing life's transience is important, but to integrate it into one's world-view too deeply is defeatist. Why pick up the rubbish if you will be gone tomorrow?

Yesterday after class, I went out into the bright day and took a taxi to visit Rumeli Hisari, an Ottoman fortress conceived to block enemy shipping to Constantinople. By (bad) luck, it was closed, but I decided nonetheless to walk around. The districts out that way, around ten kilometers north of Taksim, are beautiful. No litter in the streets. No stench of rotting garbage. Trees. Nice houses. Nice cars. Nice-looking kids leaving school or playing in the park. It looks like a wealthy part of Europe. From dogs eating rotting garbage and men pulling refuse carts in my neighborhood (it remains a mystery to me why they let some piles of garbage rot in the streets while they pick up others—probably garbage collection is a private and not a public service) to the new BMW M4 and Mercedes S-class parked in front of a trendy restaurant here. One of the edifying experiences of traveling is that the traveler can traverse the various social classes in a foreign country much more readily than is possible at home. In New York, it would be quite unlikely for me to stay in the Bronx or Harlem and eat lunch at the Four Seasons, or vice-versa. Here I am doing just that. One sees a different "Turkey" in my neighborhood than in that of Etiler or Emirgan or Rumeli Hisari. I do not regret my experience, but next time I will live in one of the nicer places.

For reasons I do not fully grasp, I have not been feeling well on this trip. My mood changes have not followed their normal cyclicality, as I have been feeling bad more often than usual. The noise and stink and ugliness bother me, but also the transaction cost each time I want to go somewhere. Ten-minute taxi rides turn into an hour, which then dissuades me from making the next visit. I'm also psychologically destabilized by my inability to rock climb. It has been more than two months now since I have climbed, due to an injury to my foot. I know it is best to let it heal, but I feel that one of the pillars of my balance and well-being has been removed. Today I had my class, came home and worked, and then sat to write this. I then went out, wandered around Taksim, and ate dinner in the Irish pub. They made a perfectly creditable steak and fries, accompanied by two draft Carlsberg beers (Guinness would have been too heavy).

FEBRUARY 7, 2015

Today is Saturday. My apartment smells of cigarette smoke again and my sinuses hurt. Yesterday, I had my final Turkish class of the week.

My progress is quite rapid, and I am convinced that I could become functionally fluent in six to eight months of full-time study. I would not be able to read complex texts except in my areas of specialization due to vocabulary, but would be able to speak well and read uncomplicated texts. I do not know if this is a goal I want to pursue. There are pros and cons. For pros, Turkish and the other related Turkic languages span a part of the world which has always interested me, Central Asia, from Mongolia to Istanbul. If I attained a decent level in Turkish I could probably communicate on a basic level with most of the Turkic people in these places. It would also advance my knowledge of the Middle East in general, constituting my second regional language. On the con side, it could distract me from my goal of writing this book. In one respect, it is an investment decision—are the years I have left sufficient to earn a return on the investment of time that learning Turkish would require? If I could only learn it at this school in this neighborhood, the answer would be a simple "no," but there are other possibilities which render it an attractive option: a better neighborhood in Istanbul, Antalya, or elsewhere.

After class yesterday I invited my teacher, Meriç, to lunch. A pleasant person and a good teacher, she is twenty-six, and said she was considering moving to Switzerland, where her boyfriend lives. I told her that in my opinion Switzerland is almost in a category by itself in human development. After lunch I looked up the addresses of the local climbing gyms. Misfortune: the nearest one was listed on Google Maps as being twenty-four minutes away by car. Using the mean of the prior ratios between estimated times and actual times spent in traffic jams yielded an estimated transit time of seventy-two to ninety-six minutes. I was demoralized. Then I thought to check if the Metro passed near the gym. So I called the gym and was told it would be easy to use the Metro. I set out, bought my Metro card from a man outside the station next to the pretzel vendors, and went into the station. Everything was clearly indicated and I assumed that the electronic machines along some of the passages would charge my card with credits. I put $8 into one, and a nice girl helped me because the "English" function didn't work. I then took the metro to Dört Levent and found the climbing gym. It was not very well-equipped, but the people there were welcoming and I climbed

for nearly two hours, taking rests and not doing anything too hard. I
have got weaker since my injury.

This morning, waking after a good sleep, I lazed around, read, then
went out for lunch and brought my Turkish language materials with me to
the restaurant, as well as the book of Ibn Battuta's travels that I had been
studying in Arabic before coming to Turkey. I was very happy with the
restaurant and will return. It did not claim to be great on a sign outside, but
its food was much better than the one that did. After an hour of studying
Turkish I turned to Ibn Battuta. Along with Marco Polo, Richard Burton,
and Sven Hedin, he is one of my archetypal travelers. Ibn Battuta sought
and found real strangeness in the world, and was moved by it. I reread one
of my favorite passages; in India he witnessed the suicide by immolation of
three widows, so shocking to him that he almost fell off his horse:

> And when the three (recently widowed) women, whom we have
> mentioned, determined to immolate themselves, they remained
> three days in singing and rejoicing, eating and drinking, as if they
> were saying "adieu" to the world. Women from all around came to
> them. And on the morning of the fourth day, a horse was brought to
> each one and she mounted it, perfumed and adorned with fineries.
> In her right hand was a coconut, with which she played, and in her
> left was a mirror, in which she gazed upon the reflection of her face.
> The Brahmins smiled upon her, and her loved ones stayed close
> by her. Before her sounded drums and trumpets and horns. And
> all of the people said to her: "When you reach the other world,
> please give my greetings of peace to my father, or my brother, or
> my mother, or my friend." She would reply: "Yes, I will," and would
> laugh gently to them.

> I mounted my horse and went with my companions to attend this
> event and see how it would occur when they would be burned.
> We went with the three women, around three miles, and stopped
> in a place of shadows, with much water and many trees, in deep
> shade. Among the trees were four cupolas, and under each cupola
> a statue of stone. Amidst the cupolas was a large basin of water,

over which the shadow deepened. The trees were dense, and the sunlight could not pass through. That place was a place among the places of Hell, may God preserve us from it. When we had arrived at those cupolas, the women descended to the basin, entered it, removed their clothes and jewellery, and made gifts of them to the other people. Each of them was given a rough cotton robe, unsewn, which was tied at the waist, at the neck, and at the shoulders. The fire had been kindled near to the basin, in a lower place. On it was poured "Kanjad," oil of sesame, which strengthened its burning. There were around fifteen men, carrying bundles of sticks. With them were another ten, carrying heavy logs, and the drummers and the horn-players were standing, awaiting the arrival of the women. The fire had been covered with a heavy cloth cover, to hide it from their view, and the cover was held in place by the men, so as not to frighten them. I saw one of the women, when she came to the covered fire, grab the cover and violently pull it from the hands of the men, revealing the flames, and saying to them, laughing, "Do you think this fire will frighten me? I know that it is a fire burning." Then she put her hands together on her head, out of respect for the fire, and threw herself in.[5]

When I first read this account I was transported into a world where there are still unknowns, where all knowledge is not available at the touch of a button. Where moral priorities have not all been agreed upon, where the least common denominator of material well-being does not rule. A wilderness of the soul, with all of the glory and disaster of real wilderness. I long for this place. I imagine that I was there in some unremembered past. Early in 1988, at the end of my long voyage, I spent every evening for a week sitting above the burning *ghats*[6] in Varanasi, India, watching the corpses burn, the large embalmed logs perfuming the night air but not completely covering the smell of burning flesh. Ibn Battuta may also

---

5. Harb, p. 430. Author's translation.

6. *Ghat* is a Sanskrit word denoting a series of steps along a riverbank. In Varanasi along the banks of the holy Ganges river, bodies are burned for purification and then the ashes released into the river. Cows, deemed already pure, are dumped in the river to rot whole.

have seen this during his travels among the Hindus, and wondered, calling into question his own beliefs, or at least marvelling at those of others. This is becoming harder and harder to do in our time. Everything is being reduced to similitude. From a state of greater diversity and distinct order, we are descending to a state of homogeneity. Entropy is increasing. From multifaceted brilliance and richness of color we are becoming gray. This is an immeasurable loss.

People can believe absolutely anything. There is no limit. The women in Ibn Battuta's account were not forced to immolate themselves. They decided to do so after their husbands were killed in battle. What kind of world-view can lead a person to make such a decision? What level of courage must one have to be able to carry it out? Surely nothing we see very often. The fine spiritual structure underpinning our lives is arbitrary. Physical laws govern our techniques only. They do not govern how we use these techniques. Nor do they govern our priorities. Nor our inner adaptations to physical reality. Nor the meaning we project onto our lives. Technological progress is orthogonal[7] to moral progress. The British soldiers at Omdurman at the close of the nineteenth century were lesser, not greater, warriors than the Mahdi's men. They burned their fingers on their gun barrels, while 10,000 swordsmen and lancers across the field from them met death straight-on, drawing it to them like a bride and hugging it in their arms.[8]

FEBRUARY 8, 2015

I am wondering whether studying a language and writing are two incompatible and mutually exclusive activities. Between getting up early, four hours of Turkish, coming back to the apartment, doing some obligatory work, and having lunch, only around three hours of daylight

---

7. "Orthogonal" is a mathematical term used for two perpendicular axes which are completely independent of each other. Movement along one axis has no bearing whatsoever on movement along the other axis. The X-Y axes of the Cartesian coordinate system are examples of orthogonal axes.

8. Though the Sudanese outnumbered the British by roughly two to one, they suffered nearly *sixty times* the casualties and *two-hundred times* the deaths suffered by the British, who also executed hundreds of wounded men, according to eye-witness journalistic accounts, including that of young Winston Churchill. See Churchill, Winston, *The River War*. London: Longmans Green, 1899 (First Edition), Volume II, pp. 195-7.

remain. Given that going anywhere takes a certain amount of time, this limits what I can see. Why my daily life would be worthy of interest, I am not sure.

"On the way to Turkish class today, the pile of garbage rotting on the street corner north of here has rotted a bit more, and I think a cat has gutted one of the trash bags in search of another putrefying morsel. The mud in the street has been imprinted with new tracks, of vehicles and of men, and the disgusting odors emanating from the garbage sorting warehouse were strangely different from yesterday..."

Today, I finally did something like I ordinarily do when I travel. I took the Metro to Sultanahmet. When I was here in 1987, there was no Metro. I remember taking, I think, a bus across from Sultanahmet to Galata back then, with the Turkish youth I had met, Akin, and eating with him on the Galata side in a run-down neighborhood. Now it is very different. From the Taksim Metro station there is a sort of subway they call *Funicüler* (*funiculaire*, a French word), though I cannot see any resemblance to a cable car, and the grade it goes down and up is not very steep. Anyway, at the bottom of it is a modern tramway station with a tram going to Sultanahmet. The entire trip was rapid and cheap, taking half the time it would take in a taxi. Viewed from the tram crossing the bridge, the Sultanahmet neighborhood is very impressive and one can see that this place was the center of the Muslim world for centuries. It is rich with history and architectural beauty, but strangely, at least one past visitor disagreed with this assessment. Chateaubriand, the early nineteenth-century French author, wrote: "The stay in Constantinople weighed on me. I only like to visit places embellished by the virtues or by the arts, and here I found...neither the first nor the second."[9]

With all due respect, Chateaubriand was either blind or a man so bigoted that he couldn't see beauty if it did not wear the same clothes

---

9. Chateaubriand, *Itinéraire de Paris à Jérusalem*. Paris: Garnier-Flammarion, 1968, p. 207. Author's translation.

he did. I wandered in the park near the Sultanahmet (Blue) Mosque, wondering at the splendor of the surroundings. People were sitting, talking, walking, men and women enjoying the weekend outside. No such place exists in Egypt nor in any Arab country I know. Perhaps such places used to exist in Syria, and I know they did in Lebanon before their civil war when Beirut was the "Paris of the Middle East."

I walked around the Sultanahmet Mosque. The interior courtyard failed to impress me and I didn't visit the interior of the mosque itself this time, as it was closed for prayer, and I had visited it in 1987. Looking at it from afar, it has the characteristic quality of Turkish mosques, resembling a multi-pooled waterfall descending from the top down towards the ground in rounded arcs. The minarets are so fine and elongated that they almost look like missiles taking off. I wandered further in the park, saw the German fountain, a nineteenth-century gazebo of ornately inlaid stonework made to commemorate the German Emperor Wilhelm II's visit, then entered the underground Basilica Cistern. This is roughly one hectare in surface and eight meters high so held around 80,000 cubic meters of water back in the sixth century when it was built. Apparently it became a dump for dead bodies and other detritus and was only cleaned in the 1960s and then renovated. It opened to visitors one month after I was here in 1987. It was worth the visit, not for its beauty, but for its eerie quality and as an engineering marvel from 1,500 years ago.

Leaving the cistern, I headed towards Hagia Sophia. I didn't feel like going inside it now so walked around it. Behind the Hagia Sophia proper some of the outbuildings have been converted into a carpet museum, where I was the sole visitor. Then a little further uphill is the entrance to Topkapi Palace. I remember enjoying this place in 1987, relaxing under the plane trees in the heat of August. Then I couldn't read Arabic, but now I read the inscription to the right of the gate, a Prophetic *hadith*: "The Sultan is the shadow of God on the earth..." To the left of the gate, in a separate medallion, it continues: "...and all the oppressed take refuge in him." Our Western political systems really have evolved and improved, whereas in its nature as a nearly absolute monarchical system that of the Ottomans was not so far from that of the ancient Egyptians or the Hittites, though it was far more complex on an administrative level. Presently Turkey seems to be moving back towards the ancient model.

I wandered in Topkapi's garden but didn't enter the palace itself, still remembering it well. I descended towards the Galata side and caught sight of the Istanbul Archaeological Museum, which I did go into. It is a magnificent museum, much more complete than Ankara's, and contains exhibits from all over the Near East, from Neolithic all the way through Roman times. In four hours, I hadn't enough time to do it justice, but was impressed all the same. The more I see and learn, the more I feel disoriented by history, by the names of the civilizations that have succeeded each other on our earth. I had no idea that Troy was inhabited from 3000 BCE onwards, but it was. There were so many such cities, such wars, but just that one was preserved in an epic poem. What of the others? How to make sense of so many lives gone past? How does mine fit in? Where is the modern world going? How can it hold the aspirations of so many?

FEBRUARY 9, 2015

After the weekend it was good to start the rhythm of classes again this morning. We started looking at verb tenses other than the present, just as an introduction. Turkish has a very developed verbal system. And the strangest thing about the language is the way words are formed, agglutinated together (Turkish is an agglutinative language). Negation, for instance, is denoted in a verb by adding a "*mi*" sound in the middle of it. And other elements such as the object of the verb are also simply tacked on to the end of it, so you can end up with impossibly long single words which have the meaning of full sentences.

I returned home by the same route as usual, running the gauntlet of aimless refugees smoking, and rotting garbage in the muddy streets. I had been told that this neighborhood had evolved from one of homosexual prostitutes and heroin addicts into that of the Syrian refugees. My apartment smelled of cigarette smoke again. I decided I would leave this place tomorrow. I wrote a detailed and rather aggressive email to the apartment's owner, complaining that he and/or the language school had swindled me on the price of the apartment (I was paying a higher rate than the one I found on a website) and listing the reasons for my dissatisfaction with my accommodation. One of these was that I had already written two messages to him previously, which he had ignored. This time I threatened to express my annoyance in an online review, and he duly replied. I also suggested that he and the other businessmen nearby set up a local fund to finance rubbish collection for the entire neighborhood, and mentioned that municipal collections had existed at Mohenjo-Daro in 2500 BCE, with this part of Istanbul a little late in adopting "modern" innovations. I'm not sure he appreciated this last point. In any event, I demanded (and received) a refund for the unused days at the apartment when I left.

FEBRUARY 10, 2015

I left my apartment in the morning, gave a small gift to Anas in appreciation of his diligent help, and walked for the last time through the muddy streets to Taksim Square. I left my suitcase at the hotel I had reserved and went to the language school. After class, it was a relief to return to a clean space with a pleasant view and with no stale smell of cigarettes. I did some work and scheduled two meetings for later in the week, one with a language school serving corporate customers in an upmarket area of Istanbul I had passed through last week, Etiler, and the second with an American academic and director of a research institute, who had spent most of his life in Turkey. In the evening, despite the change of environment, I was quite sad.

FEBRUARY 11, 2015

In class today, Sanaa, the Libyan woman, and I had to do a short skit. I tried to make it as funny as possible, with the two of us meeting in a bar and flirting. She went along with it even though it was somewhat risqué for an Arab Muslim woman, and Meriç, the teacher, laughed a lot. After class, I immediately took a taxi to Etiler to visit the other language school. Its director was very professional and polite. She described a number of options from which I could choose if I decided to return here and study Turkish further. It was significantly more expensive than my present school, but in a better area and with greater resources as well. If I continue studying Turkish, I will attend this school. After the meeting, I had lunch in a local restaurant, then wandered around the neighborhood for an hour before the weather deteriorated.

FEBRUARY 12, 2015

After class, I went out to Boğaziçi University, on the Bosphorus in the affluent area near the language school from yesterday. Boğaziçi is one of the most prestigious universities in Turkey. I met Dr. Tony Greenwood, director of the American Research Institute in Turkey. I had contacted Tony through a mutual friend and was very happy to meet him since he has lived most of his life in Turkey and is extremely knowledgeable. I told him about my plan to write a book and asked him many questions, centering on the safety, or lack of such, of traveling to points further east, near Syria. His general outlook was that there was a certain degree of danger but that it could be managed by an experienced and careful traveler familiar with local cultural mores. I also asked about the possibility of enrolling in an intensive language program offered by the research institute.

Tonight, I contemplated my future, as I have always done. Future languages to learn, countries to explore, adventures to recount. The paths trodden by Charles Doughty and Richard Burton in Arabia beckon. And Iran, to live there, learn its language and understand its mysteries. And closer to home, the past glory of Andalusia, inhabited by luminaries of Islamic intellectual history, Ibn Rushd, Ibn Arabi, and so many others, land of tolerance and union until the Reconquista. It is easy to map one's future with silent wonder and a glass of wine.

FEBRUARY 13, 2015

Today was the last day of class. I thanked Meriç for her help, and invited her for a drink after class, then returned to the hotel. I made a one-page summary sheet of everything I had learned in two weeks of studying Turkish. Cramming all of this onto one page was a task, but it came in handy in my further travels in Turkey, enabling me, along with the use of a dictionary on my phone, to make all of my needs known and to engage in basic communication with people I met. Most of my abilities revolved around the present tense of verbs and a simple understanding of nominal case endings so a potential listener could tell whether the noun I mentioned was the subject or the object of the verb. It is surprising how much can be communicated using such rudimentary language skills and a little patience.

FEBRUARY 14, 2015

I had resolved to visit Rumeli Hisari again, as it was closed the first time I tried a week ago. Rumeli Hisari is a fortress on the European side of the Bosphorus built by Mehmet the Conqueror, matched with another fortress on the Asian side. Together, they were intended to control naval access to Constantinople, but the city was taken by Ottoman forces before the fortresses played their full role. I took a taxi out along the Bosphorus, leaving behind the crowded and rough neighborhood of Taksim for the wealthy areas of Etiler, Bebek, and Rumeli Hisari. This time the castle was open, and along with two young Lebanese women, I was the only visitor. I entered and walked along the lower levels, then climbed up onto the ramparts for a better view, not really part of the normal itinerary. After the ramparts and the top of the hill, I wandered down and chatted with the Lebanese women near the top of a vertical shaft pierced through the rock of the mountainside. Speaking Arabic, they told me they thought it was an air shaft. But I looked at it more carefully, and noticing the vertical stone slabs on each side of the cylindrical hole with a hollow to hold a transversal axis, I concluded it was a simple water well, dug very deep as we were quite high above the water level. The axis was no longer in place, but once I had explained it they agreed with my interpretation.

I strolled along the Bosphorus before taking a taxi back to the Taksim neighborhood, where I headed for the waterfront near the hotel and decided to visit the Dolmabahçe Palace. Dolmabahçe had replaced Topkapi as the home of the Ottoman Sultans in the mid-nineteenth century. One of my Saudi friends had recommended Dolmabahçe to me, but I was very disappointed with it. Like a protruding foreign carbuncle on the native Muslim body, gilded and gaudy and gross, it suggested the arrogance of Europeans working for people who wanted more than anything else to be European when they were not. A tawdry version of Versailles, its only authentic aspect was the very large area of the palace devoted to the Sultan's harem. At least that was true. Atatürk chose a small room here to die. The clock in his room still reads 9:05 AM, the time of his death in 1938.

FEBRUARY 15, 2015

I visited the Hagia Sophia today. In 1987 I had done so hurriedly because it was overflowing with tourists and I was impatient. Today it was nearly empty and I took my time. The Hagia Sophia was built in the sixth century CE by the Byzantine Emperor Justinian as a Christian basilica. For nearly a thousand years, it remained the world's largest cathedral and one of its largest and most magnificent buildings. In 1453, after the conquest of Constantinople, it was transformed into a mosque, and then into a museum by Atatürk. I spent a long time looking up at the central dome, trying to decipher the Quranic inscription there. I turned slowly around a point directly below the apex of the dome, gazing intently upwards until I became dizzy parsing the calligraphy:

"God is the light of the heavens and the earth. The parable of His light is as if there were a niche, and within it a lamp, the lamp enclosed in glass, the glass as it were a brilliant star, lit from [the oil of] a blessed olive tree, neither of the east nor of the west, whose oil would almost glow even if untouched by fire." Q 24:35.

Ibn Arabi entitled his beautiful selection of *hadith qudsi* after this *ayat, Mishkat al-Anwar*, "The Niche of Lights."[10] The apse mosaic of the Virgin and Child is magnificent, radiating innocence and purity down

---

10. Ibn Arabi, Muhi al-Din (Arabic text and translation by Stephen Hirtenstein and Martin Notcutt), *Divine Sayings, 101 Hadith Qudsi*. Oxford: Anqa Publishing, 2004.

94

through the centuries. It is from the ninth century, apparently replacing one from the sixth century which was destroyed by the Iconoclasts. The *mihrab* is offset from the cardinal orientation of the building so as to face Mecca, as it must. On leaving this part of Hagia Sophia, I touched the "weeping pillar" brought from the now impoverished Temple of Artemis at Ephesus. I put my finger in the slimy hole, as have done so many millions of other people hoping for a healing miracle, but I made sure to wash my hands afterwards. Upon exiting, I saw the Beautiful Gate of bronze from second-century BCE Tarsus. The Byzantines brought many marvels here. Outside on the grand esplanade where the central area of the Hippodrome once stood in ancient times were an obelisk from ancient Egypt, other pillars, and the bronze Serpent Pillar from the Temple of Apollo at Delphi, made in the fifth century BCE from melted Persian armor and weapons and brought here by the Emperor Constantine the Great, founder of Constantinople. Wandering further, I found the remnants of the Milion Stone, also set up by Constantine in the third century, in imitation of Rome. The stone is the point from which distances to destinations near and far were measured to New Rome, Constantinople. I also noticed that Talaat Pasha's mansion, across from the Basilica Cistern, had been preserved and memorialized for the tourists, leaving out the established historical fact that he was a genocidal murderer somewhere between Pol Pot and Hitler in the number of victims attributed to him. I will visit his tomb tomorrow.

I walked aimlessly through Sultanahmet, the park, the grandiose monuments, the small winding streets. My eyes settled on Pierre Loti Street. Pierre Loti was a French author, traveler, naval officer. He lived in Istanbul for a long time and wrote a book, *Les Désenchantées*, about an affair between a French diplomat and a Turkish noble woman, in which the latter aspires to modernity and the freedom it represents but is nonetheless trapped in the ancestral female role assigned by her patriarchal society. Some years ago, I read this book and discussed it in depth with several Saudi princesses. I took a taxi back to the hotel. While we were stuck in traffic the driver called out to a street vendor who brought him food, which he generously shared with me.

I moved to a nicer hotel this evening and was filled with a strange glee at this, the precursor of my return home. The view from my room over the Bosphorus was beautiful and the ships passed by before me in the never-ending transience of life. On the nightstand was a book, *Lost Horizon*, by James Hilton, which recounts the story of Shangri-La, in the Kunlun Mountains of Tibet, a place where time slows down and life is prolonged, cut off from the rest of the world. I lay down on the bed and began to read.

FEBRUARY 16, 2015

There remained one more sight to see, the Abide Hurriyet, or Monument of Liberty, built to honor soldiers killed defending the Ottoman parliament in 1909 against a coup that attempted to restore the Sultan's absolute power. But the objects of my interest were the tombs at the same location of the Young Turks Enver and Talaat Pasha, architects and executors of the Armenian genocide, and two of the Three Pashas[11] who effectively steered the Ottoman Empire from 1908 to its destruction in World War I. I found the site, whose only entrance was through a guarded gate since it was within the grounds of a government building. As I entered the cemetery, a guard eyed me suspiciously. I saluted him and said, in Turkish, "historical monument, Sultan Abdulhamit," and he let me proceed. Abdulhamit was the last Ottoman Sultan to hold absolute power. I was surprised by the attention of the guards, who watched me as I stopped in front of each tomb. At that of Talaat Pasha, I was able to pay my disrespects in the manner I had intended, though observed from afar by a guard. At the tomb of Enver Pasha, however, an employee was cleaning the tomb and the guard walked up a few meters behind me and stood there, forcing me to abandon my original plan. "Insulting Turkishness" is a crime here, so I was discreet, though I imagine that a good lawyer could make a pretty strong argument that these two were

---

11. The Three Pashas were Enver, Djemal, and Talaat. All three were sentenced to death by a Turkish military court set up after the war, and all three rightfully died violent deaths. Enver was the only one of the three to escape retribution by relatives of the victims of the Armenian genocide, dying in battle in Russian Central Asia. Djemal was assassinated as part of Operation Nemesis, by avenging Armenian agents, in the Caucasus, and is buried in Erzurum. Talaat was assassinated in broad daylight in Germany by Solomon Tehlirian, who gave himself up, was tried, and was found innocent by reason of temporary insanity by a German court, after recounting the horrors he and his family suffered during the genocide.

not the flower of Turkishness in any case. They almost had their country entirely destroyed and dismembered, which it would have been but for the heroic and brilliant intervention of Atatürk. Despite my discretion, I have the feeling that the guards read my thoughts. I cannot be the first such visitor. Aside from the Anıt Kabir, Atatürk's monument in Ankara, this was the best guarded monument I have seen in Turkey. Shameful. My mission completed, I left as I had come and took a taxi back to the hotel, getting stuck for forty minutes in awful traffic.

Once back in the room, I felt disoriented, tired of traveling, near the end of the trip, and pleased by the progress I had made so far in doing what I had set out to do: writing this journal. I picked up *Lost Horizon* and read more. I found myself feeling sad while reading it. When I crossed the Kunlun Mountains into Tibet in 1987, I believed in places like Shangri-La, where the evils of the world could not follow, where there was real wisdom. I sought these places. I did not find them and I no longer believe in their existence. I finished the book, nostalgic for the spiritual travels of my lost youth. Tomorrow, I go home.

FEBRUARY 17, 2015

Time to leave. The worst taxi in all my traveling here. Stinks. Dirty. Falling apart. Driver coughing, driving with one or no hands on the wheel. Texting, talking on the phone, snorting like a pig. Coastal road. Following the old Byzantine city walls. Protecting slums now. A strange and contradictory feeling, desire to go home but disdain for those who never leave home. Dissatisfaction with the whole wide world.

4

FROM ANTALYA TO THE WEST

I AM UPSET, DISORIENTED, AND CONFUSED. A week ago today, France, my home for the past twenty years, was attacked by Islamic State murderers, "Soldiers of the Caliphate." They attacked the Bataclan concert hall and several other public venues, killing 130 and wounding over 400 people, Christians, Muslims, atheists, white, black, brown, unarmed men, women, and children. Wanton murder. Though we may not have realized it until now, Islamic State considers itself at war with France (and with much of the rest of the world). Can a landless terrorist group such as Al-Qaida legitimately be at war? Islamic State, though recognized by no one but its supporters, for now does have the basic requirements of a true state: territory which it controls, laws which it enforces, and an administration which taxes and regulates its population. Its objective status as a state is moot in any case—it believes itself at war with France and that is enough. Should we be surprised at their manner of attack upon us? I believe not. Deliberately murdering civilian populations is part of war. Why would we hold these particular primitive enemies to a higher standard than that to which we held ourselves, for example, in World War II?[1] What is surprising

---

1. Lindqvist, Sven, *A History of Bombing*. London: Granta Books, 2001. Some 50,000 German civilians were killed in Hamburg in 1943 and double that number in Dresden in 1945, deliberately, by the British and American air forces, whose leader, Arthur Harris, stated his goal as "…the obliteration of German cities and their inhabitants as such." This is in sections 202 and 205, with bibliographical references to other scholarly historical works. There are written

is that the individuals who carried out the Bataclan attacks had grown up in Europe, maladjusted sons of the very society they attacked. And also surprising, the religious justification which impelled them to this act. All of my years of studying Islam do not enable me to resolve and understand how the modern jihadists have hijacked this honorable faith tradition, how they have become, *de facto*, its foremost representatives to the rest of the world, and how the billion other Muslims simply remain silent and allow this to happen, while mouthing excuses like "They are not Muslims…" when, yes, they are Muslims, as uncomfortable as this fact may be to their brethren of faith. There is much to be said on this subject, and though the course of action to correct it would be simple (a military invasion and the physical destruction of Islamic State's "Caliphate," preferably invoking Article 5 of the NATO Treaty[2]), understanding and explaining the underlying religious justifications of Islamic State and similar movements is fairly complex. I cannot pretend to do justice to such a subject here, but I will mention some of the relevant religious considerations.

The Qur'an, like all ancient religious texts, and in fact like all texts, contains elements taken from the society and the historical period in which it arose (leaving aside the question of its origin, divine or human). This is apparent in many instances in the Qur'an, but one which is logically irrefutable concerns the rules on fasting during the month of

records of Harris' exchanges with the British civilian authorities, who were uncomfortable with his forthright statement of his goals, despite having accepted the goals themselves. And the Germans bombing London had the same goal. In the Asian theater, Operation Meetinghouse, the deliberate incendiary bombing of residential neighborhoods of Tokyo, is thought to have killed more people than either of the two atomic bombs dropped on Japan, on the order of 100,000 in one night. In the words of General George C. Marshall: "Flying fortresses will be dispatched immediately to set the paper cities of Japan on fire. There won't be any hesitation about bombing civilians—it will be all-out." (http://marshallfoundation.org/library/digital-archive/robert-l-sherrod-memorandum-for-david-w-hulburd-jr/). And of course Japanese troops deliberately killed civilians in China and other conquered countries. Statements that modern armies do not deliberately kill civilians in war are lies.

2. Article 5 of the NATO Treaty is the article which specifies that an attack on one member of the Alliance is an attack on all of them. It has been invoked only once, after September 11, 2001. I felt strongly that it should be invoked in this case, as did Admiral Jim Stavridis, Dean of the Fletcher School of Tufts University and former Supreme Commander of NATO, whose opinion I sought about this situation. Stavridis, James, "NATO's Turn to Attack," *Foreign Policy*, November 14, 2015. Unfortunately, President Obama and President Hollande apparently disagreed.

Ramadan. These rules are based upon sightings of the day and night. During the period between dawn and sunset no food or liquid of any kind are to be consumed. For Muslims living above roughly fifty degrees north or south latitude, following these rules when Ramadan occurs in the summer would cause dire and dangerous physical hardship. And above or below the Arctic or Antarctic Circles, following the rules would nearly without doubt result in death. Clearly, this does not seem to be what God could have intended. And yet it is extremely uncommon for Muslim thinkers to state clearly and categorically that the Qur'an or the *Sunnah* must be logically interpreted or limited in scope due to historical factors such as, in this case, ignorance of the phenomenon of the "midnight sun" at high latitudes. Most Muslims will not acknowledge that the Qur'an can be incorrect or even dependent upon the historical context in which it was revealed. This abdication of intellectual responsibility leaves an open door for ignorant traditionalists to live in the Middle Ages.[3] Islamic State, for example, in its *Dabiq* periodical, describes the division of war spoils in a manner that is taken almost verbatim from a work of Ibn Taimiyya, a medieval Islamic legal scholar.[4] Its views on enslaving "infidel" women and children are likewise firmly grounded in medieval Islamic law, in which slavery was permitted, and in which sexual relations with enslaved women were also permitted.[5] Finally, Ibn Taimiyya's fourteenth-century *takfir* fatwas, which he wrote in reference to the Mongol invaders who later converted to Islam in a manner which he personally judged to be insincere, opened Hell's gates in our time by

3. Medieval world-views are not limited to the religious authorities of Islamic State or Al-Qaida. A few decades ago, the late Sheikh Abdulaziz Ibn Baz, the Grand Mufti, or supreme religious authority, of Saudi Arabia, for example, asserted that the sun revolves around the earth (and not vice-versa). Christian creationists likewise propound ludicrous views contrary to established scientific fact.

4. *Dabiq*, Issue 4, pp, 10-13, and *Dabiq*, Issue 3, p. 30. Taimiyya, Taqi al-Din Ibn, *Al-Siyasa al-Shar'iyya Islah al-Ra'i wa al-Ra'iyyah*. Beirut: Dar al-Kutub al-'Ilmiyya, 1988, pp. 41-3 (in Arabic).

5. The Qur'an itself specifically permits sexual relations with female slaves by their owner, in a number of instances (Q 4:24, Q 23:6, Q 33:52, Q 70:30), in largely identical language, referring to them as "that which your right hand possesses..." The issue of the extent to which such sexual relations must be consensual is more complicated. Biblical citations also condone the taking of sex slaves (Numbers 31:18) or even selling one's own daughter into slavery (Exodus 21:7-11). Human rights are not the strong suit of ancient texts.

empowering individual Muslims to assert that other Muslims were not in fact Muslims, meaning that they were apostates (*murtadd*), subject to a death sentence. This legal innovation was adopted by many extremists in the Islamic fundamentalist movement, enabling them to define virtually anyone outside of their own closed fanatical religious sect as apostates, and condemn them to death.[6] Islamic State holds that probably more than half of the *billion* Muslims in the world are apostates and deserve death, from Turkish and Saudi soldiers to virtually all of the 200 million Shi'ite Muslims, to their very own next-door neighbors if these latter refuse to submit to the "Caliphate."

It ought to be clear from the above discussion that Islamic State and other Muslim extremists take a good deal of care to found their policies and practices on serious medieval Islamic legal bases.[7] Statements about such jihadists by modernist Muslims with no knowledge of Islamic law that "they are not Muslims" are clearly irrelevant and counter-productive. What is needed is a full re-examination of the original sources by rationalist but religious Muslims. There is no shortage of texts from the Qur'an and the *Sunnah* supporting the liberation of slaves,[8] supporting the rights of religious minorities,[9] and supporting freedom of religious conscience.[10]

---

6. *Takfir* means to assert that another Muslim is an apostate, which Ibn Taimiyya did of the Mongol rulers. He modified his views on this matter near the end of his life, but the genie was out of the bottle, as his earlier written opinions survived him. French translations of relevant parts of the fatwas on the Mongols can be found in Michot, Yahya, *Textes spirituels d'Ibn Taymiyya, XI, XII, and XIII, Mongols et Mamluks.* Oxford: Le Chebec, 2002.

7. Certain of Islamic State's actions, however, demonstrate such extreme barbarity as to be beyond the pale of any standard interpretation of Islamic law, such as when they burned a captured Jordanian pilot alive in a cage, though even this they attempt to justify on Islamic legal grounds (See *Dabiq*, Issue 7, pp. 5-8).

8. "To free a slave, or to give food in the day of hunger, to an orphan near of kin or a poor person in misery...such are the Companions of the Right Hand." Q 90: 13-18.

9. "Say, 'O unbelievers, I do not worship that which you worship. Nor do you worship that which I worship...To you your religion, to me my religion.'" Q 109:1-6. Medieval Islamic law and practice allowed the coexistence of Christians and Jews under Muslim rule in a way which was much more tolerant than that practiced by medieval Christian rulers. Muslim Spain, for example, was multi-cultural but when the Reconquista was completed Jews and Muslims were treated much worse than Christians and Jews had been treated under Muslim rule, often facing expulsion or forced conversion.

10. "There is no compulsion in religion. The right way has been made clear from the wrong." Q 2:256. How far removed is this from forcing people to pray in the mosque?

To resolve this situation, what is required is a reinterpretation which uses these texts as justification, and accepts that the Qur'an was revealed in a certain societal environment, that it represented greater rights and freedom for the weaker members of society in that environment,[11] but that in modern times some pre-existing societal institutions which the Qur'an permitted, such as slavery, are immoral and must be abolished absolutely. In Christianity and Judaism, this type of reinterpretation was successful; nowadays it would be quite difficult to find a Jew or Christian who thinks his son should be stoned to death for disobedience,[12] that we should commit utter genocide against our enemies,[13] or that worshippers of other religions should be systematically put to death.[14] In fact, it is often quite difficult to convince an ordinary Jew or Christian that their respective scriptures even contain such abominations without showing them the texts *in situ*.

In the case of Islam, most Muslims are so far unwilling to place any theoretical limits at all on the validity of their religious texts, and as long as they refuse to do so, the followers of extremist organizations will have the seat at the head of the table when it comes to interpreting the religion. This is not an easy subject to discuss with Muslims, and I have not managed to have such discussions with the Turks I have met during these travels, though I have with some of my long-standing Arab Muslim friends, who generally agree with me. One of them in particular mentioned the case of the Caliph 'Umar ibn Khattab, at the beginning of Islam, who suspended the application of the *hadd* punishment[15] for stealing during a year of famine and also modified the application of some other legal injunctions. He founded this decision on his own

---

11. In pre-Islamic Arabia, slavery existed, but there were few or no limits placed upon it. The limits on slavery and other unjust social institutions set by the Qur'an were thus steps towards greater freedom and equality, and the many exhortations to charity and justice in the Qur'an and the *Sunnah* likewise.

12. Deuteronomy 21: 18-21.

13. Deuteronomy 20: 12-16.

14. II Kings 10: 22-25.

15. *Hadd* means "limit," and is a specific punishment defined in the Qur'an, such as the punishment of amputation of the hand for stealing.

interpretation of social justice and the interest of the Muslim community, not on particular religious texts. Later, as Islamic law developed, it systematically generalized the exception to this *hadd* punishment (exempting people who stole food due to need from all punishment). My friend suggested that nowadays there would be a strong basis for similar decisions, but that making them would be very difficult, as no one now has the authority of a figure like Caliph 'Umar.[16]

I am in Istanbul airport now, waiting for my connecting flight to Antalya. The mass of humanity at passport control seethes: men, women, children around me go on their ways, doing what they are told. There is a food court reminiscent of an American mall. Facial expressions, aches, pains, and joys, like my own. What I am doing here? For a moment I had a feeling of joy, alone on an airport concourse before boarding in Paris. But now nothing. Emptiness. Doubt. A refugee in spirit. After drinking a Perrier, I wander around the mall, lost in the supermarket. I notice a young woman, Turkish most likely, elegantly dressed in black slacks and a form-fitting black top. Then I lose her from view. After a while, I go to my departure gate and notice that the young woman is sitting near the gate for my flight, so I speak with her. Her name is Dilan. She is from Antalya, and came to Istanbul to take an English exam for Turkish Airlines, hoping to be a flight attendant. We spoke during the time remaining before the flight, she wrote her number in my Moleskine notebook and said to call her if I needed help in Antalya.

It was evening when I arrived in Antalya. While waiting for a taxi to the hotel, I saw Dilan come out of the arrivals gate. She stopped when she saw me and introduced me to her father, who had come to pick her up. A kind gesture. The ride to the hotel was short, and after checking in I felt I needed to do some errands. The speed with which I completed them amazed me. Unpack. Thirty seconds. Go out and change money and buy bottled water. A pleasant fifteen-minute walk. Part of the strangeness of travel is the reduced set of obligations it carries compared

---

16. In an act of supreme arrogance, in 2014 Abu Bakr al-Baghdadi, leader of Islamic State, pronounced himself Caliph of all Muslims, Commander of the Faithful. Asserting the right to modify the application of certain Islamic legal norms, if it were done by a group of respected scholars, would be an audacious act, but one far less arrogant than Baghdadi's.

to life at home. Everything that "needs" to be done in a day can be done in the time it takes to do one single household chore such as washing the dishes. The rest of the time is free. While I was out, I was struck by the familiarity of everything, as if I belonged here. Our civilizations have converged so far in recent decades that even an untraveled person will know the function of virtually every store or building seen in a foreign country. While I was walking, I heard a motorbike accelerate quickly from behind me and I moved deftly to the side. It crossed my mind that if Islamic State wanted to gun down a few foreigners here, it would be trivially easy. Turkey's ambiguous political stance in this respect probably enhances my safety here. As has become more and more clear over the past year, the Turkish government and many of the people see the Kurds as an existential threat, but do not see Islamic State as such, and even do business with them, buying oil produced in IS-controlled areas of Syria, which is trucked into Turkey. If forced to choose between one or the other, they would surely favor Islamic State over the Kurds.

Last night at dinner, I felt disappointment. Before leaving on a journey, I am afflicted with the illusion that by leaving, I will shed my old doubts, my weaknesses, my unfulfilled longings. But they remain. I am the same man as I was yesterday. Only my surroundings have changed. But at the end of the trip I will not be the same. The daily change of surroundings works slowly as an abrasive, smoothing away the roughness of my being.

NOVEMBER 21, 2015

After breakfast, I wandered, not aimlessly but in the direction of a market where I had been told I could buy a knife, one of the first orders of business at the beginning of each trip. I passed the old clock tower and part of the city walls with an Arabic inscription. I saw from afar the Yivli Minaret, which I would visit later. I walked for over an hour through the mostly pedestrian streets of the bazaar. Infinite useless articles for sale, but no knives. I came to a modern mall and went in after a fairly complete security check, metal detector and all. The stores and layout had nothing to envy a middle-class American or European mall. Yuck. Only one sporting goods store, and a mediocre one at that.

No knives. Returning by small streets, I found a hardware store and the proprietor understood my prepared Turkish phrase: "*Lütfen, biçak almak istiyorum*" ("Please, I want to buy a knife"). He pointed me to a shop not far away, and just as the call to prayer was sounding and the owner was closing up, I arrived. Now I am suitably armed for the rest of the trip. And sitting at an outdoor café drinking wonderful fresh orange juice from a tall beer glass.

Refreshed, I returned to the Yivli Minaret. It was built by Ala'eddin Kaykubad, Seljuq Sultan of Rum,[17] who reigned in these parts from 1220 to 1237. His tomb is in Konya, unceremoniously lined up next to several of his relatives in the mosque complex bearing his name. We will become better acquainted with this illustrious gentleman and his works later. The minaret itself was aesthetically pleasing, an unusual fluted column of red brick, but more so were the peaceful gardens around it and the madrasa and mosque, all quiet. The *mihrab* was cordoned off from too great a distance for me to read its Quranic inscription. Due to Atatürk's reforms, few if any Turks could read it anyway. I left the minaret and returned to my room to take stock of the day so far. After reading for an hour, working out the next phase of the journey, I set out to walk around the city again, heading south towards the harbor. Antalya is a very pleasant and beautiful city. It is also the cleanest of the Turkish cities where I have spent time, apart from certain wealthy Istanbul suburbs overlooking the Bosphorus. I came to a small square with a diminutive mosque, that of Ahi Yusuf ("Brother Yusuf"), dating from the thirteenth century. It was very well executed and in perfect proportion. Size is not beauty. It reminded me of the poem "I am a little church (no great cathedral)" by ee cummings. Its postage stamp grounds contained several noble tombs, including that of its namesake.

I walked further south, following the downward slope to overlook the harbor. High limestone cliffs protect the whole coastline, but for the small harbor bay. No wonder Attalos II of Pergamon, founder of Antalya in the second century BCE, chose this site. I found and followed a wide, yellow plastic ribbon stuck to the flagstones, assuming correctly that it would lead me to the Hiderlik Tower, a fortification thought to

---

17. The Muslims referred to the Byzantines as Romans, and to Byzantium as Rome, or Rum.

date from Roman times (second century CE). Undergoing renovations, it is a squat, ugly citadel, as if it had once been tall and fine before a giant stepped on it. It may have been used as a lighthouse. The yellow plastic path having disappeared, I navigated by map towards Hadrian's Gate along Atatürk Street, having turned back towards the north. Everything in Turkey is named after Atatürk. I even saw a larger-than-life bas relief of his face on a government building. No wonder Erdoğan keeps naming things after himself.

Hadrian's Gate is a strange sight. A fine Roman monument executed with great skill set into a wall of unprepossessing masonry, rough-hewn from a kind of stone so porous that it resembled hardened foam. I am a rock-climber but I am unfamiliar with this stone. Perhaps a very low-density type of volcanic pumice? I was left to wonder if the barbarous masons erected their wall before or after Hadrian. I presume after. Civilization does not always go forward, upward, from worse to better. Often it goes the other way, as seems likely to happen in the next few centuries. I considered the gate as well as several inviting dihedrals leading up the walls nearby. These could have been climbed safely without equipment, but I refrained. Then I passed through the gate and stopped on the other side to consider it from that vantage point. Just as a flock of Chinese tourists arrived, I spied a ruined wooden staircase leading to the top of the wall, which I hurried to mount. It provided a view over the top of the gate and the wall and served in lieu of a recycling bin for Turkish beer bottles. Perhaps young Turks bring their girlfriends up here. On my way back to the hotel I sat at an outdoor terrace and had an Efes beer with some olives.

I ate dinner at a Turkish Mexican restaurant. The margaritas were excellent, which was a surprise to me, and the food was good. I was impressed that of the people eating there, ninety percent appeared to be locals. A young couple sat next to me, Jamal and Dilşa. The latter is, I think, a Kurdish name. They were both highly educated and had both lived in the US as students, he in Virginia and she in Seattle. From what he said, Jamal found Virginians hospitable and generous but had a low opinion of their educational level. I told him that in my opinion the US demonstrates that the systems of a country (economic, legal, administrative) are more important than the inhabitants themselves. The US has an extremely well-educated elite, but a large part of the population is grossly ignorant and would compare poorly with socio-economically similar inhabitants of France or other European countries. Many educated foreigners are astounded when they meet ordinary Americans who do not even know on which continent the foreigners' country is situated.

I discussed Islam and politics with Jamal, and he was a supporter of Erdoğan's AKP party, so a person who sees Islam as having a role in society. But he was clearly a reasonable man, hoping for a negotiated peace with the Kurds and a resolution of the civil war in Syria. He was drinking Johnny Walker Black Label. And it seemed that virtually every other table was also partaking in alcoholic beverages, as was I. Islamic State could just as soon murder fifty or a hundred people here as they did in Paris, for they would consider Turks who lead secular lives as apostates deserving of death.

NOVEMBER 22, 2015

My plan for today is to visit the Antalya Museum and to make arrangements for onward travel, leaving tomorrow. I want to see several sites at some distance from Antalya and make it to my next destination, Çıralı. The only way to do this is to hire a car, either with or without a driver, as bus transportation to these places is irregular or non-existent. I prefer a car with a driver because I neither have to bring the car back to where I started nor drive. I asked the hotel reception as well as a man at the nearby taxi stand, using my limited Turkish and the vocabulary from my Turkish dictionary. The taxi was cheaper, but I felt that the man proposed by the hotel was more likely to act in good faith, so I chose him.

I went to the tramway stop near the clock tower to take the tram to the museum. A nice lady I asked told me it was the last stop. As I got off the tram and headed toward the museum, she walked with me. It turned out she worked there. I was the only visitor, though a few more arrived later. The museum is organized chronologically from the Paleolithic to Neolithic, to Bronze Age and then more recent periods. There is a huge technological leap from the Paleolithic to the late Neolithic, the Neolithic Revolution, during which mankind learned agriculture and animal

FROM ANTALYA TO THE WEST

husbandry, considered the requirements for sedentary civilization. After
the late Neolithic, technology continued to improve (for example metal-
working, bronze first, then iron), but for the life of me I couldn't see
any aesthetic improvement at all in the artifacts left by the different ages
post-Neolithic. To my untrained eye, the finest examples of late Neolithic
pottery are as pure and as beautiful as those of Greek or Roman pottery.
Perhaps I am just ignorant of these matters, but the older periods had
examples of such beauty and perfection of execution that it would be
difficult to assert that they were less refined than those produced 3,000
years later. Over a historical time scale, techniques evolve. Aesthetics
change but do not evolve. People remain the same.

Apparently Neolithic sites such as Çatalhöyük, which I saw near
Konya, abound in Turkey. Most are still unexcavated tells, mounds of dirt
and rubble. The same abundance exists in civilizations themselves, waves
successively washing over the Anatolian land: Hatti, Hittite, Phrygian,
Lycian, Lydian, Pisidian, Persian, Greek, Roman, Arab, and now Turkish.
Travel is a strange school. I am an educated person, but I do not really
know what to make of the ebb and flow of cultures and civilizations
over the centuries and millennia, though I have thought long on the
subject. Culture seems to move through the medium of humanity the way
a wave propagates through matter. For the most part, the matter does
not move—the wave moves through it. The people remain—genetically
and geographically—the same, and are in turn Hittite, then Lycian, then
Roman subjects, then subjects of the various Muslim rulers. There are
exceptions to this when large scale physical population transfers take
place (the Mongols and the Turkic-speaking peoples moving westward
in the last thousand years come to mind), but it seems that this is a minor
means of cultural transmission, "flow transmission" as opposed to "wave
transmission," which seems to be the dominant means of cultural transfer.

Jamal, of dinner company last night, owns a construction company,
and told me that wherever he digs here he unearths artifacts. The
plethora of ancient ruins was also illustrated by the vast collection of
Roman statuary in the museum, mostly from Perge, one of the sites
I will visit tomorrow. There were over 100 life-size or larger marble
statues, mostly from the second century CE. The most beautiful were

of Nemesis, the adolescent goddess of divine retribution, but there were also many emperors, including Hadrian, all depicted in armor and bearing certain symbols to denote their imperatorial status. I saw nothing from Termessos, a site also on tomorrow's itinerary, apart from a few coins. It seems it has never been excavated. As I was almost ready to leave, I came across an old French man deeply focused on photographing ancient coins in the display cases, some of them from Termessos. With his intensity and scholarly mien, I thought he must be a professor of numismatic history or some other highly specialized academic. I wish I hadn't spoken to him, as this professorial image was shattered. He was just as interested in photographing the collection of Byzantine women's clothing and did not remember the names of the ancient sites he had visited during the past week. The last impression I gleaned in the museum was from some Arabic calligraphy, illuminated manuscripts of *hadith*, sayings of the Prophet Muhammad.

I ate dinner in the hotel restaurant, apparently the most expensive in Antalya but similar in price to an ordinary restaurant in France. The food was good, though perhaps a little too complicated for the abilities of the chef. I grant the gastronomy award in Turkey to the restaurant I frequented in Göreme during my stay there, which was simpler but truly excellent. I again engaged a couple in conversation, this time a Turkish man with a Russian woman. She had lived here for five years. It seems that there is a large Russian expatriate community, mostly serving Russian tourists. It appears, then, that Turkey provides better economic opportunities than Russia. The discussion with them was less interesting than that with the couple of last night, so I retired to my room.

NOVEMBER 23, 2015

Today was a busy day. Yasin, who was to take me to Perge, Termessos and Çıralı, worked at the hotel but took a day off to drive me where I wanted to go. He had a soft voice and spoke good English. He was also a very timid driver, unusual for someone here. He had a friend with him, Ali Reza. Both of them had worked on cruise ships, and Ali Reza still did, while Yasin had opted for a more sedentary career in the past few years as a receptionist. The three of us set out in Yasin's car for Perge. Yasin told me that his name was taken from the Qur'an and was surprised when I quoted the first lines of the eponymous *surat*: "Ya Sin, by the wise Qur'an, truly you are among those who have been sent..." Q 36:1-3. Yasin had worked for a number of years in Germany as well as on cruise ships, but he chose to work in Antalya to be closer to his family.

The layout of Perge was difficult to visualize, but there was scaffolding around twenty-five meters high around one of the Roman gates. The metal stairway only started on the second story, so I climbed to it and ran quickly up the six flights to the top. Yasin wisely distanced himself from me to avoid being questioned if I was caught, but no one saw me. From the top, I had a commanding view of the entire city, better than a map. It was quite extensive, though not laid out like a normal Roman town with Cardo Maximus and Decumanus Maximus perpendicular to each other.[18] According to Hittite sources, Perge predated the Romans by well over a thousand years, which explains its more complicated and organic urban planning. Our visit lasted around an hour and was enjoyable, but Perge harbored no transcendent moments for me. As we left I asked Yasin to stop the car so I could see the stadium. It was huge, able to seat 12,000 spectators. The neighboring theater was closed for renovations. I hopped the fence quickly (and quite gracefully, I think, for my age) and entered the theater through a tunnel, coming out near the stage. It was an impressive sight, and the bas reliefs carved into the lower walls to my left were ornate, the objects of the restoration. Then I hopped back out and we drove to Termessos.

Termessos was a Pisidian city north-west of modern Antalya, founded by the Solymoi. These latter are mentioned in the *Iliad*, and were reputed to be tough enemies; after killing the Chimera, the hero Bellerophon was sent to fight them: "Next after this he fought the glorious Solymoi, and this, he thought, was the strongest battle with men that he entered."[19]

---

18. Roman towns were laid out on axes based on perpendicular grids aligned to the cardinal points of the compass, and the two names mentioned are the main north-south and east-west roads in the Roman architectural template.

19. Homer, Richmond Lattimore, translator, *The Iliad*. Chicago: University of Chicago Press, 1951,

Indeed, Termessos is one of only two cities to have successfully defied Alexander the Great during his campaigns in the fourth century BCE. It also had the honor of becoming an ally of Rome rather than being subjugated as a vassal state, and minted its own coinage for much of its history. As we approached it by car, the reason for this independence became obvious. Termessos sits on top of a mountain pass, impregnable. It receives a stream from one of the summits above it, enabling the founders of the city to create a voluminous cistern to serve the population's needs and to withstand almost any siege. And the approach is not one that an army would want to make, even now. At each turn in the road the defenders hold the high ground and in some places sheer cliffs overlook the road so that boulders pushed over them would devastate the would-be invaders. This is my kind of city, an ancient Switzerland of sorts!

After the nine-kilometer access road, it is a half-hour hike to the main area of the city of Termessos. The stonework is impressive, more so than at Perge and most other sites I have seen in Turkey. The Termessian masons cut their blocks of limestone with exacting precision. From the upper walls of the city, still intact, out of which flows the stream (probably once acting as a sewer), I can imagine Alexander's troops stationed below in humiliation, hoping that the order would not come to storm those walls. It did not come. Arrian, in his biography of Alexander, mentions Termessos, which Alexander left alone, venting his frustration on the easier target of Sagalassus nearby: "The people of Termessos are an Asiatic race of Pisidian blood; the town stands on a lofty and precipitous height, and the road which leads past it is an inconvenient one."[20]

Aside from its historical significance Termessos is a wonderful site to visit, not least because one has the illusion of being the first person to discover it. No excavations, no fences, few signs, just a wondrous ancient city exposed to the elements on a distant mountaintop.

In addition to being a mountain fastness with a theater literally perched on the mountaintop and offering, even in the absence of actors, a spectacle to arrest the senses, Termessos is also impressive for another

p. 176 (Book VI, lines 184-5).

20 Arrian, *The Campaigns of Alexander*. New York: Penguin Books, 1971, p. 96.

reason: it looks as if large parts of it had literally been thrown to the ground by giants in a fury, and not been troubled since. And for some reason the pottery is not scattered over the ground as is so often the case. Apparently the city was actually destroyed in a violent earthquake in the fifth century CE, ruining the water-supply system which gave life to the city and rendered it impregnable to attack. Perhaps when they felt the earth tremble the nearby barbarians, always waiting on the borders of civilization for their moment to come, guessed that the impenetrable fortress would fare less well than their own primitive dwellings. Maybe they took the pottery. Above the city itself, on the way to the mountaintop, is a vast necropolis with hundreds of giant sarcophagi, each weighing several tons, thrown down in a jumble on the hillside. All fell prey to tomb robbers. Perhaps they overturned some if the earthquake failed to do so. Others had their monolithic lids pried off by levers, while yet others had holes smashed in their sides to extract the contents. In a different location, a kilometer from the others, however, was another tomb, nobler and built into the mountainside. It was adorned with a beautiful bas relief sculpture of a mounted warrior, an eagle above the tomb, and a blazon which was later defaced by vandals. This, it seems, is the tomb of Alcetas, one of Alexander the Great's generals and successors, who sought refuge in Termessos from his peer and enemy, Antigonus. When Alexander died, at the age of thirty-two, it is said that when asked which of his generals should succeed him, he answered, "The strongest." This led to a period of internecine war during which Alexander's empire collapsed into constituent parts, each ruled by a general. Alcetas was one of these. The elders of Termessos granted Alcetas sanctuary, only to violate their word when threatened by Antigonus' army. The young men of Termessos quit the city in protest, wanting to honor the promise of sanctuary granted to Alcetas. This latter, rather than be delivered to his enemies, committed suicide. Termessos delivered his body to Antigonus, who mutilated it and left it unburied until the young men built for him the magnificent and noble tomb I saw. A superstitious man could be forgiven for thinking that the calamity of utter destruction visited upon this city later was a just punishment for violating the sacred commitment of sanctuary.

I am sitting by the main street of the ancient city of Olympos. Before me the stream, bridge foundations still intact, but spans collapsed of old. Behind me ruined structures fading ghostlike into the lush vegetation. Strewn everywhere, potsherds, the extinction of ancient civilizations always occurring in an orgy of smashing pottery. I walked here from the Edenic garden of the guesthouse where I am staying in Çıralı. Along the beach, past a submerged path with a large sign: "Olympos." I went further to the beach's end and into the dense underbrush replete with ruined ancient buildings. Rough-hewn stones with massive lintels over the windows. Contemporary of Olympos, I imagine. And of course the broken pottery. I can imagine the barbarous yobs smashing everything joyfully after having sacked the city. Alas, their tribe has not died out. Having concluded that these jungle-bound ruins were not the right way to access the city, I returned on my tracks and asked two men whether there was a way to Olympos which did not involve wading or swimming a hundred meters through the water. They replied in the negative and said the water was not very deep, so I followed their suggestion and removed my shoes, rolled up my trousers, and waded through the tidal lake to the ticket booth, which I saw once I rounded a promontory. Olympos itself is not remarkable: structures mostly from the Roman period, first to third century CE, and not built with massive cut blocks like Termessos or Perge, except for a few of the buildings such as the theater. This structure gives an impression of ageless ruin, the lower slabs of the seating having been quarried by the Byzantines for use in other buildings.

The weather is bright and warm and there is a breeze from the sea, but even so the humidity is stifling due to the dense vegetation, and I am sitting in the shade of a low wall as I write this. Olympos was part of the Lycian League, a sort of ancient United Nations—or rather United City States—in which the larger cities had more votes but in which all were represented. Other major Lycian cities were Xanthos, Patara, and Pinara, which I missed, and Telmessos (modern-day Fethiye), which I visited. Lycia sent troops in support of Troy and is specifically mentioned

114

in *The Iliad*. Alexander the Great conquered this entire region, largely without a fight.[21]

After leaving Olympos, I wandered through Çıralı town and saw a sign advertising massage, as this is a beach resort in summer. Now it was empty. But by luck, the Thai masseuse was present, and her husband showed me to the back of their small shop. It was not an auspicious place, dirty with many cats, and the rickety house itself seemed ready to collapse. But her massage was excellent, every bit the equal of that I had in a luxury hotel in Paris before leaving, and which cost ten times more. Her name was May, and she had a small daughter whom I had seen on entering her shop. She had been five years in Çıralı, but when I asked if she liked it, she said "no." She had no friends and missed Thailand and her family there. It was not my business to ask how she had ended up here, but I felt sorry for her, nearly alone in a foreign country, with very little contact with the outside world and probably looked down upon by the local population.[22] I thought of Baudelaire's swan.

I walked several kilometers in the direction of the Chimera, a natural site in the mountains where methane gas seeps out of the rocks and burns in eternal flames. At night, Chimera's flames are visible from the sea, and ancient mariners used them as a navigational landmark and invented a mythological creature as their cause. The mythical Chimera is described as being a terrible tripartite hybrid creature—lion, goat, and snake—and breathing fire. It succumbed to the hero Bellerophon, rider of the winged Pegasus, who also tamed the Pisidians. Some ancient historians identified the location of the flaming rocks here as the origin of the myth. Freya Stark saw it from her boat when she traveled here. After walking a few kilometers, I hadn't reached the Chimera path and went back to the guesthouse, where the owner, Bülent, arranged for someone to drive me there in the evening. Just after dark, Ibo picked me up and drove me to the base of the mountain. No one else was there except for a man in charge of his café. I set out alone walking up the hill.

---

21. Arrian, pp. 91-2.

22. Masseuse would not be thought of as an honorable profession in a Turkish village, even though it is purely therapeutic.

The moon was out and near full, so I didn't use my headlamp. I have an innate desire to pass unseen, whereas using a light in darkness is like a neon sign advertising one's presence to all. From hunting as a child, I also learned that to listen one must stop moving. My father, who did research in neuroscience, said that listening is based in a part of the brain near that which controls movement, and that moving prevents listening. Thus, every so often while walking I stopped to listen to the night. I crossed two groups of people coming down from the mountain, having spotted them from several hundred meters away. One was a large group of Germans, noisy and discourteous, and they declined to return my "*Merhaba*" greeting. The other group was composed of Turks and was more polite.

The path was much shorter than I had been told, taking me twenty minutes as I picked my way carefully in the moonlight. I saw the Chimera flames from below, at which point the path ends, and made my way even more carefully amidst the jumbled blocks of stone overgrown with weeds. Even by the firelight, I could see that some of these blocks had formed an ancient structure. By chance, I was alone. There were three or four main "hearths" and a strong smell of natural gas and tar in the air. I picked the largest flame and sat next to it, slightly anxious that a new flame might kindle under me.

By the wavering light of the Chimera, I write. I am seeking my own chimera, like the Spirit Spout, ever changing and ever moving before me. I seek it around each bend, just behind those trees, beyond the fog of distance, always out of my reach. Distant voices and lights. For now, I am alone here with the flames. And my chimera.

When one is alone in the night there is no appeal. The firelight and the darkness reflect our inner cares, our fears, our dark memories. There are no distractions from real inner life. Once in my early twenties, I camped alone in the woods, in mid-winter, in France. I had camped alone many times, but this time I had smoked a great deal of marijuana and squatted on my haunches for several hours watching the fire. The extent of its circle of light defined civilization. Beyond it was only darkness. This experience is primordial and must be close to what our early ancestors felt. Here at Chimera, it was less absolute since I could see quite far due to the multiple gas flames, and there were other people not far away. I imagined the ancient mariners on the sea below, navigating by the light of these same flames. Which of them let fly his unbridled imagination to create Chimera, the mythical beast? After fifteen minutes or so, a large, noisy group of Turks arrived, and I began my descent. Overstaying a moment which has passed cannot bring it back.

At the guesthouse, Bülent made me a very enjoyable dinner, with pomegranate fruit taken from his garden. I was the only guest, while he was accompanied by his mother and a boy who helped with the chores— not his son. Bülent was originally from the Euphrates Valley in Turkey, north of Iraq. He was, I think, Kurdish, and was an accomplished traveler. He had looked at my small backpack when I had arrived and later told me that he took a pack slightly larger than mine for six months each year. He would work six months at his guesthouse, then close it for the winter and leave to travel all over the world. A good life, as Wilfred Thesiger put it, *The Life of My Choice*.

NOVEMBER 25, 2015

I woke up in the night feeling upset. The strange, dark surroundings bothered me. It was cold in my bungalow and I had been sleeping with my down jacket on. Why did I come here? I have a perfectly nice home. Why leave it? What am I doing here? One of the advantages of travel is that, when sick of a place or sick of his own inner state, the traveler can leave. Unfortunately, some ills are harder to ditch than others. It was time to leave Çıralı. Bülent organized a car for me to the bus station in Kumluca, south of here. He accompanied me part of the way and we wished each other safe travels. I bought my ticket to Fethiye, waited an hour, then took the bus. The view of the coast was magnificent. Under the sun, orange limestone cliffs fronting the sea of hammered bronze. Islands, peninsulas, wild coastline, with every so often a cove, sandy beach, and turquoise bay, all this below the winding road. In contrast, the towns and bus stations were like refuse from some landfill, marring the landscape like scars on a young body.

A few hours later, the bus arrived in Fethiye. But first, a stop in Kaş, the bus station a pit, surprisingly worse than many even though Kaş is a luxury beach resort in the summer. Change of bus, a half-hour wait, fresh orange and pomegranate juice. The pomegranates here, from Çıralı in particular, have the darkest red seed fruits I have ever seen, along with those from Taif in Saudi Arabia. If it is the fruit of the underworld, then the juice from these is the blood of Hell's creatures. In Fethiye, I took a taxi from the bus station. Everything passing by the window seemed normal to me. But what is normal? Our minds are relativistic entities. After a few days, surroundings become "normal," whether that means rubbish in the streets, war, famine, or paradise. I believe that humans are simply incapable of holding a steady, firm idea about anything except perhaps the most absolute moral norms. Actually, evidence bears out that even these cannot be held firmly. A dirty street of half-built buildings is normal if that is where I am.

NOVEMBER 26, 2015

Thanksgiving. I am not there. My wife and grown children are with my mother in America, celebrating. I am here, where no one cares if I wake or sleep. Nor where I will go tomorrow. We define meaning in our lives in an arbitrary manner. One of the greatest sources of meaning is fulfilling a categorical imperative, a duty. I am a soldier, thus I must fight. I am a father, thus I must provide for my family. These duties bear no uncertainty, and fulfilling them proves a person's mettle and gives value to his life, value that virtually any person, from any culture, would recognize. Many people are never granted the privilege of passing beyond the obligation of ensuring the material wellbeing of themselves and their families. For those lucky enough to surpass this constraint, the search for meaning becomes more complex. In my case, I have an acute need for meaning and an equally acute awareness of what is truly an obligation or duty and what is not. My familial duties are a joy to me, as when I advise or assist my children, I know that I am doing right and good. On a trip such as this one, even an unforeseen professional obligation can be welcome, because the rest of the time I have no obligations, no constraints, only that I told myself I would write this book, and that I am now doing.

Today was relaxing. I walked around Fethiye and saw literally nothing of interest. It seems to be a destination for culturally vapid beachgoers. I had a fresh juice (again a mixture of orange and pomegranate) near the city's main mosque, made and served by a very courteous man. Generally, the Turks are very polite people, though strangely I find street vendors and taxi drivers to be more so than the staff of high-end hotels. I returned to my room because it was raining intermittently and I didn't have the energy to walk up to the local Tomb of Amyntas from the fourth century BCE. At dinnertime I went and had a drink at a locally famous bar, where I asked and followed the recommendation of the waitress for a restaurant and had a good meal, octopus and sea bass wrapped in vine leaves. Then back to the hotel just as the rain started again. I drank some whisky bought in a small liquor store for an exorbitant price, and thought of my journey so far.

NOVEMBER 27, 2015

This morning, I woke early, refreshed and not hungover despite several glasses of whisky last night. I was the first person in the hotel restaurant for breakfast, and modified my usual olives and cheese in favor of round bread with fresh honeycomb and butter. Then I arranged a taxi to the tomb of Amyntas. This is one of the finest examples of a Lycian rock tomb, carved into the limestone face of a cliff in the fourth century BCE when the city of Telmessos existed on the present site of Fethiye. Amyntas is a Macedonian name, so perhaps a comrade of Alexander the Great was buried here, or at least a Macedonian who came to Lycia and was a prominent citizen. He does not seem to have been an important historical figure. Though the tomb is highly photogenic and appreciated by travelers past and present, including Freya Stark in *The Lycian Shore*, it was defaced with graffiti by adolescent lovers and badly maintained with one of its limestone columns crumbling. The ruins of the local castle were even less inspiring. Presumably most of ancient Telmessos must be underneath present-day Fethiye. Even the theater was uninteresting, most of it newly "renovated," that is to say rebuilt and not seeming ancient or authentic at all. Tourists may enjoy it for five minutes on a rainy day away from the beach. Back to the hotel, packed my things to leave, and caught up on writing. Off to Bodrum now for the next stage of the journey.

The ride from Fethiye to Bodrum took slightly over three hours, and the scenery was spectacular, the highlight a broad and fertile valley whose river emptied into the sea at Akyaka. The mountains here come right down to the sea abruptly, with peninsulas, large islands, and also tiny mountaintops barely surpassing the water level. Freya Stark visited this region in the 1950s by boat, when there were few roads, and commenting on an ancient port and on the successive ancient sailors who passed through it, wrote:

> Each in their turn passed through the narrow opening and felt the sudden calm. In these places, the natural features have remained unaltered; the moments that visit them, fashioned to one pattern by nature itself, drop like beads on a string, through long pauses, one after the other, into the same silence.[23]

Strangely, midway through today's journey, I noticed that the geology had changed. The overlooking mountains were the same fine limestone I have seen here all along, but the lower foothills were of a kind of fragmented sedimentary, slate-like, unclimbable rock. Nobody looks at rock the way climbers do, probably as sailors look at waves in the sea or as pilots look at clouds and the air currents they can depict. To go deeper into a particular aspect of nature is to learn to perceive an extant beauty that others do not perceive. Would that I could perceive all beauty!

Tomorrow, I will visit Bodrum and plan the remaining days of the trip. I long for open travel, where I do not have a counted number of days. My present family and professional obligations render this feasible, but I have not done it yet. To travel and not know when I will be home. It can be frightening. What home? Perhaps I will try. Looking at the map at the beginning of this trip, reaching Gallipoli seemed feasible, but it is not. I will return in the future and go from Izmir to Istanbul. Before that

---

23. Stark, Freya, *The Lycian Shore*. New York: Tauris Parke, 2011, p. 101.

the Black Sea Coast. And the south-east, near Syria, my most dangerous and daunting objective, which I will still undertake as I feel that I must. As Bernard Moitessier, the great French solo navigator, wrote, about watching his sailboat founder after having been washed off of it by a rogue wave passing the Cape of Good Hope:

> And I could see that page of *Terre des hommes* about destiny, about the absolute need to follow one's destiny, whatever the result. I too, I would end like Saint-Exupéry's gazelle, whose destiny was to bound under the sun and to die one day under the lion's claws. But I regretted nothing, in that water, warm and so light, from which I readied myself to leave peacefully on my final voyage.[24]

NOVEMBER 28, 2015

Last night, I had dinner in the restaurant of the hotel in Bodrum. I spoke with two Turkish ladies at the table next to mine, and they invited me outside when they went to smoke a cigarette. They were both doctors, former colleagues. One had moved to Istanbul and was back here visiting her friend. In Arabia, such an anodyne event would probably never have occurred, innocent as it was. In twenty years of regular stays in Arabia, the closest I came to being invited to sit with a female stranger was a sultry look from under the veil of a lithe and beautiful (I imagined) woman. The name of the younger woman here was Talia, and the older Nilufar, from Persian for "water lily," passed into French as *nénuphar*. Both were divorced, Nilufar twice and Talia once. According to Nilufar, Talia still had plenty of time to divorce a second time, being younger. Nonetheless, they seemed to maintain cordial relationships with their ex-husbands. Both of them spoke English quite well. We spoke about Islam, but they knew little about it even if they were interested. Atatürk's reforms have created a situation where educated Turks know so little

---

24. Moitessier, Bernard, *La Longue route*. Paris: Flammarion, 1986, p. 84. Reproduced with permission from Flammarion and Rowman & Littlefield. Translation by the author. An English translation of this work is published by Globe Pequot as *The Long Way*.

about Islam that they cannot even discuss the topic with *takfiri*[25] Islamists in the same language, the religious language which the subject requires.

When I woke up this morning, I could hear a storm raging outside. I opened the curtains and saw the wind bending the trees sideways and blowing rain onto my balcony, which looks over Bodrum from on high, down to the castle on the sea. Sea birds were flying in this storm. Why? The only reason would be for the fun of it, to test themselves against nature. They could not see far enough through the rain to look for food and were clearly not bound for any particular destination. And surely they could have found a place to shelter from the wind, so were just soaring in the turbulence for fun. I will not go out in this weather at all, and unless it improves this day will be spent reading, writing, and relaxing at the hotel. No refugees could have left Turkey's shores for the nearby Greek islands in this storm, or if they had, they would have drowned by now.

The storm abated after breakfast, and by coincidence, I left the hotel at the same time as another guest, a Westerner like me. Ordinarily I would have kept my distance, but for some unknown reason I started talking to him. His name was Andrew and he was working in Tarsus as headmaster of a prestigious school. We walked through Bodrum together, dodging raindrops, and looked at all the major monuments. The fourth-century BCE Mausoleum of Mausollos, one of the Seven Wonders of the World, though ravaged by ignorant knights in the fifteenth century who took its stone to build their castle, was nonetheless interesting. There were drawings on placards of what the mausoleum (this word owes its origin to the name of Mausollos) looked like, based on a very detailed description written by Pliny the Elder.[26] It is a terrible shame that the barbarous knights destroyed this monument, leaving only the Great Pyramid at Giza from the original Seven Wonders of the Ancient World. Their spiritual descendants continue to cause mayhem today. Islamic State destroying Palmyra in Syria; the Taliban demolishing the Buddhas at Bamiyan in Afghanistan; the British

25. As discussed earlier, *takfir* is an Arabic word and means to assert that another Muslim is an apostate, a status punishable by death. Islamic State, Al-Qaida and other modern jihadist organizations take this right as self-evident, to decide that people who profess to be Muslims are not so, and thus deserve death.

26. This is based on a text at the site of the mausoleum, which seemed quite academic in tone.

122

railroad engineer dismantling 4,500-year old Harappa, sister city of Mohenjo-Daro in Pakistan, to use the fired bricks as ballast for railroad tracks; and continuing back to the Knights Hospitaller of the fifteenth century here in ancient Halicarnassus (present-day Bodrum).

Leaving the mausoleum, we wended our way to the Myndos Gate, guarded by an obnoxious huckster. We declined his services and poked around the ruins, also built by Mausollos in the fourth century BCE. The gate is all that remains of the city walls of Halicarnassus. The moat where Alexander lost many troops, as recounted by Arrian, was still visible.[27] The walls were made of large blocks of andesite, a seemingly granitic rock, but more porous. One of the interior corners of the wall formed a very satisfying dihedral, with large protuberant blocks providing ample hand and footholds. While Andrew watched, I carefully climbed it to the top, eight or nine meters, and was rewarded with the view of the surrounding ruins and ancient battlefield. We then headed for the theater in the rain. I thought it was unremarkable, having seen several such Roman theaters, none of which can compare to that of Termessos alone on its mountaintop, but Andrew seemed to appreciate it. We left the theater and walked to the port, stopping for beer and a good discussion. I do not know what it is that makes a man who has passed most of his life in one place decide to up and leave and begin to explore the wider world. I made this decision aged nineteen, involuntarily pushed by factors beyond my control, partly to escape an unhappy childhood and partly to mollify my own personal demon, which has not left me.

I parted from Andrew at the castle, reserving it for tomorrow, and walked back through the town. I read and planned the rest of the trip. Not much remains. Two weeks are long in experiences but short on time. I know that I could travel longer. When in the middle of a trip I have no idea whether it is a success or failure. I have a vague sense of *mal-être* interspersed with glorious feelings of freedom, and moments when I feel that I am beginning to grasp what the history of our world is about. But then the feeling subsides like a wave withdrawing from the sand, and I just see chaos all around, murder and destruction visited on innocent people.

---

27. Arrian, pp. 85-9.

I read the newspaper this morning. Disheartening. Six refugee children died at sea two days ago in the terrible storm I witnessed from my balcony. China is forbidding the teaching of the Tibetan language in schools, attempting to carry through to conclusion the destruction of the Tibetan culture and nation. Closer to where I am, the Russian jet shot down by Turkey on Erdoğan's orders, for a seventeen-second territorial encroachment. Such an event had never happened before in fifty years of cat-and-mouse games between NATO and the Warsaw Pact. It is a bad idea to maintain a defensive alliance with a country run by a hothead. The Russians noted that he named his son-in-law as Minister of Energy.[28] So Turkey is moving towards being a dynastic dictatorship.[29] And it has now imprisoned journalists who reported on the government delivering arms to Islamist rebels in Syria. And what of the 500 oil trucks traveling to Turkey from Syria, recently destroyed by the Americans and the Russians? They were trading Islamic State oil to Turkey. Whose side is Turkey on?[30] And in the most recent outrage, a Kurdish human rights activist was assassinated. How could the government not have had a hand in this? Perhaps Turkey is not so different from its neighbors after all.

Thoroughly disgusted by the bad news of the world, I walked into Bodrum again. I went more slowly than I did yesterday, and because I was alone, I was more observant. I left the main thoroughfare, passing through small streets and alleys and listening for people speaking Arabic. I wanted to see if the refugees who depart from these shores on rafts bound for the nearby Greek islands were still here as they were in the summer. I walked down an alley between two buildings to a pebble beach on the sea. There was

28. He has since been named Minister of Finance.

29. Since this comment was written, the United States has also moved in this direction, with the son-in-law and daughter of President Trump (that phrase still sticks in my craw) named to important positions, and with the latter using the White House staff as advertising agents for her fashion brand.

30. As of my last visits, in late 2016, Turkey had chosen sides against Islamic State, aided by the latter's murderous attacks on Turkish citizens. Turkey is also, and even more strongly, still against the Kurds, both those in Turkey and those in Syria, and the Turkish Army has shelled several of its own cities, reducing some neighborhoods to rubble.

a group of young men sitting together, speaking neither Turkish nor Arabic, clearly not from here and clearly migrants. By the look of one of them, I guessed he was either Afghan or from the Northwest Frontier Province of Pakistan. I sat at a respectful distance on the beach after greeting them and looked out over the sea, wondering if the land in the distance was the Greek island of Kos, and wondering too at the journey these young men had made to get here. The call to prayer sounded, balancing tremulously over the cyclical sound of the waves. I felt sad for the men but I know that I would do what they had done if I were in their position. No one can blame them for taking destiny into their hands and leaving war, famine, corruption, and death. If there is no hope where you are, you move. *Fortuna audentes iuvat* ("Fortune favors the bold").[31] When they rose to leave, one of them, perhaps sensing my compassion, put his hand to his heart and nodded his head to me. I remained, staring out to sea.

I carried on and saw no more young men, walking to the end of the concrete jetty protecting the marina. This is where I would sit if I had nowhere to go. There was a group of Turkish friends there and a couple of old men taking their constitutional walks. I returned to land to see the Museum of Underwater Archaeology. In front of the entrance gate was a statue of Herodotus, born here in the fifth century BCE (when Bodrum was known as Halicarnassus, part of ancient Caria). I knew he was referred to as "the Father of History," but did not know he was also a great traveler, having visited many of the places he wrote about. As elsewhere in Turkey, there were a great many stray cats here, several of which were kittens. A little girl, two or three, stumbled after them, calling my attention to her parents. I greeted them in the same manner as I had the young men, and they returned my greeting. They said they were Syrian, and I think they were planning to try to make it to Europe, though they did not say so openly. So many young children, and some adults as well, have drowned simply because life preservers are rare on the refugee smuggler boats. The rubbish bins in front of the museum were lined with heavy-duty plastic bags that could have been made into serviceable emergency life preservers. I should have told them to take bags like those for their journey.

---

31. Virgil, *The Aeneid*. Book X, line 284.

The museum was remarkable, opening my eyes to a whole part of archaeology that I did not know: the excavation of shipwrecks. The man responsible for excavating most of the wrecks in the museum was George Fletcher Bass, founder of the Institute for Nautical Archaeology and "Father of Underwater Archaeology." Some people have the fortune to lead lives where a governing passion rules what they do, where the vast majority of their time and life energy is devoted to that passion, where they meet with nearly unmitigated success, and where they literally enjoy everything they do. George Bass seemed such a man, the epitome of a successful life. The shipwrecks themselves shed light on the complexity of ancient trade relations (back to the sixteenth century BCE), including ingots of iron and bronze, exotic woods, and amphorae of oil and wine being traded. And I noticed an anecdote in one of the texts accompanying an exhibit: in the ancient realm of Caria, of which Halicarnassus was the capital, tax evaders were sold as slaves to foreign powers. And we think our legal system is harsh.

NOVEMBER 30, 2015

I woke up earlier than usual today, well-rested. I read the news, answered some emails, showered, and had breakfast. I then read about the Bodrum Peninsula in preparation for my drive around it today. The driver, Deniz, was polite, but his car smelled like an ashtray. We drove to Ortakent, then south, and followed the coast. The whole place was empty. The coastline was beautiful but scarred by quick and cheap development. The Greek island of Kos, to which I had flown several times on my way to climb on the neighboring island of Kalymnos, was just across the water, such a short journey causing the deaths of so many. No migrants at all were here now. Deniz said that there were many during the summer. Continuing around the coast and turning north at the end of the peninsula, the island of Kalymnos came into view. It is one of the finest sport climbing destinations in the world, with myriad stalactites on overhanging limestone.

We continued to Gümüşlük, and I asked Deniz to stop at Myndos, site of a city of ancient Caria which played a role in the wars between Greece and Persia in the fourth and fifth centuries BCE. Its main claim to fame was having been mentioned in various ancient historical and geographical texts (Strabo, Arrian). Now it has no claim to fame at all. Deniz called a friend of his who said there was nothing to see. I thought he was just being lazy, and insisted, so he took me to a small port with plenty of fish restaurants and no clients. The whole place stank of rotting fish. There was a small island nearby with a few ancient ruins and a sign about them, but nothing more. Deniz asked a man inside the police station. I do not know exactly what was said, but if one were to try to construct a Platonic form of stupidity, it would look like that guy. We continued on the road around the peninsula and saw hollowed out rocks nearby as well as a large section of green land between the road and the sea. This was the protected site of the ancient city of Myndos. Little could be visited, but Deniz turned into a dirt track with a brown government sign that read, "*Hammam*" ("bath"). The track was nearly impassable, but in a field to the right were the ruins of a monumental building complete with sections of fluted marble columns and monolithic blocks. We passed the structure and reached the end of the track. Our immediate problem was then that there was no way to turn around. The road ended in the sea, with little left of the good harbor mentioned by ancient historians, and a van in front of us, driven there for whatever reason by an incompetent, had become stuck turning around. I got out and left Deniz to help him in order to escape from the asphyxiating stench of burnt rubber as he spun his wheels, mercilessly trying to gain purchase. Along the coastline, I walked among large lintel stones from ancient buildings lying along the shore and in the sea. Finally, Deniz managed to extricate us from this parking predicament by turning his car around on the dirt track itself, and we left the van driver to his own devices. On the way out, I stopped and looked more closely at the monumental ruins. Not much left.

The drive back to Bodrum was uninteresting, even depressing, due to shoddy development. First, wonderful hills despoiled by thousands of tourist bungalows resembling small white boxes, as if some passing giant airplane had dumped a rubbish bin full of empty packaging on the hillsides. And then a long section of strip mall that would have fit perfectly in the ugliest parts of New Jersey. We arrived at the hotel and I paid Deniz, giving him a significant tip in appreciation of his good faith and effort in trying to find Myndos (and probably ripping various parts off the bottom of his car in the process). I arranged for him to drive me to Ephesus the next day, with stops along the way to explore, hopefully, sites more interesting than Myndos.

I have just finished lunch at a restaurant in the port of Bodrum. The first lunch of the trip so far. I am feeling depressed, unsure of the value of what I am doing, and even more unsure of what I will do next. I will not study Turkish any further unless I decide to make a three- or four-month full-time commitment. Studying for a few more weeks is useless since I can already make simple sentences, and another few weeks would not advance my abilities much further. I miss home, am bored, and feel lonely. I doubt I could travel for six months on end as I did when I was young. I will go back to the hotel. Maybe I can find a dumb TV show to watch. I have not watched anything in ten days.

DECEMBER 1, 2015

This morning, I leave for Ephesus, stopping to visit the ancient ruins of Priene on the way. I just finished breakfast. Olives, a variety of Turkish cheeses, bread, scrambled eggs with tomatoes and peppers, and some pomegranate seeds for dessert. I have felt disoriented for this entire trip. I presume it is a feeling shared by many of us in Europe since the Bataclan attacks. Disoriented that we were attacked by Muslim extremists, killing 130 of us, mostly young people, for nothing. Disoriented that the weak and incompetent leaders of our countries failed to stop these attacks and have refused to do anything serious to avenge them. (We bomb Islamic State oil trucks now, on their way to Turkey to sell their oil. Why did we not do so before?) Disoriented that any hope of cooperation with Russia against Islamic State is now shattered. Disoriented that the democratic institutions of our civilization are being weakened and may not survive intact.

Deniz came to pick me up at 11 AM and we left, heading north towards Selçuk, near the site of ancient Ephesus. This will be the last stop on my journey before flying to London for a meeting of the Fletcher School European Advisory Group. Along the road, the view of the coast was magnificent. Steep mountains covered with evergreen forests falling into the wine-dark sea. Turkey truly is a beautiful country. Unlike the Bodrum Peninsula, the coastline here is undeveloped, much more to my liking. Along the way, Deniz asked if I would like to stop at Euromos, an ancient temple. Of course I would, though it was not mentioned in any of the preparatory reading I had done. We were the only ones there. Not much of a city, but a temple of Zeus, much better preserved than other temples I had seen, with most of its columns still standing and joined by enormous rectangular blocks on top of them. I pondered a while, considering my privilege to travel freely in this manner and see these places. But I felt disoriented nonetheless.

We continued on towards Priene. Deniz asked if I was married, and I said that I was. Deniz was not married, he said, having been in two relationships that he found difficult. He told me that his main pleasure in life now was drinking two beers each evening after work, to relax, and on the weekends drinking *raki*[32] and talking with his friends. At Priene, Deniz went to have tea while I walked around the site. Priene was a small city (3,000 to 6,000 inhabitants) from the fifth century BCE until the tenth century CE. It overlooks a broad plain leading to the sea, which, at the time of the city's initial settlement, was the sea. The silt deposited by the river filled in the coastline over the years, but initially Priene was a port city. The Meander river has reclaimed up to a hundred square kilometers in the past 2,500 years, the seacoast moving steadily further west. Priene is said to be one of the earliest examples of urban planning with perpendicular city streets, a technique said to have been invented by Hippodamus of Miletus. Miletus is another ancient city contemporaneous with Priene, and just to the south of here. Unfortunately, whoever made the assertion that urban planning was invented here was wrong, as the architects of Mohenjo-Daro predated Priene by 2,000 years and embraced absolutely modern city planning.

Whatever the case, Priene is a beautiful city, with a well-preserved theater, and its Temple of Athena, started by Mausollos, is impressive, five

---

32. *Raki* is a hard liquor made from anise, such as exists in many Mediterranean countries. It is similar to *ouzo* (Greek), *'arak* (Arabic), and *pastis* (French).

of its columns still standing. The others have been thrown down by the rough hand of Time, enormous fluted disks previously stacked upon each other to form the columns now strewn in a grove of pine trees and mixed with enormous blocks fallen down from the mountain above during the earthquake which seems to have wrecked the city. I wandered over the entire site, around 40 hectares of walled area of which twenty-seven were urbanized. It has been excavated by a team of German archaeologists who prepared a map and signage in German and Turkish but not English, thus excluding almost all foreign visitors from reading them. As was the case with the other places I saw, Priene had very few visitors.

We continued on towards Selçuk, where we located my hotel and parted, wishing each other safe travels. From the room in Selçuk, I spoke with my son for nearly an hour about an economics paper he had written. It felt strange to be discussing something like this with him, strange to see how he has grown up. I felt cut off from my past, his past. I ate dinner in an ordinary Turkish restaurant where I was the only foreigner. This place was empty now, no tourists at all. I sat for a drink in the hotel bar and had an interesting conversation with Mursalin, a man of Kurdish ethnicity who works in the hotel. His name is an Arabic word meaning "those who have been sent" and comes from the Qur'an, in *Surat Ya-Sin* (Q 36:2, quoted earlier), so two names of people I have met came from these few *ayat*, Yasin and Mursalin. Years ago, despite his own Kurdish origins, Mursalin was a Turkish Special Forces soldier fighting against the PKK in eastern Turkey.[33] He had some unusual views about relationships between men and women, notably that if a man seeks sex with other women while he is married, it is the fault of his wife. I argued that if a man does this it is his own decision, his own responsibility, and therefore his own fault, not that of his wife. The world-views of Turkish men appear to be less modern than the country's infrastructure, as was previously hinted to me by Talia and Nilufar, the two divorcées I spoke with a few days ago in Bodrum. After a second drink, I went to bed, gazing briefly from my window onto the sole standing column

---

33. The PKK (Kurdish Workers' Party) is a group fighting for an independent Kurdish state. It is classified as a terrorist organization by Turkey, the EU, and the US, and hostilities have recently recommenced between it and Turkey after relatively successful negotiations led to a few years of peace.

of the Temple of Artemis, illuminated in the night. Two days later, Mursalin drove me to the airport and I gave him my knife, for which he thanked me.

DECEMBER 2, 2015

I am sitting on the top of Ayasoluk Hill writing. Here, John the Apostle is said to have written his Gospel. He is also said to be buried just down the hill, and Emperor Justinian built a basilica over his grave in the sixth century CE, which was thrown down in ruins (still extant) in the early fifteenth century, apparently by the Mongols, but was recorded for posterity by Ibn Battuta shortly before its destruction, thus:

> The Friday Mosque of this city is among the most beautiful mosques of the world. There is no comparison to it in beauty. It was a holy church for the Byzantines, who came to see it from far countries. When the city was conquered, the Muslims made the church into the Friday Mosque. Its walls are of multi-colored marble, and its floor of white marble. It is roofed with lead and has eleven different cupolas, under each of which is a basin of water. [34]

John the Apostle would have sat here looking over the sea, the world rotating around him as around an axis, but the sea is more distant now and the rotation has quickened, spinning out of control. All of the things I see escape me. I seize only a moment, and another and another in the sweep of history, but it is much too great for me. I am not able to comprehend its ebb and flow, its storms and cataclysms, what rises and what falls, and how it will be for us. A lifetime of searching and I have found nothing but wonder. But I imagine that I can feel the foundations of our civilization trembling. The collapse is far off, that day when we will follow the others, leaving traces and mysteries for the future, but the cracks now appearing in the edifice are real. Can the citizens of an aging civilization feel the onset of its decline? Or is it my own personal, irrevocable, mortal, and banal decline which I detect?

---

34. Harb, p. 318. Author's translation.

I had breakfast this morning, spoke with the owner of the hotel, then left to visit the ancient sites. I walked to the Temple of Artemis, now a malarial mud hole with a sole mottled column, fragments of stone disks held together by splotches of sloppy cement like a Viagra-erected dick, artificial and disgusting, stuck into the surrounding swampland. Around it lay the remains of a fractured monument, broken stone insufficient to form prayers to. This temple was one of the ancient world's Seven Wonders. The rest of the stone must have been quarried for use elsewhere. Aside from the general worthlessness of the site, it is infested by touts, fake guides, and souvenir sellers. It is the worst place I have been in recent memory. As I left, I was aggressively approached and offered the services of taxi drivers, but I declined for fear that the foul memory of this place would follow me like a bad smell. I stationed myself on the side of the road to Ephesus and stuck out my thumb. The third car stopped for me, a poor man in a rundown vehicle who spoke no Arabic, French, or English. I told him in Turkish, "I would like to go to Ephesus." He left me at the intersection and I walked two kilometers to the lower gate.

Ephesus is an impressive ancient city, with nearby settlements apparently dating back to the early Bronze age and attested to in Hittite texts, though the present vestiges are Greek and Roman. It is also one of the ancient Christian outposts to which the Apostle Paul wrote his epistles. That to Ephesus was one of the "Epistles from Captivity," of great theological significance as they define the relationship of the Church to Jesus and other matters. Its theater is the largest I have seen aside from the Colosseum in Rome. There were busloads of tourists here, apparently brought in from elsewhere since they were not to be found in the hotels or restaurants of Selçuk. It was a simple matter to walk a few meters away from the major sights to be rid of them. The city was imposing for its size, and for the famous Library of Celsus, but more interesting to me than the monumental structures were the terraced houses from the third century BCE, in which wealthy Ephesians lived. The archaeological effort put into excavating these houses, undertaken by the Austrian government, must have been Herculean, and the result is exceptional, a true window onto the lives and homes of wealthy people from almost 2,500 years ago, particularly their aesthetic sense expressed in the design of their interiors.

This part of the site is subject to a small additional fee, and for the nearly forty-five minutes I spent there, I was utterly alone. It takes so little to escape the mass of humanity.

After three hours, I left Ephesus quickly from its upper gate, striding like a soldier to dissuade the touts from bothering me. I set off on the road towards Selçuk, took a minute to find my bearings, then continued walking. I had not taken any water with me and was thirsty. An orange grove across the road contained a tree with branches overhanging the fence, and I took the liberty of reducing its burden by two mandarin oranges. Glorious primordial citrus! They quenched my thirst and provided me with a sensation that I still vividly remember. I reached the main road and again stuck out my thumb to hitchhike. I feel a curious freedom when I do this, from some unfathomable source, the freedom of the road. In the ancient Arabic *hadith qudsi*, mentioned earlier, the poor wanderer is called "son of the road."[35] Thirty years ago, leaving Mount Kailash in Tibet just before the onset of winter, I spent three full days by the road waiting for a truck to pick me up. One finally did on the fourth day. This time I was much more fortunate and, as earlier, the third passing car stopped for me. The driver worked in tourism and spoke good English. After a pleasant conversation, he dropped me back in Selçuk, from where I climbed the hill to the ruined Basilica of St. John built over the Apostle's tomb, then the castle above it, and within its walls reached the summit of Ayasoluk Hill, from which point all may be seen. I sat on a block of ancient stone, a ruin from a past time, in the warm sunlight and meditated on John the Apostle writing here, at the axis of the world, at the end of his own life. Did he take the just measure of the events which he had witnessed and recorded? Did he know that they would be read for two millennia by millions unknown to him?

---

35. The *hadith qudsi* referred to is in the entry for February 4, 2015. This phrase "son of the road" also occurs in *Surat al-Baqara*, "They ask you what they should spend [in charity]. Say, 'Whatever you spend for good is for parents and relatives and orphans and the needy and the son of the road. And whatever good you do, verily God knows of it.'" Q 2:215.

5

FROM ANTALYA TO THE EAST

FEBRUARY 10, 2016

I AM IN THE PLANE TO ISTANBUL NOW. I often have trouble explaining to people why I have made the changes in my life that have enabled me to travel, and why I would even want to do so. I bear a sort of societally inculcated guilt at having decided to work less, to earn less money, and to be freer. Last April I visited my wife Hélène's nephew, Yann, at the end of a rock-climbing trip to Spain. When Yann was a child, around twelve years old, he and his family came to visit us for two weeks in Cairo. I took them to the Pyramids, but also to Saqqara to see the Step Pyramid of Zozer, emanating hoary antiquity. We went also to the Serapeum, a vast underground gallery containing dozens of massive sarcophagi for the burial of the sacred Apis bulls, mummified by the Ancient Egyptians. The Ancient Egyptians mummified virtually everything, from cats to ibises, from bulls to themselves. For some reason, on the day of our visit the electricity was out, and the guard refused us entry. I explained to him that I had already been four or five times to this place and knew the simple floor plan by heart, and moreover that I had a small flashlight for the six of us. This information, and a bribe, earned us entrance, and we explored the "bull mausoleum" in the dark. As we left, I bribed another guard to allow Yann and me to descend a long ladder into an as-yet unexcavated tomb currently being examined by Egyptologists. Yann's eyes were filled with wonder at these sights. When I visited him recently, he was no longer twelve but in his mid-thirties, with a family of his own, living near Barcelona. I explained to him, trying to employ the tenuous reasoning I use when I justify to "adults" my choice to travel and write, when Yann interrupted me and said, "You don't need to explain or justify why you made these decisions and want to travel. That is what you are, a traveler. That is just what you do." I felt vindicated that someone who had known me when he was a child harbored no ambiguity concerning my decision.

Now I am starting a new phase of my travels. I have spent ten weeks traveling in Turkey. Four in 1987, two in the fall of 2014, two in Istanbul in early 2015 to study Turkish, and two from Antalya to Izmir last November. I will make three more trips: this one to the south-east near Syria; one to the Black Sea coast, probably in June; and one from Izmir to Istanbul, probably next autumn. That will be sixteen weeks. Is this enough to "know" a country? This present trip is the crux of the journeys. It is the most dangerous of them due to the war in Syria and the various groups of Syrians in Turkey, some of whom would surely wish me harm. Before I left, my daughter Marianne expressed concern about my plans, and I wrote this reply to her:

> I thank you for your concern for me. Your brother Alexander also expressed a similar concern when we spoke tonight. I am not a foolish person, nor do I seek risk for its own sake. But sometimes in life you have to make decisions based on your own nature. Before you were born, I was a real traveller, almost an adventurer, and I am still such a man now. If there is such a thing as destiny, it is my destiny to travel to places that are far away, different, and sometimes potentially dangerous. I have fixed myself a goal, to write a travel book. This goal calls me to go to certain places, which are close to, but not in, danger. I will go. I will not go blindly or ignorantly, and each step of the way I will look around me and assess the conditions. If my judgment tells me I can go forward, then I will.

In the book by Bernard Moitessier I read last summer, *La Longue route*, while drawing what he believes are his last breaths before drowning, he remembers an excerpt from *Terre des hommes* by Antoine de St. Exupéry about the absolute need to follow one's destiny. St. Exupéry describes this need in gazelles, raised from their birth in captivity but longing for the open desert: "You know that which they seek. It is open space which will complete them. They wish to become gazelles and to dance their dance. At 130 km/h, they wish to know rectilinear flight, broken by leaps and bounds, here and there, as if flames were bursting forth from the desert sand. And what of the jackals, if the Truth of gazelles is to taste fear, which alone can push them to surpass themselves, and draw from them their noblest maneuvers! And what of the lion, if the Truth of gazelles is to be ripped open by its claws under the sun!"[1] I knowingly accept the risks of what I do. I will go, and I hope to bring back something worthy.

I have prepared more for this journey than for the others. I read the relevant chapters of *The Fall of the Ottomans*, an excellent academic work on Ottoman history by Eugene Rogan, a professor at Oxford.[2] I also read in full Franz Werfel's *The Forty Days of Musa Dagh*.[3] My goals are ambitious. To look over the sea from the slopes of Musa Dagh, where in 1915 Armenian villagers fought for their lives and won them against the overwhelming forces of the Turkish Army, withstanding their assaults long enough to be rescued by the French Navy. To see Tarsus, Antakya, and Şanlıurfa. To experience Göbekli Tepe's 12,000-year-old temple, which turns our view of Neolithic history upside down. And to stop and visit Andrew, whom I met on my last trip in Bodrum, and who lives in Tarsus. Most of these goals are in places marked either red or orange on the color-coded travelers' advisory website of the French Foreign Ministry. All of them are under travel advisory by the US, American consular services being always more timid than those of

1. Saint-Exupéry, Antoine, *Terre des hommes*. Paris: Gallimard, 1939, pp. 167-8. Translation by the author.

2. Rogan, Eugene, *The Fall of the Ottomans*. London: Penguin Random House, 2015.

3. Werfel, Franz, *The Forty Days of Musa Dagh*. Boston: Verba Mundi, 2012.

European countries.[4] So I will proceed with prudence, stay vigilant, and turn back if I feel in danger.[5]

The connection in Istanbul was smooth, as was the flight to Antalya. After landing I took a taxi. On the road from the airport to town, a deep depression descended upon me. I do not know why. Travel should be liberating, and it often is for me. Maybe life is just passing by me too fast. No matter what I do, how intensely I concentrate on it, I feel that I am somehow missing it. The taxi driver did not know the exact route to the hotel so I gave him the phone number and he called. From last November, I vaguely remembered a street and an old clock tower, but I couldn't tell if this memory was from here or from some other place in the past. Our reconstructions of reality are often both inaccurate and ephemeral, but in this case I was right. I took my room, unpacked in a minute, and came to the restaurant in which I sit now, where I had dined once on my previous visit to Antalya. This time I will not delay, but will head east.

FEBRUARY 11, 2016

Today was physically tranquil but morally trying. Work responsibilities required my time and attention, and I was unable to free my mind from them. I did, though, manage several crucial errands. I arranged to go to Alanya tomorrow with Yasin, the same man with whom I traveled to Perge, Termessos, and Çıralı last November. By chance, I had seen him while going to the hotel reception. I then had breakfast. My "traditional" Turkish breakfast includes several eggs made to order, many olives,

---

4. This greater timidity is not the only difference between US and Western European consular services. In my experience, many US diplomatic personnel are grossly incompetent compared to their European counterparts. In Cairo when I was a Fulbright Scholar, I learned that six of the 600 US Embassy staff posted there spoke Arabic well (one of those six was studying with me, and told me). At the same time, Hungary had around thirty Embassy staff, and I learned that six of them also spoke Arabic well. In Saudi Arabia, as a dual US/French citizen, I registered with both consulates. In 2002–03 when a spate of terrorist attacks against foreigners occurred in the Kingdom, the French Consulate asked me to provide them with an accurate map to my apartment location, and also sent me regular security information and requests for confirmation of the dates of my presence. Nothing similar from the US side.

5. I also took the additional precaution of informing a close Saudi friend and business colleague of my itinerary, and telling him that if I ended up kidnapped by jihadists then I counted on him to enlist the help of his government's intelligence services to get me released!

several types of both green and black ones, at least four or five types of cheese, and fresh-squeezed orange juice. This, followed by coffee and a small piece of bread with honey or a piece or two of fruit, sets me up for the day until dinner, with either nothing or a small snack at lunchtime. I then walked to the bazaar area of town and changed money, then followed the tenuous thread of my memory through the winding streets of the bazaar back towards the knife shop I had patronized the last time I was here. I did not make it there, finding another store where I methodically considered the various knives and chose a fairly well-made one, for which I overpaid because the owner was something of an "operator" and I liked him. Even so, I haggled him down by twenty percent from his initial price, which was probably fifty percent too high.

On the way back to the hotel, I wandered through the bazaar, passing shops containing nothing I would want. I passed by the Yivli Minaret. It was beautiful, as it was a few months ago and, as I presume, it has been for the past 800 years. I stopped next at the Tekeli Mehmet Pasha Mosque. Inside, supporting its domed cupola, a hexagonal base with six Arabic medallions high above, one for Allah, one for the Prophet, then one for each of the first four "Rightly-Guided Caliphs" of Islam: Abu Bakr, Umar, Uthman, and Ali. It was under the reign and on the orders of the Caliph Uthman that the accepted codex of the Qur'an was compiled from existing fragments and from memory, and all variants destroyed.

Tomorrow, Yasin and I will leave at 9 AM drive first to Aspendos, then Side, then Alarahan (and its nearby castle) and finally to Alanya, where Ibn Battuta landed by sea on his way from Latakia (in present-day Syria) in the year 1332. Today I practiced being alert as I walked through the bazaar. Gaze moving, not resting too long on anything (pretty women are the main distraction to overcome in this regard—here many are veiled). Keep at a fair distance from others. Notice if their gazes rest upon me. Prefer one side or the other of the pavement to the middle. Navigate with a certain degree of unpredictability. And do not look at my phone unless I have a wall behind me. Threats seem general from afar, but from up close each one is specific. Urfa is not potentially dangerous by nature. It is potentially dangerous because certain individuals there might wish me ill, and might act on that wish.

The terrace at which I am now sitting and having a beer while writing this is surprisingly full of people, as the weather is chilly. They are all locals, ordinary people. Playing backgammon or cards with friends, talking, drinking tea or beer. Those drinking tea apparently feel no urge to kill or otherwise molest those drinking beer. Yet a few hundred kilometers from here lies the Islamic State. How can these Muslims accept modernity, tolerance, and individual choice, and those not? The theological issues have not been resolved. Here they live and let live without requiring theological certainty.

FEBRUARY 12, 2016

Today I awoke with my alarm at 7:15 AM. I got up, showered, and went to breakfast. I had the usual, with even more olives and olive oil on bread, in keeping with a *hadith* of the Prophet Muhammad: "Eat the oil of the olive tree and anoint yourselves with it, for it is a blessed tree." Western scholarship considers many if not almost all of the *hadith* apocryphal, a view which is intellectually grounded,[6] but for a student of Islam the *hadith* literature has another role, which is to convey the concern of Islam for the right ordering of life and for the respect for life and for other people which underlies much of the Islamic religion. After breakfast I packed my things, unusually stowing my journal in my backpack, which I locked, and putting my headlamp, binoculars, and a small bottle of water in my small pouch to carry with me.

I met Yasin in the restaurant after checking out of the room, but as I arrived there the manager was leaving. I said goodbye to her, but realized that Yasin must not have told her he was going to drive me to Alanya, and so I avoided mentioning it. We waited for a friend to bring his car and talked. He had married his girlfriend of four years, Sabina, in January, between now and our meeting last November, and was happy. What's more, Sabina was to join us today for part of the drive so she could visit a friend in Manavgat, a town on our way. We left Antalya, got stuck in

---

6. For more on Western critical views of Islamic law and the historical veracity of the *hadith*, see Schacht, Joseph, *An Introduction to Islamic Law*. Oxford: Oxford University Press, 1964. Also other works by this author.

traffic, picked up Sabina, got stuck in more traffic, and finally made it out of the city. Sabina is from Turkmenistan near the Caspian Sea. I expressed interest in visiting her country, having been in Azerbaijan, across the Caspian from it, in 1985, but she disappointingly informed me that it was closed to tourism, like Saudi Arabia. The first site we arrived at was Aspendos, an ancient Roman city. Its main, or I could say only, attraction was its very large theater, though it has been restored with little attention to preserving its authenticity. Yasin, Sabina, and I climbed to the top level of the theater, and three New Zealander women, slow and annoying at the ticket window ahead of us, redeemed themselves by singing verses of Leonard Cohen's "Hallelujah." The acoustics of such structures are remarkable. I wonder if there are any extant Roman scientific writings on this subject, or if they had only practical expertise.

I decided to quickly explore the rest of the site and left the theater, following a path upwards towards the acropolis. My attention was drawn to a woman screeching in a loud and shrewish voice ahead of me. The crone was berating two men, perhaps relatives of hers, who seemed to be souvenir salesmen. She had given me a head-start on them, but I still wished she would shut up. I accelerated my pace and left the tourist predators behind. The acropolis was disappointing, just nondescript ruined buildings. One small area was fenced off and marked, "No Entry," predictably attracting my curiosity. It had been excavated to around two and a half meters below ground level, and I scanned the dirt below, hoping to see a Roman gold coin uncovered by the recent rain. Deciding to play a trick on a future traveler, I tossed a Turkish half-lira coin to the bottom of the pit. It stuck nicely in the dirt as if to say to the perceptive visitor, "Here is your prize! I have waited these 1,800 years for you to climb down into this muddy pit to find me!" Sometimes I have a hard time understanding my own actions.

We left Aspendos and drove to Side, a great ancient city covering several square kilometers of a peninsula jutting into the sea. After running a gauntlet of completely empty tourist traps we visited the Temple of Apollo at the extremity of the peninsula, the marble columns standing near the sea. And below, washed by the waves, stone slabs cut to fit into each other, an ancient dock for ships crossing the Mediterranean from the Greek islands, Syria, or Egypt. Most of the remaining ruins were sadly off-limits, but we observed them through a fence and I climbed over a wall quickly to get a closer look. We then made our way back to the theater, near the car. I paid the fee to enter and was glad since this theater was smaller but much more authentic than that of Aspendos with its concrete renovations. Access to the entire upper tier was forbidden but I climbed a steel structure supporting it and went to the very top, on the slanted and unequal rows of limestone seats. I was rewarded with a glorious view all the way to the sea and over the rest of the extensive site. Two Turkish girls looked askance at me upon my illicit perch, so I climbed back down and left.

We returned to the car and drove towards Alarahan, dropping off Sabina on the way to visit her friend. A short time later we reached our destination at the point where a river valley narrows and becomes largely impenetrable. A steep spike of rock at this point is the site of a castle built by Ala'eddin Kaykubad, Seljuk Sultan of Rum, in the thirteenth century. Apparently, Seljuk power reached its apogee under him. Ala'eddin surely deserved to be proud of himself for having expanded his domain at the expense of his neighbors, but, as we will see, his success seems to have gone to his head, as witnessed by some of the dedicatory inscriptions to his own glory with which he graced his monuments (all written in Arabic, not Turkish). After all, he was not quite on the level of Alexander the Great, nor even Mehmet the Conqueror. Below the fortress, which looks quite impregnable (it is—I verified this later), lies the Alarahan caravanserai which this Seljuk ruler also built. Above the door was one of the inscriptions of which Ala'eddin Kaykubad was so fond, naming him "…the most august…exalted King of Kings, the Master of the Necks of the Nations, the Lord of the Sultans of the Arabs and the Persians."

The caravanserai was built of massive blocks of cut limestone, abutting on the east side against a hill. Due to the excessive humidity, the interior felt like a cave, so much so that eight centuries of condensation and resurgence of rain water had traced runnels and miniature stalactites on the inside faces of many stone blocks. Though I have been in far older stone structures than this one, I have never seen this phenomenon inside a building before, only inside caves. This degree of humidity cannot have been good for the travelers staying here, especially in winter, and I imagine that some of them left sick but nonetheless relieved to leave these damp lodgings behind.

I chose to visit Alarahan to follow in the footsteps of one of its most illustrious guests, who left in sufficiently good health to travel onwards for another twenty years, covering much of the known world at the time: Ibn Battuta. I came here to see what he had seen. In his travel journal from 1332, Ibn Battuta writes that he left Latakia, on the Syrian coast, by sea and landed at "Al-Ala'iyya" before traveling north into Anatolia. Al-Ala'iyya is none other than modern-day Alanya, so named by Atatürk for unknown reasons (one source claimed it was a spelling error between Ottoman and modern Turkish), changing the name from Al-Ala'iyya, derived from our friend Ala'eddin Kaykubad. Given that Ibn Battuta traveled to points north and west of here from Alanya, and that the Alarahan was a mere century old when he did so under the reign of a descendant of Ala'eddin Kaykubad, Yusuf bin Qaraman (1292–1337), it is a virtual certainty that Ibn Battuta stayed here. For his sake, I hope they gave him a room away from the east wall, or his blankets would have been soaked. He did, however, marry local women during his travels, and also purchased slave girls, so perhaps he had company to keep him warm in the cold chambers of Alarahan. As they say in French, Ibn Battuta was quite a "hot rabbit," as we see from this anecdote he relates from his stay in the Maldives:

> On this island...from the coconut and from the species of fish which they eat, the inhabitants acquire uncommon manly vigor, and are remarkable in this respect. I myself had in this country four wives, besides my slave girls, and each day I was able to make the rounds of them all, and spent the night with her whose appointed turn it was, and I remained there like this for a year and a half.[7]

Now that I have established in whose footsteps I follow, I will recount a minor adventure which Ibn Battuta's good sense may have spared him.

---

7. Harb, p. 581. Author's translation.

As I mentioned, the caravanserai is overlooked by a spire of rock on which Ala'eddin Kaykubad erected an impregnable fortress. This impregnability would also apply nowadays in the era of firearms, so long as artillery and aerial bombardment were not available to the attackers. The effort expended in building this fortress is quite incomprehensible, as only the caravanserai was in need of protection, and it seems unlikely that any enemy would have been well-organized or numerous enough to justify the construction of such a citadel. My opinion of Ala'eddin had started to take form, and he seemed to be given to overkill. This was to be borne out later.

The fortified rock pinnacle was 150 to 200 meters above the valley floor. Yasin had initially not planned to accompany me to the top, but I could feel, as he translated the instructions of the café owner near the start of the path, that he was catching the fever of adventure which inhabits all men (though in most it lies dormant). In this case, Yasin, a kind and mild-mannered hotel receptionist and young newlywed, decided to climb the mountain. We set out along the path, followed by a gentle old dog, crossed paths with a younger and nastier compatriot of his, then reached an official sign which pronounced our endeavour both dangerous and forbidden. Needless to say, we ignored it. I stifled my impulse to take a photo of us next to the sign, deciding that such a photo would be more reasonably taken after victory, not before. How embarrassing it would be to have such a photo noted in my autopsy by the Turkish authorities, should I fall off the cliff…

We proceeded on a rough path to a tunnel entrance. This one had collapsed and looked unsafe, and Yasin said that the man from the café had told him to use the second tunnel entrance. Continuing upwards we found it, though the opening only existed because the roof of the tunnel had caved in some centuries earlier. The tunnel was roughly 150 meters long and very steep. It was utterly dark and the rough-hewn stone steps were wet and slippery, as were the walls. I had a headlamp, but Yasin did not and could not use his phone's light, as he needed both hands to steady himself. I led and he followed. At tricky sections where the steps had broken I shined the light back for him. Out of the tunnel we followed a path and had still 100 meters of elevation to go. Some of it was easy (grade three) rock climbing. It was never technically difficult, nor even frightening for an experienced climber, but certain sections were exposed to a dangerous fall. Yasin was a beginner, and rather intimidated, but he did very well and said he had never climbed something so hard.

We reached the summit and admired the view. There were ruined buildings at the top, a cistern, barracks, and, of course, a Turkish flag. What any invading thirteenth-century army would have sought here is beyond me. They could never have made it past the tunnel and first set of walls in any case, even if they outnumbered the defenders twenty to one. After taking in the sheer drops and the 360-degree panorama, we began to retrace our steps down. As is usually the case, the descent was more dangerous and more stressful, as well as less interesting, than the ascent. At the bottom we took photos of each other in front of the "Forbidden and Dangerous" sign and I suggested that Yasin could bring his friends to the summit when they came to swim in the river in the summer. He said that none of his friends would do it, but he was happy that he had. On our way back Yasin spoke to some locals who were harvesting bay leaves for cooking. I am often impressed by how cordial relations are here among strangers. They gave him a bunch of bay leaves and I took one leaf, crumpled it in my hand and savored the olfactory moment. We then sat on cushions in a veranda of the café and drank a beer, toasting our exploit and thanking the proprietor for his guidance.

We then drove to Alanya. From afar I saw a promontory 200 meters above the sea of sheer cliffs with a crenellated defensive wall at the top. I commented to Yasin that whoever built a defensive wall at the top of a cliff fronting the sea was someone who wasted resources and was probably paranoid. The author of those walls was none other than Ala'eddin Kaykubad, Master of the Necks of the Nations…

FEBRUARY 13, 2016

Today I woke early but after a fairly good sleep. It would have been really good, but some unknown and accursed insect stung me on my left wrist and right bicep. I took a shower (cold, unfortunately), made coffee in my room, and read, mostly about Musa Dagh. This is the most important and most complicated objective of this journey. I made a list of the others (Tarsus, Urfa, Antakya), but it is first. I am considering how to get there without taking unnecessary risks. While having the beer with Yasin yesterday and discussing the next phase of my voyage, he called a friend who lives in Hatay Province, who said the "road" along the coast from Arsuz south to Çevlik, at the foot of Musa Dagh, is impassable for ordinary vehicles. It also has a second disadvantage, being at sea level while Musa Dagh's summit at 1,355 meters is too high for a "lightning" up-down hike carrying almost nothing. With this coastal route hence excluded, I must travel via Antakya, near the Syrian border, and with a dominant Sunni Muslim population. The villages near Musa Dagh are partly inhabited by Arabic-speaking Alawites, the mortal enemies of Islamic State, so it is unlikely that they would be hostile to Westerners. In Antakya this would be less certain.

There are different manners in which to approach risk and, of course, different types of risk as well. One way is to take a fatalistic approach whereby when one decides to do something one simply accepts the risk and accepts that there is nothing to be done to reduce it. We all adopt this attitude when we fly in a commercial airliner since there is literally nothing within our power to reduce the risk we undertake. On the other hand, risk in sports activities or in traveling to unstable destinations can and should be actively managed, not passively accepted. I will do my best to manage risk by making prudent decisions about where and how I travel, and then when I am there by using the utmost vigilance.

After considering my future itinerary, I went out, following the narrow cobblestone streets down towards the sea, passing first a cannon emplacement and then taking a marked path towards the Ottoman shipyard and the Red Tower. I was completely alone. The cannon emplacement was uninteresting, but not so the shipyard which was composed of a series of five or six "bays" opening onto the water and covered above by a vaulted ceiling. In the ceiling were a number of holes, for workers to lower themselves or items of equipment down onto the ships. There was also an example of an Ottoman ship and a winch in which one or two men would walk in a sort of human-sized hamster wheel, which through the use of an axis and pulleys could lift objects weighing several tons. This type of mechanism apparently dates from antiquity. I walked slowly through the shipyard, still alone, and came past the gate to a ticket booth. I had seemingly approached from the wrong direction, with no ticket booth where I had entered. I nonetheless bought a ticket. Ala'eddin Kaykubad had (again) adorned the gate to the shipyard with an inscription extolling his myriad qualities. His megalomania was starting to wear on my nerves.

I was now in a public area, with a path along the ramparts leading to the Red Tower, perhaps 700 meters away. I walked slowly, stopping to look at the sea, and was surprised that a man was walking behind me at an equally slow pace, stopping when I stopped. I looked at him and he looked away. But I could feel that he was staring at me when I resumed walking and he followed. I stopped abruptly at a place where the path made a right angle, turned to face him, leaning on the barrier, and pretended to fiddle with my phone. He looked at me and remained immobile long enough to seem truly suspicious, then came towards me. I put my right hand in my pocket on my knife, phone in my left hand held chest-height in front of me, and turned slightly sideways to him as is my instinct in such situations. I watched his every move. He approached and passed, but then waited for me further on. I passed him, in a state of alertness. Again he followed. Then he used his phone to call someone, speaking in Arabic. I paused again facing him near a replica of an ancient catapult, and he went past me, heading towards the entrance to the Red Tower, where he presumed (correctly) that I was going. So I changed my course, leaving the path and rapidly climbing a very steep hill, coming out above the tower to have a dominating view of the area. I waited and surveyed the area below, but didn't see him again. In such situations I am never certain whether I am paranoid or whether the subject of my suspicions is truly ill-intentioned, as I rationally believe he was in this case. (I think he was an ordinary thief.) Being quite alone, it is better to be prudent.

I waited for some time before descending to the Red Tower. It was not particularly interesting, a utilitarian military structure, but the view from the top was commanding. And there was an expanded image of one of Ala'eddin's ubiquitous inscriptions: "...*Ala' al-dunya wa al-din*...King of Kings, Master of the Necks of Nations..." Here he takes a certain poetic license, modifying his Arabic name "Ala' al-Din," which means "Nobility of the Religion," to title himself "Nobility of the World and of Religion," there being an opposition of *din* (religion) and *dunya* (world) in the Muslim world-view. Perhaps he had forgotten something of his own religion of Islam: "Walk not upon the earth in arrogance, for thou canst not rend the earth asunder, nor equal the mountains in height." (Q, 17:37).

I came down the tower stairs, took a taxi five kilometers up to the citadel, and explored the last of Ala'eddin's works which I would see. The citadel occupies a high (200- to 250-meter) promontory and contains a ruined church (pre-dating the present citadel) and some other unremarkable structures including several cisterns, crucial for a citadel. But the best aspect of it was the view. From one corner of the citadel, the full westward coastline was laid before me like a patchwork quilt of colors, and to the south the crenellated wall surmounting the cliff. This was not only vertical, but was largely composed of rotten limestone. Not even the most expert rock climber would have attempted it. Ala'eddin was indeed either deeply paranoid or an effete aesthetic perfectionist who couldn't bear the idea of an incomplete wall for his citadel, even when it didn't need one.

I walked slowly down from the citadel on a footpath, steeper than the road that it crossed periodically. There was a mosque from the sixteenth century. Walking. Inner silence and the call to prayer. A cemetery near the mosque, some tombs inscribed in the Roman alphabet, others in Arabic script. Forgotten lives, the smell of burning plastic and the breeze from the sea. And the faithful walking gladly to heed their call. I descended by a sinuous footpath to my hotel through rough hillside and then the old town, then spent several hours reading and writing. I was very fortunate concerning Musa Dagh. A photo on Wikipedia of the summit monument was credited to a man with a German name, André Thess, so I looked him up and found someone of that name, an accomplished professor and director of a research institute in Stuttgart. I wrote to him and he replied that he was indeed the author of the photograph, and he gave me some practical information about visiting Musa Dagh, very helpful because nothing of the sort was available on the internet. I was determined to go, regardless of the ease or difficulty, guided or not guided, even to the point of camping on the mountain if necessary, but André's help eased my way. As William H. Murray, of the Scottish Himalayan Expedition put it:

Until one is committed, there is hesitancy, the chance to draw back, always ineffectiveness. Concerning all acts of initiative (and creation), there is one elementary truth, the ignorance of which kills countless ideas and splendid plans: that the moment one definitely commits oneself, then Providence moves too. All sorts of things occur to help one that would never otherwise have occurred. A whole stream of events issues from the decision, raising in one's favor all manner of unforeseen incidents and meetings and material assistance, which no man could have dreamt would have come his way.[8]

FEBRUARY 14, 2016

Today I woke early, ready for a long trip. I took a shower, hot this time after complaining yesterday, then settled my bill and left for Mersin with Ibrahim, a chauffeur, teacher of Turkish traditional dancing and friend of Koray, the owner of the hotel where I stayed. I had been misled by the simplicity of my map. A large-scale map indicating a straight road actually contains very little information. The scale means that if the road snakes back and forth across a mountainside innumerable times, limiting the feasible speed to thirty kilometers an hour, this will not be apparent from the map. So it was today. The drive from Alanya to Anamur, barely 100 kilometers, took over three hours. Mountain passes, narrow road, precipitous drops into the Mediterranean blueness. It was a beautiful journey, but long and sometimes frightening. In my active management of risk, I forced myself to remain alert, a sort of co-pilot to Ibrahim. At one point this may have saved our lives, when a Mercedes M-Class driven by someone wealthier than he was careful took the wrong lane

---

8. Murray, William H, *The Scottish Himalayan Expedition*. London: JM Dent, 1951.

out of a construction area and came at us head-on. I cried out a warning and Ibrahim swerved off the road to avoid a collision. This was the most dangerous moment of this entire book, one of a handful of such moments in my life. We continued on and descended from the high mountains to an open and fertile valley. I noticed some strange-looking fields, as if a whole plantation of scrub palm trees had been blighted by desolation, shrivelled up, and died. I asked Ibrahim what these were and he said, "*muzler,*" Turkish but cognate to the Arabic word *muzz*, bananas. He explained that this devastated appearance was a normal stage in the life of a banana plant, and that the plastic bags on some of them covered bunches of bananas yet to be harvested.

We reached Anamur, an ancient city founded by the Phoenicians but whose present ruins are Byzantine. The Byzantine stonemasons were far inferior to those of Termessos or of the Roman cities, building their edifices not of cut stone blocks but of fieldstone and mortar, much less noble. The city as a whole, however, is very impressive. In a wonderful site fronting the sea, it extends over several square kilometers, with a fortress on a hilltop to the south of the main city. There were several churches, a long section of wall ten meters high, serving what purpose I know not, a ruined theater, and a well-preserved Odeon, a sort of mini-theater used for presentations and democratic meetings, with seating for several hundred citizens. We left Anamur and continued along the coast, stopping at Mamure Castle, conquered from the Armenian kingdom of Cilicia in the thirteenth century and rebuilt larger by Mahmut Kaykubadoğlu, Mahmut, son of Kaykubad. Mahmut's brother Yusuf seems to have been ruler after him, when Ibn Battuta landed in Alanya in 1332. The castle was undergoing renovations and was closed, but Ibrahim and I examined it in detail from the shore, a high crenellated wall and towers abutting the sea, certain parts of clean cut masonry blocks and others of lesser quality stone and mortar. We then drove to Kızkalesi, turning north for a few kilometers to see the caves of Heaven and of Hell. These were grottoes, perhaps 150 meters of compact limestone, untouched by climbers' hands. The difficulty grade would be high with few holds. I went down into the Chasm of Heaven and followed it (with my headlamp) to its extremity, the cave of Typhon, which, according to legend, joins the River Styx of the underworld. The descent and subsequent ascent took twenty-five minutes, and the Chasm of Hell, from a viewing platform, another few minutes. Ibrahim was planning to drive the seven hours back to Alanya tonight, so I did not want to delay him unnecessarily. We stopped to catch a sight of Kızkalesi (the Maiden's Castle) on a nearby island.

The final approach to Mersin was in itself a descent into hell. Interminable. A twenty-kilometer corridor of apartment blocks, all similar, all new. Where did their inhabitants come from? Sucked out of the idyllic village life to live in these barrens of the mind, complete with electricity, hot water, and satellite TV? I swear on my life that I would prefer a log cabin in empty wilderness, like Richard Proenneke, who built a cabin in the Alaskan wilderness and lived alone in it for thirty years.[9] Modernity of this type is dehumanizing, an asphyxiation of the soul. I could hardly breathe as we penetrated further and further into this metropolitan heart of darkness.

FEBRUARY 15, 2016

Last night I had two drinks in the hotel bar, and wrote. For my second drink I asked the young bartender to make me a dry martini and taught him how to do it, enhancing his future repertoire. I also spoke with two foreigners, one Canadian and the other Welsh. I told them I was traveling alone, further east, and they admitted that they were already very frightened even to go out shopping here in Mersin, the two of them together. They are here for work, to install some kind of mechanical system for a company. They described how every man in the shopping center they visited seemed hostile to them. I really cannot imagine this being true, having been all over Turkey and never felt the general hostility they described even if I have faced isolated instances of hostility from specific individuals. I think they simply felt extremely out of place, different, and surrounded by others whom they presumed were hostile

9. Proenneke, Richard, *Alone in the Wilderness: An Alaskan Odyssey*. Anchorage: Alaska Northwest Books, 1999.

when they really weren't. They thought I was out of my mind when I told them my next destinations, Antakya and Şanlıurfa, and the area around Musa Dagh, near Syria.

I read and considered my future route, had breakfast, then left at noon by car for Tarsus. The driver was an older gentleman named Talaat. His company offered to drive me to Antakya, so that could be a possibility if Andrew cannot find someone to drive me. By coincidence, Talaat used to drive children from a local well-to-do family to the Tarsus American College and thus knew exactly where I was going. The American College is an oasis of green and relative calm in the busy city of Tarsus. Andrew is its headmaster, a position he took after a successful career as a teacher and high-level administrator in the school system of British Columbia, Canada. He wanted to see more of the world. As I arrived at the school gate the security guards were expecting me. Andrew's assistant led me to his office and he stepped out of a meeting to greet me. We had a quick lunch with some of the teachers, then Andrew showed me around the well-organized and pleasant campus. Many of Turkey's elite were schooled here, including Muhtar Kent, former chairman and CEO of Coca-Cola, and the alumni are apparently fiercely loyal to their school. Andrew then showed me to his house within the school grounds and we arranged to meet after he had finished work. I unpacked my things in one of the rooms and set out to explore Tarsus on foot.

I walked around in a state of alertness, but in the course of the whole afternoon I felt no hostility from anyone. I first visited the Ulu Mosque, wandering around the grounds and briefly entering. Some men were praying so I didn't linger. I then looked at but could not enter the (closed) Kubat Paşa Madrasa. In front of it, a group of young people were roller-blading, including a statuesque young woman with beautiful dark hair. I continued on my way, relying on the GPS navigation of my phone to lead me to St. Paul's Well, but instead I penetrated deeper and deeper into a sort of primitive industrial slum. Not the apocalyptic vision of endless identical apartment blocks seen yesterday on the approach to Mersin, but a more personal sort of hell: exhaust fumes, rundown buildings, stray dogs eating rubbish, and dust containing the refuse of centuries and of yesterday. Finally, having looped twice around the GPS "location" of St. Paul's Well, I concluded that it had been razed and replaced by a spanking-new Total station. I inquired of several mechanics, first in my broken Turkish, then in Arabic, as to where it was. One of them came towards me and said, "Are you Arab?" His rotten teeth and garlic breath almost knocked me back, but he pointed me in the right direction (which was where I had come from) and said it was quite far away.

So I retraced my steps, inquired again and received help again. At this point I came across the so-called tomb of Daniel, the biblical Prophet. A Roman bridge had been discovered when consolidating the structure of a mosque there in 2006, and a full excavation was done under the mosque building, reminiscent of similar but larger below-ground-level excavations in several Spanish cities (Barcelona, Valencia, Zaragoza). It is impressive and instructive to see the structures of a past civilization literally covered by those of subsequent civilizations. Finally I asked help yet again to find St. Paul's Well, an ancient well near the supposed location of St. Paul's house, and continued on my way to this chimerical monument. I was following the road among a flow of pedestrians, when past me glided the wondrous form of the Roller Blade Girl, probably on her way home. I imagined that I could smell her perfume, which lingered in my mind after she faded from my sight amidst the crowd.

I then asked again about the well and was pointed towards the excavations of the Roman Road, three meters below the present ground level, made of large cut blocks of black basalt. I then eventually found the actual well, the only visitor and outnumbered by five staff members. I loitered there, looking through the glass panes onto the excavated level two meters below. A polite employee offered to draw water for me from the well, roughly twenty meters deep according to him. I looked down into the well when he lifted its cover, but declined to drink for fear of catching ancient amoebic dysentery. Then I returned to the Tarsus American College for a few drinks and dinner with Andrew and his colleagues.

FEBRUARY 16, 2016

Andrew had already left for work this morning when I awoke. I read and prepared the trip to Antakya tomorrow, choosing a hotel and organizing transportation from here to there, and from Antakya to the area around Musa Dagh mountain. I requested a driver to take me on a tour of the sights nearby without mentioning that I intended to stay the night in Vakıflı, on the mountainside. Then at 10 AM, as planned, Barry and Azzam, two of Andrew's acquaintances married to two teachers at the school with whom we had had dinner last night, arrived and we went out walking in the city. We had an interesting discussion. Barry, in particular, has traveled to many places, including Egypt in 1989, just a year before Hélène and I spent two years there. We visited Cleopatra's Gate, apparently also known as "The Gate of the Bitch," (*Kancık Kapısı*), which gained little from being seen up close as opposed to the way I had seen it the day before, from a moving car. We then went to the Eski Mosque, shaded and cool. The Quranic inscription above the *mihrab* was difficult to read, but Azzam, who is Pakistani, read it aloud with ease though he didn't know its meaning. It was the 37th *ayat* of *Surat Al 'Imran*, "Whenever Zechariah entered upon her [the Virgin Mary] in the prayer chamber, he found her with provisions." In the *surat*, Zechariah asks her where these provisions come from, and she replies: "It is from God. Verily, God provides for whom He wills, without account." Q 3: 37.

After this old mosque we went to Tarsus' famous waterfall, which is pleasant enough and cools the air, but is otherwise not worth the ugly walk through the city to get there. All the same, being in the company of Barry and Azzam was enjoyable, and we turned back towards the school, having had our fill of dust and exhaust fumes. We walked around ten kilometers during the morning and in this time we crossed the path of only one person who seemed genuinely hostile to us as Westerners. I noticed him from afar, a tall and wiry young man with a measured gait and a straggly untrimmed beard, the mark of a *Salafi* Muslim. *Salafi* means a Muslim who sees himself as following the example of the early Muslims (*salaf* means "predecessors" in Arabic). Whether these people actually follow this example in a proper manner is a wholly different question. I doubt that the Companions of the Prophet would have burned a captured adversary alive in a cage and filmed it, as Islamic State recently did to a Jordanian Muslim military pilot. This young man crossing our path looked at me with a burning gaze of hatred. I watched him carefully as he passed, and the meaning of his gaze was unmistakable. Afterwards I observed him discreetly over my shoulder as I walked, to make sure that he continued on his path. Neither of my companions noticed his hostile look. Perhaps my association of him with the *Salafi* movement, indirectly responsible for much of the wanton violence committed in the name of Islam, made him appear threatening in my eyes when he was not. But I doubt it.

Andrew and I had a hearty dinner in the same restaurant as last night, an excellent Turkish restaurant with various kebabs and appetizers. Turkish cuisine, as elsewhere in the Mediterranean, is generally healthful and tasty. I can eat it throughout my trips without becoming tired of it. Andrew and I enjoyed each other's company, conversation, and camaraderie. We spoke of our families, our careers, and our adventures, and I invited him to visit me at home in France. I read before sleeping but had a troubled night, alternating between visions of sensual female bodies, and a dark disquiet about my trip tomorrow, heading towards Syria and into the red zone on the travel advisory maps.

FEBRUARY 17, 2016

I am having dinner in a restaurant in Antakya. This morning the driver arranged by Andrew, Muaffak, picked me up at the school gate. The drive was pleasant, with attractive scenery for part of the way. Turning south, we were near the border with Hatay Province. In 1271, Marco Polo landed near here at Laïas, now the modern town of Yumurtalik, and then began his overland journey to China. Laïas was an important port city of the Armenian Kingdom of Cilicia, to which Polo referred as "Lesser Armenia," until the area was conquered by the Seljuk Turks about a century after his passage. He has this to say about the place:

> There is on the sea of the said province a city named Laïas, prosperous and large, and active in commerce, because you must know that all the spices and textiles of the Euphrates are carried to this city, and all of the other precious things...And the

merchants of Venice, Pisa, and Genoa, and those of the other land-locked cities come here to buy and sell ... [10]

From here Marco Polo traveled north to Sis, the capital of Armenian Cilicia, and then to Kayseri, which I passed both in 1987 and in 2014 on the way to Göreme. He continued on to central Anatolia and points east, not returning home for twenty-four years, curiously the same length of time away as Ibn Battuta sixty years later.

There was no red line across the highway marking "Red Zone, Travel Advisory" as we entered Hatay Province. My greatest anxiety occurred when I saw snow on the northern slopes of a mountain range to the east of Dörtyol. I checked carefully on the map, and these summits are at 2,200 meters, whereas Musa Dagh is only 1,355 meters. Further south, a summit at 1,800 meters was clear of snow, so Musa Dagh should be fine, though a little *névé* would not stop me.

I need to determine an estimated scale for my two maps. The best topographical map I could find of Hatay Province seems to date from the French colonial period after World War I, when Hatay was part of French-administered Syria before being ceded to Turkey in 1939. After yesterday's debacle I am not likely to put much faith in GPS, though around Musa Dagh the map is all blank anyway. There seem to be no roads. The satellite imagery is slightly better, but it is very hard to navigate by this alone. It occurs to me that the unpaved part of the Arsuz-Çevlik coastal road is barely more than twenty kilometers long. Perhaps I will walk it after coming down from Musa Dagh. I check, and it is broken by two riverbeds that are probably only in flood on rare occasions, and ought to be passable on foot. I feel good looking at the landscape play over the windows, and I ask myself if this is the life I want to lead. I think it is.

We arrived in Antakya and I helped Muaffak find the hotel. On first approach, Antakya, ancient Antioch, appeared a dirty, dusty, and noisy city. I checked in, paid a deposit, and occupied my room. It was actually a small suite, very nicely decorated with original Ottoman features such

---

10. Polo, Marco, *Le Devisement du monde: le livre des merveilles*, I. Paris: Éditions La Découverte, 1982, p. 68. Translation from French by the author.

as the black and white tile floor and carved wooden paneling. I read about Antakya, then went out, taking a taxi to the Church of St. Peter. This cave church is quite simple and according to legend belonged to the Apostle Luke and was frequented by him and the other Apostles. It may be one of the earliest Christian churches in the world. Above the renovated stone façade is some wonderful fluted limestone, which could be climbed if it were in a less holy place. I was alone in the church. At the back is a baptismal font fed by drops of water resurging from within the mountain. This was cordoned off by a red tape barrier. I watched the guard as he was pacing outside while speaking on his phone and timed my incursion based on the frequency of his passing in front of the door. I crossed the barrier, said a prayer and tentatively baptized myself with the water from the mountain in this ancient font. I have no idea what I am. Christian? Muslim? Confused mystical pantheist? "To God belong the East and the West: whithersoever ye turn, there is God's face," from the Qur'an (2:115) becomes, in *The Interpreter of Desires* by the twelfth-century Sufi mystic Ibn Arabi[11]:

My heart has become capable of every form; it is a pasture for gazelles and a convent for Christian monks. And a temple for idols and the pilgrim's Ka'aba and the tables of the Torah and the book of the Qur'an. I follow the religion of Love: whatever way Love's camels take, that is my religion and my faith.[12]

Ibn Arabi gives an even more explicit description of his pantheism in his *Mekkan Revelations*:

Glory to God who brought all things into existence, being himself their substance. He is the substance of every object in manifestation, although He is not the substance of objects in their essences.[13]

---

11. About Ibn Arabi, see footnote in the February 4, 2015 entry, above.

12. Arabi, Muhyi al-Din Ibn, *Tarjuman al-Ashwaq* ("The Interpreter of Desires"), Arabic text with translation by Reynold Nicholson. London: Royal Asiatic Society, 1911, preface to first edition.

13. *Ibid.*

These views reflect Ibn Arabi's doctrine of "Unity of Being," *wahdat al-wujud*, according to which there is only one Being, God, and all existence is nothing but this Being's outward manifestation.[14] Such views would be considered heretical by much of Islamic orthodoxy but I see them as the logical extension of the idea of *tawhid*, the Oneness of God, so not heretical at all, just easily subject to misunderstanding.

I left the church and went by taxi to the Antakya Archaeology Museum, which had moved from its old location to a magnificent modern building on the road to Syria. During the drive I could feel the proximity of war and death, the fragility of all life and thus its flickering worth. Emotion, compassion, visions of tragedy. This is what it is to be alive. I am not afraid. The museum was surprising, truly excellent. And empty. An elderly Arab couple and I were the sole visitors—three visitors as opposed to the fifty or sixty staff. I learned that there were stamp seals from the sixth millennium BCE, earlier than I had thought, and fine pottery. But I knew that already. Refinement in physical form seems to be primordial for humans, innate from the very moment we are able to shape clay. I learned of the city of Alalakh, from the second millennium BCE, near here, which was subject to the Hittites and later to Mitanni. Mitanni was a Hurrian kingdom ruled by a class of Indo-Europeans judging from their names, discovered at Nuzi by Professor Edward Chiera, "Illustrious Scholar and Teacher, Discoverer of Nuzi, and Inaugurator of the Nuzi Names Project."[15]

The site of Nuzi is in present-day Syria. I would have liked to see it because I wrote my master's thesis in linguistics on the Nuzi Names, their demonstration of an earlier and broader Indo-European presence in the Near East than was previously thought, and on the tenuous possibility that the older sites of the Indus Civilization in Pakistan might possibly have been Indo-European as well.[16] Where is Indiana Jones to resolve these queries about our past? There were also many Hittite lion

---

14. Chittick, William, *The Sufi Path of Knowledge*. Albany: SUNY Press, 1989, p. 79.

15. Gelb, Ignace; Purves, Pierre and Macrae, Allan, *Nuzi Personal Names*. Chicago: University of Chicago Oriental Institute Publications, Volume LVII, 1943. Dedication page.

16. Ray, Nicholas, *Indo-Aryans in the Ancient Near East: Linguistic, Archaeological, and Historical Considerations*. Rochester: University of Rochester, unpublished master's thesis, 1989.

figures, and I realized that the bas-relief lion face symbol of the Alarahan caravanserai I visited a few days ago is none other than a flattened frontal view of a Hittite lion. So the Seljuk masons must have seen some of these Hittite statues without knowing their ancient origins. The museum was organized chronologically, from the Paleolithic to the medieval. There were Hellenistic and Roman mosaics, many of them, some very large. I was impressed by them but not touched. Some art forms are not immediately tangible, requiring study to be appreciated. There was an ancient Arabic inscription of the *Ayat al-Kursi* with no diacritical marks at all, reminiscent of the Arabic on the *Masjid al-Aqsa* on the Temple Mount in Jerusalem, one of the oldest extant examples of Arabic writing.

I then went to Habibi Neccar Mosque, named after a figure from the turn of the (first) millennium who apparently believed in Christianity and the Apostles. He, as well as several prophets and John the Baptist, is reputedly buried under the mosque. I find this claim dubious since John the Baptist seems to have peregrinated a good deal after his death and been buried in many places (though the bodies of saints were often dismembered and various parts found their ways to different locations as holy relics). There was a Quranic *ayat* above the *mihrab*: "From whencesoever thou startest forth, turn thy face in the direction of the Sacred Mosque" (Q, 2:149).

I left the mosque and wandered for over an hour in the covered bazaar until I felt so claustrophobic that I started imagining how people could escape if there was a fire. They couldn't. I also bought walnuts and dried fruit in case I had to spend the night on Musa Dagh. I will do so if I cannot find a guide to take me up and down in a day. Tomorrow is a big day. I go forward without knowing what is before me, as I did when I was young.

FEBRUARY 18, 2016

Yesterday in Antakya I was in the highest possible state of alertness, walking in a meditative state. All thoughts calm and noticing every movement around me. The child straying from his mother. The cat watching from the roof of a shack overlooking the bazaar alley where

I walked. The movements of the spice sellers filling bags of wondrous essences for their customers. I felt no hostility or undue attention at all from anyone, but remained on my guard. Islamic State has a significant presence here, as has been described in numerous articles in the press, and a number of journalists were kidnapped nearby in Syria, at least one of them having been brought there from here in Antakya.[17] In Şanlıurfa a few months ago Islamic State beheaded two journalists with impunity.[18] I will go there too. Knowing about this potential danger, I was ultra-careful, even going to the lengths of scoping out an escape route from my room yesterday before bed and blocking the flimsy door with furniture.

Now I am off to Musa Dagh. Another arbitrary quest, seeking something nearly invisible, an evanescent shimmering realm that does not fully exist but which is created by my journey towards that untraveled world. I am tilting at windmills. Part of the greatness and the modernity of *Don Quixote* derives from its recounting imaginary adventures, not real ones. Or rather real adventures where the signifier is real but the signified is imaginary, where meaning is invented. For Cervantes' noble knight, the windmills at which he tilts *are* giants.[19] The meaning of the events in our lives is inside us, not outside. Musa Dagh is my windmill, and I will tilt at it.

The road to Samandağ passes through the drab, dirty, dusty towns of the Orontes plain. The landscapes of the imagination are so often purer and more beautiful than real physical landscapes. I felt a strange anticipation of Musa Dagh, as if it were an important place for me, which now it is. My driver's name was Ahmet. He was Turkish but spoke excellent Arabic, more fluent than mine. Our first destination was the Titus and Vespasian Tunnel at Çevlik, a marvel of Roman

17. A very large number of recent press articles discuss the situation in Antakya and other areas of Turkey bordering Syria. One excellent and in-depth article is Wright, Lawrence. "Five Hostages," *The New Yorker*, July 6 and 13, 2015. Another is Padnos, Theo. "My Captivity," *The New York Times*, October 29, 2014.

18. Stack, Liam. "ISIS is Said to have Killed 2 Activists in Turkey," *The New York Times*, November 2, 2015.

19. "Signifier" and "signified" are linguistic terms defined by the great linguist Ferdinand de Saussure, mentioned earlier in the context of the Hittite language. The signifier is the windmill. What it signifies, to Don Quixote, is a giant.

engineering which took a century to build with slave labor, starting in the first century CE. Its purpose was to divert the Orontes river and prevent it from flooding Seleucia Piera, for a time the capital of the Seleucid Empire founded by Seleucus I Nicator, another of Alexander the Great's generals (fourth century BCE). This empire held dominion over territories from Sardis in Western Turkey to Samarkand in Central Asia, almost 4,000 kilometers from here. I followed the tunnel for its full length, around a kilometer, and Ahmet accompanied me until it became pitch dark (the first part of it is a deep channel rather than a tunnel). At certain points the Judean slaves cut and removed solid limestone to a depth of over twenty-five meters. On the way back the batteries of my headlamp waned, leaving me to navigate several hundred meters of wet, slippery rock with only a dim red LED.

After visiting the Roman necropolis nearby, I reconnoitered the slopes of Musa Dagh above with a view to prepare my ascent. This is a propitious place to briefly discuss Musa Dagh and how it attracted my interest. I grew up in America with several Armenian friends. I had visited Soviet Armenia in 1985 on the only organized tour I have ever taken (which also included Azerbaijan, Georgia, and Ukraine) and was lucky to see Erevan and Echmiadzin before the devastating earthquake of 1988. Though I had visited Armenia, at the time I had not heard of Musa Dagh. But last November, just after returning from the trip described in the previous chapter, I met Admiral Jim Stavridis, former supreme commander of NATO and now Dean of Tufts' Fletcher School (my alma mater), in London. I have known Jim since he became dean a few years ago and I value his deep knowledge and experience. Jim's family is of Greek origin, and his ancestors fled Turkey (from Smyrna, present-day Izmir) during the tragic years of the collapse of the Ottoman Empire, rife with ethnic cleansing, murder, and the genocide of the Armenians and Assyrians. Jim recommended Franz Werfel's book to me, and I read it in preparation for this trip. When I sent Jim a photo of myself from the summit of Musa Dagh, he replied that it was time for me to go home!

Six Armenian villages existed on the flanks of Musa Dagh (*Musa Ler* in Armenian, meaning Mount Moses). In 1915, these villages received their deportation orders from the Young Turk government later than others and so the villagers knew from watching the fate of other villages the real aims of the Young Turk leaders: the extermination of the Armenian population in Ottoman lands and the expropriation of their property. The majority of the villagers, 4,000-strong, decided to defy the deportation order, entrench themselves on the heights of their mountain and fight. They did this despite having only five or six hundred men of fighting age, the rest of the population being women, children, and old men. They also had many more men than rifles, most of which were antiquated hunting guns. Yet their infinitely superior knowledge of the difficult terrain of Musa Dagh, and the Turkish military's dismissal of them as inconsequential adversaries, enabled them to defeat successive waves of Turkish attackers, each time reinforcing themselves with captured rifles and ammunition. After fifty-three days, however, the Armenians on Musa Dagh were starving and running out of ammunition. It was just then that the French warship *Guichen* spotted the white flag they had raised on the mountaintop, emblazoned with a red cross and the message, "Christians in Distress: Rescue!" Several ships of the French Navy shelled the Ottoman troops, forcing them to withdraw, and then rescued all of those on Musa Dagh, 4,058 people[20] in five ships, taking them to Port Said in Egypt. Eighteen men died on Musa Dagh defending their families. In my own mind, Musa Dagh thus became the archetype of righteous entrenched resistance against overwhelming odds, more real than Kurosawa's *The Seven Samurai* and Clint Eastwood's *The Outlaw Josey Wales*, and more inspiring (due to its happy ending) than Leonidas at the Battle of Thermopylae or the Americans at the Alamo. So I resolved to go there. And here I am.

Back to the reconnaissance of Musa Dagh. A seemingly obvious line of approach would be directly from the coast, as by this path the summit or areas near it would remain visible most of the way due to the absence of trees on the upper slopes. But this approach would add hundreds of meters of elevation. Our next stop was the village of Vakıflı, the only remaining Armenian village in Turkey. Professor André Thess, mentioned earlier, had

20. This figure of 4,058 people saved occurs in a number of sources, including this one on the site of the Armenian Genocide Centennial: http://armeniangenocide100.org/en/forty-days-of-musa-dagh-part-4-2/

kindly given me the name of the man who had guided him up the mountain the previous September, on the hundredth anniversary of the rescue of the Musa Dagh Armenians by the French Navy. Amazingly, nobody was there on that historic anniversary except André, his wife, and their guide from Vakıflı, Mr. Toros Manca. When I arrived in the village my first priority was to find him. I had already decided that without a guide I would set out today with the intention of camping the night on the mountain and finding the site the next day. I had limited equipment, a tarp for shelter, and clothes warm enough to spend the night outside. I also had my walnuts and dried fruit. Going alone was definitely not my preferred option, not least because Musa Dagh is covered with thorny brush and scrub trees, and its topology is abrupt. It is a place in which, despite superior numbers, invaders ignorant of the terrain can be impossibly trapped by well-prepared defenders. It is crisscrossed by footpaths made by generations of shepherds and woodcutters, many of which do not really have a particular destination. Not a good place to get lost.

Arriving in front of the Armenian church in Vakıflı, I asked someone where I could find Mr. Toros Manca. We had stopped in the street, blocking a red Citroën behind us. As Ahmet was moving our car out of the way it occurred to me to ask the driver of the Citroën, so I waved and smiled and he opened his window. I addressed him formally in Arabic, "Peace be with you," and he replied with the formal reply, "And with you be peace." Many people in Hatay Province speak Arabic and few speak French or English. I then asked the driver if he knew Mr. Toros Manca, and he replied in relatively fluent Arabic, "He is my brother-in-law." When one is on the Straight Path everything happens for the best. But he then also told me that Toros' mother had passed away yesterday, and her funeral was today. Even so, he called Toros, who was kind enough to come and meet me. I spoke Arabic to Ahmet, my driver, and he translated into Turkish for Toros, then repeated the process in the other direction. Toros promised to do his best to find someone else to guide me tomorrow. I awkwardly presented my condolences to him. Realizing that I did not know how to do this in Arabic, I later enquired of an Arab friend, and she told me, "May God have mercy on your mother," or, more beautiful, an *ayat* from the Qur'an, "Verily to God we belong and verily unto Him we are returning." Q 2:156. Facing death, these simple words hold more power than all of our science. Science can help us make life better, make it longer by forestalling death, but science cannot speak to death. This *ayat* speaks to death. Such words are a blessing upon us, like the 23rd Psalm. Toros left us to attend to the funeral arrangements of his mother, and I saluted him as he went, hand on heart. He agreed to call Ahmet at 14:00 to tell us if he had found a guide for me or not.

There were several hours to wait until 2 PM, so I decided to work on the assumption that I would not have a guide and would have to leave this afternoon and camp on the mountain. I asked Ahmet to drive me to Hıdırbey, where there is an enormous tree which, legend has it, grew from the staff Moses planted there while resting. We then went further to Yoghonoluk, a few hundred meters higher and thus possibly a better starting point for the hike up Musa Dagh. Yoghonoluk is also the home of the (fictional) hero Gabriel Bagradian from Werfel's book, patterned after the real-life hero Movses Der Kelousdian, one of the leaders of the Musa Dagh resistance.

Yoghonoluk was an unremarkable village and I quite easily found the mosque (formerly an Armenian church) and above it a path leading out of town along the mountainside. This would make a good approach point, except that it was seven kilometers from Vakıflı, where I had taken a room in the guesthouse and left my things. I had to find a closer approach point. By this time, Ahmet was wondering about my intentions, as I had booked his services for a "day tour" of the sights here and return to Antakya. I explained to him that I intended to stay the night either on the mountain or in the guesthouse, and climb to the top of Musa Dagh, but would need to go tomorrow to Iskenderun, and today wanted to reconnoiter the entire area in preparation for climbing the mountain. I compensated him for his extra time.

We returned to Vakıflı and I visited the church. It seems to date from quite recently, probably after the genocide of 1915. I spoke with the lady in charge of it and with an elderly parishioner, again both in Arabic. The elderly lady spoke very well. In the church I sat in a pew and said a prayer, then lit a candle and made the selfish wish that events like those which happened here, and which are happening now a few kilometers to the south of here, would never overtake my own children. It is beyond my ability to understand such events. One can only know that they happen, and draw the inevitable logical conclusion that at certain times, under certain conditions, the majority of human beings lose their humanity, cease to be bound by any moral norms whatsoever, and commit acts of real evil. These acts are such that any rational person, even any child, would realize that they do not conform to the "Golden Rule," that what they are doing to others, violating, demeaning, annihilating them, they would never want done to themselves. What is more, this collective psychosis, if such we can call it (it may well be a simple return to our primal, basic, *normal* state) appears so strong that many of the individuals under its sway have no difficulty considering themselves "good Christians," as did some of the Nazis, or the American cavalrymen who massacred women and children at Sand Creek, or "good Muslims," as did the Turkish *zaptiehs* (members of a hybrid police-military force) and soldiers. A long shift at the Auschwitz gas chambers followed by helping the kids learn their catechism after dinner. A tiring day slaughtering Cheyenne children with the trusty cavalry saber, then back to the barracks for a beer and a steak with the guys. And a tiring march on the deportation path, beating old Armenian women to death with cudgels because they could not keep the pace, followed by evening prayers at the mosque and a relaxing *shisha*.[21]

Still uncertain of the availability of a guide, I decided to retain Ahmet longer in order to further reconnoiter the approaches to the mountain. We drove down again to the coast, near Çevlik and the Titus and Vespasian tunnel visited this morning. I wanted to ascertain the route by which the Musa Dagh Armenians had walked down to the

---

21. Perhaps it is my own morbid nature, but I have read fairly deeply on this macabre subject. The "Rebellion" and "The Grand Inquisitor" chapters of Dostoyevsky's *The Brothers Karamazov* constitute the best treatment I have ever read of the inexistence of divine justice and the moral impossibility of either forgiveness or just punishment. Historically, Primo Levi's *If This is a Man*, to which I allude again below, describes the author's experiences at Auschwitz. Historian Dee Brown's *Bury My Heart at Wounded Knee* examines the genocide of the Native Americans through direct testimony of American soldiers who participated in it, and others. Sven Lindqvist, a Swedish historian, examines the origins of the idea of genocide in *Exterminate all the Brutes*. And, of course, Joseph Conrad's *Heart of Darkness*, and the film it inspired, *Apocalypse Now!*, treat aspects of this issue. A *shisha* is a "hubbly-bubbly" water pipe in which flavored tobacco is smoked.

French warships which rescued them. I also continued to entertain the idea of walking north along the roughly twenty-kilometer coastal track leading to Arsuz, where it becomes a road again. Physically, with my light equipment, this would have presented no difficulty. Yet my adventurous soul was quelled by a sign bearing the symbol of the Turkish *Jandarma* (Military Police, from French, *gendarmes*) with a large word in bright red, "*HIRSIZLIK.*" I asked Ahmet what it meant, but he hadn't noticed it. I asked him to go back, with misgivings that the word might have been important. We went back and he said it was Turkish for "highway robbery" or "banditry." I duly gave up the idea of walking the "Bandit Coast" alone, but asked Ahmet to follow the road by car until it became impassable, to see it. The coast was wondrously beautiful and remote. No buildings, no mobile telephone service, an occasional parked car, its denizens silently contemplating the sea from rocky promontories or hidden coves. Not a single car crossed us going the opposite direction (south, as we were proceeding north). There was a dramatic view up to the line of cliffs protecting Musa Dagh from this direction. As we were driving, shortly before turning back due to fallen rocks which had blocked the track around ten kilometers from Çevlik, we witnessed something exceedingly strange. A small boat, manned by two individuals, landed on the beach below, and a fit, bearded man wearing a full camouflage wetsuit ran up the hill and crossed the road in front of us, carrying a hand saw. I turned as we passed and watched him cut down a small tree and take it back to his boat. We were around twenty kilometers from Syria, so close that I received a welcome text message from the Syrian mobile telephone operator. I could see the whole flat pan of the sea before me, broken only by a few fishing boats, no military vessels. This coast would be a perfect place for smugglers to bring people or weapons to or from Syria. Or to smuggle scrub trees cut from the side of the road. On our way back I could see the small boat quite far offshore as well as the tree stump left by camo-diver's sawing.

We returned the way we had come, after having stopped some minutes to admire the coast. I saw the tip of the peninsula south of Arsuz in the distance. And I noticed that the rock here is a sort of gneiss or granite with inclusions of quartz, not the limestone found higher up on Musa Dagh. Having pored over maps and satellite imagery of this area for more than an hour, I asked Ahmet to return to Vakıflı by a smaller road, rising steeply out of Çevlik at first and then following the slope of Musa Dagh on an approximate iso-altitude curve. I thought this road would provide a good starting point if I had to start the hike alone today. I saw several dirt tracks heading north (uphill) from this road, and indeed it was one of these which we used the next morning, so my reconnaissance was worthwhile.

In Vakıflı, Toros Manca was receiving family members after the funeral. I left him in peace and sat drinking tea with Ahmet at a table in front of the guesthouse (where I was the sole guest). An hour or so later we spoke briefly with Toros and he said he had found a man to guide me up Musa Dagh the next morning. He also very hospitably invited me to dinner at his home tonight, which, since there are no real restaurants in the village, allowed me to dine on something more than the iron rations I had bought in Antakya. I let Ahmet drive home, arranging for him to come back tomorrow afternoon to take me to Iskenderun. He was very helpful, translating my Arabic into Toros' Turkish and vice-versa, and generally looking out for me, even to the point of bargaining on my behalf lower prices from people we met, which I asked him not to do.

I had a few hours to while away before dinner time, so made a hotel reservation in Iskenderun for the next night using a cellular data connection, as there was no Wi-Fi anywhere in the village, nor, it appears, any landline internet service. I examined my room in the guesthouse, an old stone building probably from the town's original Armenian period. The people living here now, like Toros and his family, are Armenian and speak Armenian, but also speak Turkish seemingly as native speakers. The room was clean and pleasant, if Spartan and unheated. I showered and from my limited choice of clothing selected the most formal funeral attire I could, my dark hiking trousers with a lightweight black wool sweater. Then I went down to the little shop downstairs and bought some bottled water. I spoke in Arabic with the young woman there, named Marie, who was from Syria, but I was struck dumb by her beauty and could do little more than babble like an idiot.

I could not sit long and so decided to walk around the village for an hour before going to Toros' home for dinner. First, I confirmed that I could find his house by going most of the way there. Then I wandered and went towards Musa Dagh to look up at the mountain. I heard distant percussions, shelling in Syria perhaps or an evening craftsman hammering metal far below in the valley. And deeper ones, rumbling like thunder. I passed near the cemetery and started to read the inscriptions on the graves. Some of those buried here had died as babies, some as young men and women. My disembodied mind floated back to the British Cemetery in Florence in 1985, on one of my very first trips, where I stood solemnly before the tomb of a young man dead at eighteen, inscribed, "Blessed are the pure in heart."[22] Vakıflı has its share of these and more than its share of unmarked graves and ditches between here and the desert wasteland of Deir al-Zor, illusory goal of the deportation death marches whose only goal was death itself. But there were also those who traversed this period of madness in its entirety. Iskuhi Babeck, 1904–1983. She must have seen it all. Or Boğos Kus, 1889–1988. Perhaps he fought on Musa Dagh and returned here to his ancestral home. Then a fresh grave, a palanquin of roses and two candles burning. Toros' mother. I said a prayer for her in a vague feeling of confusion and anguish, as if this place, or my knowledge of it, were demanding answers to questions which I cannot answer. Why have I been so lucky? How can these things happen? What do such events mean for our own morality and belief? What are we? If this is a man…then what? I pulled myself together and walked to Toros' home for dinner.

As I came down the road to his house the pungent farm smells drew me out of my reverie. And I felt alone, going to dine with people I do not know, in a place far from my home. But all of them were kind and welcoming. Two older men, one of them Mihran, the driver of the red Citroën I had so fortunately stopped, spoke Arabic and we communicated in that language. They asked me about my family, my home and my travels. I told them that thirty years earlier I had

---

22. *King James Bible*. Matthew, 5:8.

visited Erevan, the capital of Armenia, and Echmiadzin, the seat of the Armenian Christian Church, as well as the ancient Armenian site of Ani in eastern Turkey. My having been to the important places of their nation disposed them well towards me. A young man named Aram had played in a basketball championship in Erevan some years before. There were also three young women, shy and retiring, and it was only at the end of the meal that I learned that they spoke English quite well (especially one of them, Nora), better than my Arabic, and lived in Istanbul, where they would return early tomorrow, having come here only for the funeral of their grandmother. Over dessert I spoke mostly with them and then again with the men for the three glasses of *raki* we drank in honor of Toros' mother's passing. While drinking I listened intently to the conversation in Turkish and was generally able to parse the flow of sound into Turkish words and even to seize the meaning of some of what they said. But I didn't speak, just absorbed their language, present in their company. I was at home among strangers, filled by my journey.

FEBRUARY 19, 2016

Toros had told me to be ready at 6:00 AM. I had a terrible time sleeping. From 9:00 PM when I returned to my room to 2:00 AM I dozed fitfully while a nearby dog barked. At first he was answering a compatriot from afar, which I could barely hear, but from time to time he would launch into a frenzied soliloquy of barking perhaps aimed at his interlocutor. These frantic howls woke me from my light sleep each time they occurred. A certain degree of worry possessed me as well, being in a remote place near the Syrian border in an empty guesthouse. Around 2:00 AM the dog fell asleep for good. I know because I slept little after that. At home I have allergies which appear each year, usually in March for around two weeks, but being here further to the south I will have to bear them twice this year. I got up at 5:00 AM instead of 5:30 for which my alarm was set. I didn't shower but ate some cookies, walnuts, and dried fruit, and drank water. I double-checked my pack, which Toros had burdened the night before with four big oranges and a half-liter of *raki*, making it weigh roughly five kilos. If I had camped with all of my equipment, food, and water it would have been twice that.

At 5:30 AM I heard a car go by. Nora and her cousins on their way to the airport and back to Istanbul. Then, at 5:40 AM I heard a truck. Toros was here already. I went out to meet him and he introduced me to Abdulrahman, who would guide me. Out of courtesy I did not ask his ethnicity or religion, but his name is Muslim and I assume that he is as well, and Turkish. Abdulrahman is sixty, moderately tall, but with easily fifteen kilos in excess weight on his frame. I confess to thinking, "Damn, this guy is going to have to rest every five minutes…" but of course I kept this to myself. Toros, for his part, is clearly fit and strong, a mountain man. Toros drove us on the road I had reconnoitered yesterday, around three kilometers to one of the dirt tracks previously mentioned, and dropped us off.

We started up the track. I let Abdulrahman set the pace, fearing that he would feel bad if I did. But he really impressed me. He must have known these mountains since his youth, and despite his ample spare tire he hiked very well. The dirt track became a stony path, reddish soil with large chunks of limestone embedded in it, struck white in places by the blows of donkeys' shod hooves. Ahead of us were two of these donkeys, making very fast progress under the blows of their riders. With visions of a Persian princess being guided donkey-back to the top of Musa Dagh, I accelerated my pace and even remarked out loud, "*Mumkin güzel kız*," a mixture of Arabic (*mumkin*, "possibly") and Turkish (*güzel kız*, "beautiful girl"). Abdulrahman understood, laughed, and probably secretly thought that his client was insane. A little later, falling behind me, he exhorted me to slow down, probably with some Turkish obscenities I couldn't comprehend. Before I did we had almost caught up with the donkey riders, dispelling my fantasy of a Persian princess. They were not heading to Musa Dagh at all, but were workers going to cut wooden staves on its forested slopes. We were the only visitors that day.

After half an hour at a good pace, Abdulrahman insisted that we stop. We took a brief rest, drank some water, and arranged our packs. The donkey riders had gone west and I started to follow them, but was instructed that our path lay to the north. Another half hour of steep incline brought us to a low stone rampart. Just before this we found ourselves in a ravine filled with dense vegetation including holly bushes, and I remembered the "holly gorge" of Werfel's book, site of several skirmishes. Continuing another fifteen minutes or so brought us to a flat and broad prairie at the exit from the ravine. Here were several stone structures and a well with water in it now. I think this was the area used as pasture for the Armenians' flocks. Werfel seemingly wrote his battle scenes based upon discussions with participants or witnesses, but only visited Musa Dagh after the publication of his book. Drawing a precise correspondence between his descriptions and the actual places is not a trivial task. We wended our way across the prairie, up a small hill and down to a much smaller flat area. Here two freshly cut staves lay in an X on the ground. I took one for my walking stick, not realizing until later that I was probably pillaging the work of one of the donkey-riders, unless they had left these crossed staves for us? Further on we came to a place easily recognizable from Werfel's tale, a steep ravine sloped on the east (the direction the attacking Turks would have come from) but even more steeply sloped on the western, defending side. There were what seemed to be remnants of demolished trenches, revealed by the rectilinear way the plants grew, perpendicular to the slope. Here a careless attacking force could be destroyed by entrenched and hidden defenders.

After this ravine, the landscape opened out. We were on the Damyalik, the plateau below the summit of Musa Dagh. There were many places for huts or tents, though it was hard to imagine some 4,000 people living here. Werfel's account seems too orderly to have reflected the reality of this place. As we progressed, in one large flat area at the south end there was a low rectangular stone enclosure of perhaps fifty square meters. Abdulrahman led me there with an air of introspection and reverence and said, "*Mezarlık.*" Here in unmarked graves lay the mortal remains of eighteen men who died to save, and who did save, more than 4,000 of their community, mostly women and children. There are no tombstones, no monument, no respect, except for that in the hearts of those who visit this place. Only Abdulrahman's telling me allowed me to know the meaning of these stones. We can never know the significance of physical artifacts, what they symbolize, or what they were before we see them in their present state. *Fragmentum quod vile putas et inutile lignum, haec fuit ignoti prima carina maris* ("This, which you think a vile and useless piece of wood, was part of the keel of the first ship to sail the unknown seas").[23]

We continued upwards and I looked back on the *Mezarlık*. Those men got what they aimed for. If they could look down and see what their sacrifice had won, they would be happy. They saved their families and their friends. Can they look down? Can they sense the homage of a foreign visitor paying his respects? Soon we reached the location of the *Vapur* (steamship, because the naval vessels which rescued the Armenians were steamships, *bateaux à vapeur*), a stone monument in the shape of a steamship. The monument was erected in 1932 and later mostly demolished, presumably by the Turks. This was the culmination of the hike. We left our packs near the monument, took photos, and stretched. I looked around at the 360-degree panorama over mountains and sea, trying to square in my mind Werfel's narrative with this place. Far to the south-east was what may have been the South Bastion, probably overlooking part of our path up the mountain. Closer, just south of the ruined monument was a buttress so utterly impregnable that no enemy force would have even attempted it. This spot surrounded by cliffs had a panoramic command of the entire seacoast to the west, and it occurred to me that it must have been here that the Armenians had placed their white sheet embroidered with a red cross, and the words "Christians in Distress: Rescue!" I surveyed the surrounding mountains and sea from this vantage point, then stumbled down the hillside, my mind clouded by the understanding of what happened here on Musa Dagh. I thought of Movses Der Kelousdian, who led his people through the valley of death as surely as his namesake the prophet had done. And of Admiral Louis Dartige du Fournet, commander of the French Eastern Mediterranean fleet in 1915, who answered this call for help and thus saved more than 4,000 lives. There is a monument commemorating Musa Dagh in Toulon, France, near my home. And descendants of those rescued still go to Dartige du Fournet's grave in the Dordogne region of France to pay their respects to him for what he did.

---

23. Martial, *Epigrams*, Book VII, 19.

After some time we descended on a steep path towards the sea, roughly 100 meters of altitude loss. It was probably by this path that the Armenians started down to the ships. We reached a basin carved from the stone of the mountain, catching and keeping water from a spring. The water flowed into a stone-hewn trough for animals. This fountain of life is what saved the people on Musa Dagh. Without this water they would have had no chance of survival. This stone trough must be the same one they used then. The water was cold and clear. A little further down was a rough fire pit. We were in the shade of the high cliffs which I had seen yesterday from the road along the coast. Here we stopped and Abdulrahman began to prepare lunch, with me as his assistant chef. We gathered dry wood and made a fire, had olives with olive oil and red pepper powder, then a tasty salad of onion and fresh coriander. We added to this grilled beef sausage, all served on flatbread warmed on the fire. At the end we drank *raki* and toasted the heroes of Musa Dagh, those buried in the *Mezarlık* and those who survived. We then cleaned up, returned back to the *Vapur* monument on the summit and took some rest. I went back to the flag buttress and surveyed the surroundings for the last time. I had hoped to be able to walk down to the sea from here, but Abdulrahman said it was a dangerous hike and too far. I tend to believe that he simply preferred to stay on paths he knew well, and to not have to deal with transportation back to Vakıflı from the coast.

We hiked down the paths we had followed coming up. This time we didn't stop at all. It took two and a half hours at a steady downhill pace to reach our starting point, then three kilometers more to Vakıflı along the road. At the end, Abdulrahman asked me to give him the green synthetic towel I had used as a headscarf to absorb sweat and protect my brow from the sun, which I did, a memento of our time together. The whole hike, according to Abdulrahman and Toros, was twenty-three kilometers, and one thousand meters of elevation, and took us nine hours including almost three hours spent at the top. On returning to Vakıflı, we went to see Toros at his house so I could say goodbye to him and Abdulrahman. I did so, went to the guesthouse, packed my things and met Ahmet, who had returned from Antakya. He drove me to Iskenderun, stopping in Antakya to pick up his young wife, Pinar.

They were newlyweds and she was the receptionist at the hotel where I had stayed in Antakya. There was a moment of severe discomfort on his part when I told him where I was going to stay in Iskenderun, and he told me that he worked at that same hotel and ran his chauffeur business on the side. I settled his worry by telling him to drop me off discreetly 100 meters from the hotel. What is another 100 meters after more than twenty kilometers? I was tired and feeling sick from my pollen allergies, but I had a good dinner and anesthetized myself with abundant alcohol in the form of Turkish wine. Early tomorrow Ahmet will take me to Şanlıurfa, six or seven hours distant and the final destination of this trip.

FEBRUARY 20, 2016

The last two days have been like one long moment, with an intensity I do not remember since the journeys of my youth. I do not know if it was the scent of danger, the knowledge of present tragedy a few miles away, or my following in the footsteps of those who fought and survived. I slept relatively well last night despite my allergies and the fact that I couldn't control the temperature of my room. It was too hot but when I opened the window the traffic noise was unbearable. Ahmet and Pinar picked me up at 8:00 AM, again 100 meters down the road from the hotel so that he would not get in trouble with his employers, having taken a day off to drive me to Şanlıurfa (Urfa). We stopped at a pharmacy to buy medicine for my allergies, then drove north out of the stinking industrial zone around Iskenderun to Karatepe National Park. The landscape was idyllic, rolling hills rising into the foothills of the Taurus Mountains with pine forests and clear, cool air. After some hesitation on a small road through a pine forest we found the Karatepe (Turkish for "black hill") archaeological site.

We were walking towards the entrance of the archaeological park when a large German shepherd dog came hurtling down the path straight towards me at full speed, barking and snarling. I stood my ground and waited, sidestepped him at the last second, spun, and primed my right leg to deliver a strong roundhouse kick to the side of his head. His teeth weren't bared, however, so I held back, fearing that it might well have broken both my foot and his neck had I delivered the blow. The timing of my movement was perfect, one of those moments when one's actions are completely aligned with the flow of events. Right action. The Straight Path. But the dog continued attacking, so I delivered a hard kick to the ribs, then another to the belly as he moved away from me to turn his aggression towards Pinar and Ahmet. Now the dog was cowed and grovelled on his belly in submission before slithering away. I had "fought" with my dogs as a boy and was accustomed to how they fight. Trained dogs are truly dangerous, even to a strong man, but untrained ones are far less so. This one was extremely aggressive and deserved what it got. The museum guard apologized and tied the dog to a stake. It seems that not many people come to this site, or the dog would have learnt better manners or been euthanized after hurting someone.

After this exciting episode, the only physical aggression I have ever suffered in Turkey, we explored the site of Aslantaş, a late Hittite city from after the fall of Hattuşa. Much of the statuary had been smashed and pieced back together, and the place was overgrown with pine forest. Archaeologically, it was nothing exceptional, but the place was beautiful, cool, and overlooked the water of Aslantaş Lake, created by damming the Ceyhan river. We took leave of Karatepe and drove towards Şanlıurfa through the rolling Anatolian plains and past Gaziantep. The soil is sandy. There is no water. In the summer, it is as hot as hell. This place is basically useless. Around four hours later, we arrived in Şanlıurfa, the name meaning "Glorious Urfa," the epithet having been added to celebrate the heroism of the city's inhabitants during the Turkish War of Independence. In ancient times Urfa was known as Edessa. The prophet Abraham is reputed to have been born here, and the surrounding area has been inhabited since at least 9000 BCE. Seleucus I Nicator, whose capital was at the foot of Musa Dagh, founded the "modern" city in 304 BCE. I mentioned my visit here to one of my more erudite friends, and he replied that the philosopher Bar Daisan had taught in Urfa, he who said that only self-knowledge can allow us to escape the destiny fixed in the stars. Bar Daisan was born in 154 CE in Edessa, and his name means "Son of Daisan," the Daisan being the river which runs through Urfa.

With some difficulty, Ahmet and I located the hotel I had reserved. I had chosen it for its central location right in the old city, and because

I knew that the clientele would be Turkish, removing its attractiveness as a terrorist target. Pinar and Ahmet looked around the hotel, taking a professional interest, and also made sure that everything was right with my reservation and my room, translating my Arabic into Turkish when necessary. We sat and had tea together (I hate Turkish tea, so had Turkish coffee), chatted for some time and then they left for their long return journey to Antakya. They are a hard-working and kind young couple, and I wish them well.

I went up to my room and unpacked, then examined the room from a security perspective. Being here made me nervous. I had it on good authority that Urfa was Islamic State's largest base outside of Syria and Iraq. As I mentioned earlier, a few months previously IS had beheaded two journalists here and were not caught. Many IS fighters apparently use Urfa as a rear base for rest before returning to combat in nearby Syria.[24] So I had to be on my guard. I had had serious second thoughts about coming here at all, but really wanted to see the ancient temple at Göbekli Tepe as well as the city's Islamic architecture. The security situation of my room was not good. Exiting through the window was possible but tricky and likely to result in serious injury. To make matters worse, the door was a flimsy piece of junk that one kick would knock down. I figured out a way to wedge the desk chair between the bathroom door jamb and the room door. This arrangement would probably add two more kicks to the effort necessary to enter the room by force. As well as these physical precautions, I also adopted fairly extreme behavioral measures while in Urfa, addressing everyone in Arabic, then in French, and only then with a mixture of Turkish and broken English[25] if they did not speak the first two languages (Arabic is widely spoken here, as it is in and around Antakya). This had the effect of rendering my national origin even more uncertain than my now full beard had done. I could pass for Lebanese or Syrian, or Persian, and when I told some Arabic speakers I was French, several asked, "French, or Algerian?" I also controlled

24. Cohen, Roger, "Turkey's Troubling ISIS Game," *The New York Times*, November 7, 2015.

25. My accent in English marks me as an American, and we still top the "most hated" list among jihadists.

my colloquialisms, replacing the "hey" and "ouch" of my American upbringing with the Arabic "*ya*" and "*aie.*" This kind of practice requires considerable self-control, and I am still a novice. I can only imagine the training someone like Richard Burton must have imposed upon himself, and yet even he was almost found out as an impostor on his pilgrimage to Mecca, for being seen urinating while standing up![26]

I rested in the room momentarily, then went out walking. I moved very slowly, absorbing my surroundings. There were many mosques, several of them beautiful. I made my way across the garden representing a legend by which Abraham, the prophet of the Old Testament (and likewise considered a prophet by Muslims), had been in Urfa destroying pagan idols when Nimrod, the Assyrian king, took offense at his actions. He had Abraham immolated on a funeral pyre, but God transformed the fire into water and the burning coals into fish. Abraham himself was hurled into the air from the Citadel fortress only to land unharmed in a bed of roses. Now the Gölbası area of Urfa symbolically re-enacts this legend, with rectangular reflecting pools containing (very fat) fish, and near them a rose garden. This whole area is dominated by a sheer rock face on top of which is the Citadel. I noticed a door in one of the buildings of a mosque complex, which seemed to be an information office. I entered and addressed them in Arabic and they replied, giving me a map and some information about the city. I sat outside with my back against a wall of the mosque, unfolded the map, cut off all the

---

26. Captain Sir Richard Francis Burton, 1821–90, represents my ideal of a Renaissance man: erudite, daring, able, artistic. He knew many languages, and translated several works from medieval classical Arabic, including *The Thousand and One Nights* and *The Scented Garden*, a fifteenth-century manual of eroticism by Al-Nafzawi. I have read excerpts of both of these works in the original. Burton was also an explorer, searching for the source of the Nile with Speke, and he made the pilgrimage to Mecca and Medina disguised as an Afghan religious man. It was on this journey that he is rumored to have almost been found out due to urinating while standing up. His book, *Personal Narrative of a Pilgrimage to Al-Madinah and Meccah*, recounts this pilgrimage. Burton's religious beliefs are quite mysterious, and at least one of his biographers questions whether he deceived the Muslims by impersonating one of them on his pilgrimage, or whether he deceived the English and actually was a Muslim. Finally, he published a work called *The Kasidah* (which means "Ode" in Arabic), a poem he attributes to a Sufi Master rather than to himself, where he seems to disclose many of his own personal beliefs, including this, which I have taken as my motto: "He makes Self-cultivation, with due regard to others, the sole and sufficient object of human life." I would summarize the message of Burton's *Kasidah* in the following seven points: there is no God; there is neither Heaven nor Hell; do good because it is good, not for recompense; fight ignorance; love life; develop yourself; make and live by your own laws.

waste paper, and looked at it. Near me were two pretty but modestly dressed young women speaking Arabic. As I was reading the map, a rude young man ran by and yelled something unintelligible at me.

I soon got up to walk around, having taken my bearings from the paper map and the compass on my phone. There was more tension in the air here than in Antakya. Sometimes it seemed that there were more Syrians than Turks in the outdoor areas. I was nervous but calmed myself, and no one else showed me any hostility, though some looked at me longer than normal. I went into the Dergah mosque complex, which contains the cave in which the prophet Abraham (Ibrahim in Arabic and Turkish) is said to have been born. From a vantage point along the wall some distance away I watched the pilgrims, for this is a sacred pilgrimage site, to understand the protocol for the visit. Shoes off. Sober demeanor. Ticket. Then enter. Exit by the same door, creating a slightly turbulent flow of humanity. Thousands of people per hour were visiting this place. I advanced, removed my shoes, took the ticket, and entered, ducking low beneath the transom. There were eight or nine men in a very small room (the women had their own side, behind a thin partition), four praying before a thick glass window looking into a wet and ugly cave, and four or five waiting their turn. I waited, then took my place. I felt ill-at-ease but then realized that all three monotheistic religions revere Abraham, and Muslims would recognize this common heritage. So I knelt and said a prayer, foreshortened by the heavy stench of feet which curdled the air. Then I rose and went out.

I wandered slowly, taking in the beauty of the other Islamic buildings. The Dergah Mosque itself was large and modern, not interesting to me. Another, Hassan Padişa, was older and aesthetically pleasing with its series of low domes and its octagonal minaret. Near it was the old bazaar, which I went into, hoping to buy some tissues and a bottle of water. I must have inquired at six stores before I found tissues. Each time I spoke Arabic, and I received highly variable responses. One shop assistant even shooed me away as if I were a poor refugee taking up space in his premises. Finally I found what I wanted after having achieved my real goal, which was to see the bazaar. The crowds in such a place make personal security impossible. The best one can do is to be as alert as possible and accept the small risk. Leaving the bazaar after wandering its sinuous lanes, I sat on a bench next to a Turkish man in front of the Hassan Padişa Mosque. The man was genteel and although we did not speak we made gestures of respect to each other. As I stood up I said "*Ma'a al-salama*" "(Go) with peace," the formal and religious Muslim manner of taking leave, and he replied, "*Ma'a salamat illah*" "(Go) with the peace of God." I considered entering the mosque but had an unquantifiable feeling that I shouldn't, and I obeyed it.

Thus far the Islamic architecture of Urfa was pleasing but not remarkable, at least by the measure of someone who has seen a great deal of this architecture, including its splendid realizations in Fatimid Cairo. I found a place to sit on a sort of raised promontory overlooking the Balıklı Göl (the fish pool) from the Abrahamic legend and read the ripped out pages of a guidebook as well as the tourist office map. Three Turkish girls were playing at being coquettish near me, or rather one was, the prettiest, striking poses while her friends snapped photos of her. I told her she was *çok güzel*, very beautiful, but she knew it already. It must be intoxicating to be beautiful, to be an object of desire so powerful that it can sometimes transcend all social boundaries; witness the numerous courtesans or slave women who became official wives of kings and sultans. "Je suis belle, ô mortels, comme un rêve de pierre..."[27] The girls moved off, and two Turkish men spoke with me briefly—briefly because we had no common language which I was willing to speak. Then two other Turkish girls, *muhajabat* (wearing the *hijab*, head-scarf) sat near me. I smiled at them and they gave me two cookies. I took my bearings and was drawn to a colonnade of very unusual arches, part of the Rızvaniye Vakfı Mosque and Madrasa, a complex which forms the northern border of the fish pool. The arches were almost flowery in their elegance, as was the mosque itself. Inside its grounds there were steps down to the pool with its "sacred" carp, but there was no fountain for ablutions as there usually is in a mosque courtyard. The idea of washing in water densely inhabited by the piscine equivalent of rats did not seem religiously pure to me, but the architectural effect of the steps down

27. Baudelaire, Charles. "La Beauté", from *Les Fleurs du Mal*. "I am beautiful, oh mortals, like a dream of stone..." Author's translation.

to the water was spectacular. The inside of the mosque was very small, sober and unremarkable. This enclosure abutted against another, older, one, the Halilur Rahman Mosque. It formed the short end of the rectangular Balıklı Göl fish pool and is supposed to mark the spot where Abraham fell to the ground and landed in a bed of roses. This mosque was originally a sixth-century Byzantine church. The entire space was harmonious, the garden, the mosques, the clean rectangular lines of the fish pools, almost contemporary in their architectural purity. I can only imagine how even more beautiful had Abraham's grandiose beds of roses been in bloom. Şanlıurfa thus has one of the most stunning architectural ensembles I have seen in Turkey, apart, of course, from the magnificent Sultanahmet area of Istanbul. I returned, vigilant, to my room, had dinner, wrote, then thought about Göbekli Tepe and my visit there tomorrow.

I must admit that I was nervous about Göbekli Tepe, though it was the main reason I came to Urfa in the first place. Wandering in the bazaar and the mosques and gardens was, I thought, relatively safe because I could be careful, call for help from the police or passersby, or defend myself if necessary. But Göbekli Tepe is in an empty area, an hour from the Syrian border, and the terrain on the way to the border is mountainous with a number of small roads. What if a particularly enterprising group of Islamic State fighters decided to enter Turkey through its porous border near here, drive on small roads and waylay taxis with Western travelers bound for Göbekli Tepe? This would be an excellent means of replenishing the supply of wearers of orange jumpsuits for beheadings, as they seemed to have run out lately. Thinking about it, such a "raid" into Turkey might seem risky for the jihadis, but something they might actually do, a much more serious risk for me than being attacked in a public place in the city. If this risk ever materialized, my options would be limited: fight and get killed instead of kidnapped, or end up wearing an orange jumpsuit.

I decided to bear the risk nonetheless, as I had come far and was not willing to abandon my plan because of a tiny chance of catastrophe. I came to several conclusions on how to mitigate the risk as much as possible. First, take a taxi whose driver was well-known to the hotel. Second, email the licence plate number of the taxi and name of the hotel employee who recommended him to Hélène, so that if I disappeared the Turkish police would know whom to interrogate to find out where I had been taken. Third, study the terrain around Göbekli Tepe (via satellite imagery and maps) so as to know major landmarks ahead of time and know in which direction to run if I had to. And finally, have a plan of action defined ahead of time, meaning I would only have to execute it, not think about it. To die even in such an uneven fight is far preferable to being publicly beheaded, and I would choose that option without hesitation. Of course, before resorting to violence I would try to reason with my assailants, and would have a strong Islamic legal argument why they should leave me alone, namely that I am *Ahl al-Kitab*, one of the "People of the Book," the name Islamic law gives to Jews and Christians who are lawfully in Muslim lands, and thus my blood is *haram*, "forbidden" for them to spill. No reasonable Muslim jurist or theologian would ever refute this argument for it has been established almost since the beginning of Islam and is the reason why Jews and Christians were generally treated with tolerance throughout Islamic history. Unfortunately Islamic State seems to recruit from European-born lumpenproletariat low-lifes with little knowledge of Islamic law, and whose fondness for gore seems to come straight out of the video games they probably played instead of studying or working. One could say that they came to religion late, and by a circuitous path. Islamic State's home-grown Arab fighters are probably more decent and religious. I fell asleep thinking of these considerations and slept very badly, waking up at every creaking board or loud noise outside. On one of these occasions, around 3:00 AM, I distinctly heard two rifle shots outside. I was scared.

FEBRUARY 21, 2016

I got up, having slept perhaps four hours. I had breakfast, packed my things (as I had requested to change to a nicer room facing the mosques—this was a mistake, as I realized later), and transferred certain items from my small travel bag to my pockets. I already carry most of my cash and my ID hidden in a money belt under my clothes, but I also took a whistle and a tiny flashlight. The taxi I had reserved came on time, driven by an elderly Turkish gentleman named Saleh. I could not communicate well with him and made do by using the Turkish dictionary on my phone. I followed our progress towards Göbekli Tepe using GPS. I also, strangely, recited verses from the Qur'an to myself. I know some of the most beautiful ones by heart. This is one of my favorites, *Surat al-Doha* (Q 93), partially quoted previously, which has never failed to calm me:

> By the glorious morning light, and by the night when it is still, thy Lord hath not forsaken thee, nor is He displeased. And that which comes after shall be better for thee than the present. And soon thy Lord shall give unto thee, and thou shalt be contented. Did He not find thee an orphan, and care for thee? And He found thee lost, and guided thee. And He found thee needy, and enriched thee. So for the orphan, do not scorn him. And for the petitioner, do not repulse him. And for the bounty of thy Lord, proclaim it!

Muslims believe, almost in an axiomatic sense, in the inimitability of the Qur'an, specifically that no mortal could possibly compose words of equal beauty to those in the Qur'an. Though I have a great appreciation for poetry in all of the languages I know,[28] including for pre-Islamic Arabic *jahiliyya* poetry, which is beautiful beyond temporality, when I recite verses like those above I tend to agree with them.

We progressed towards Göbekli Tepe, but I began to become nervous when we continued further north than where GPS identified the site. Remembering the debacle of St. Paul's Well in Tarsus, I remained calm and asked Saleh why we had crossed over the highway when the site was south of it. He reassured me and said the site was north, not south, of the highway. I trusted him, as he seemed without malice. As we continued driving I saw a sign for our destination and also a sign for a place called Göktepe to the east, and in that direction spotted a suspiciously high mound of dirt. We reached Göbekli Tepe and parked,

---

28. English and French as an educated native speaker, well-versed in poetry and able to write it as well; Spanish at a moderate level; Latin as a weak reader who has to parse each sentence like a mathematical equation. And Arabic as a diligent student who has spent many years striving for a distant goal.

and I had to go the last two kilometers to the site in a minibus on a dirt track.

The existence of the Göbekli Tepe site was first noted in 1963 in an archaeological survey conducted by the University of Chicago. The exposed tops of the gigantic T-shaped monuments were thought to be grave stones, as it was not understood that they were only the tops of buried stone monoliths nearly seven meters high. In 1994, Klaus Schmidt, from the German Archaeological Institute, realized the nature of the stone slabs and began excavations at the site, which he continued for nearly twenty years until his death. The site is quite small in extent, or rather the excavated part of it is small. Professor Schmidt surveyed the entire mound with ground-penetrating radar, and it covers a surface of around twenty nine hectares, so it is actually huge. The T-shaped stone pillars are impressive, as are the animal carvings which adorn many of them. But what is utterly amazing about this place is that it dates (by multiple verified carbon-14 dates) to the tenth millennium BCE, so 12,000 years ago. That is almost back to the end of the last Ice Age. And at that time there was not supposed to be any agriculture or animal husbandry. Both religion and the physical means to construct such extensive monuments were thought to have come later, and to have required these two civilization advances which together formed the basis for the Neolithic Revolution. But here we have a massive site requiring the organization of hundreds of workers over years and relatively sophisticated engineering, in the late Paleolithic period. How could this be? The current dominant hypothesis is that hunter-gatherers were able to build these monoliths without knowledge of agriculture or animal husbandry and thus without settled civilization. Personally, I find this unlikely. There were no signs of habitations at the Göbekli Tepe site, but many bones were found of wild animals which had been cooked and eaten. Does this show that the builders had no domesticated animals or agriculture? It does not. It merely shows that they did not live on this site and that on this site they ate only hunted animals. Could this not have been part of a ritual by a more advanced people, one which possessed Neolithic-era skills and techniques in the late Paleolithic? Just because we have not found such a people does not mean they did not exist. Göbekli Tepe itself witnesses this, and its discovery has proven the dominant paradigm utterly wrong. As Ian Hodder, Professor of Archaeology at Stanford, said, "Göbekli Tepe...changes everything."[29] That the dominant paradigm needs to be revised is therefore not in doubt. But how to revise it? By attributing Göbekli Tepe to a pre-agricultural group of hunter-gatherers, as most experts seem to have agreed? Or by positing that its creators possessed settled civilization and its technologies in 9500 BCE, a couple of thousand years earlier than had been thought?

Aside from this grand dilemma and the disarray into which our idea of prehistory has been thrown, the Göbekli Tepe site also presents other aspects which are utterly bizarre, the main one being that the entire site was deliberately back-filled, buried, in the eighth millennium BCE. Why on earth would anyone have done this? Invading barbarians would have smashed it. "Normal" civilization would have re-used the stone for new constructions. Why bury it? Perhaps future discoveries will answer this question, but more likely not. Also interesting, fragments of incised human skulls have recently been discovered at Göbekli Tepe, indicating some type of religious practice with respect to the dead.[30] And a very unusual academic article has been published, asserting that the various animal figures on one of the stone pillars (the "Vulture Stone") represent astronomical constellations, and that the precise disposition of these figures constitutes a "date stamp" for an astronomical event which occurred at roughly 10,950 BCE, probably a comet impact, and which is known as the Younger Dryas Event.[31] Göbekli Tepe has thus

29. Symmes, Patrick. "Turkey: Archaeological Dig Reshaping Human History," *Newsweek*, February 18, 2010.

30. The archaeologists of Göbekli Tepe maintain an excellent website which discusses recent developments and has links to academic articles for those who are interested: https://tepetelegrams.wordpress.com

31. The Younger Dryas event saw the temperatures in the Northern Hemisphere drop suddenly by several degrees at the end of the Pleistocene Epoch, ushering in our own Holocene Epoch. In order for the creators of Göbekli Tepe to have been able to know to record the locations of constellations at the time of that event, they would have had to understand the precession of the earth's axis, probably requiring thousands of years of observation, which seems highly unlikely. That said, the authors of the cited article argue that the accidental organization of the animal forms representing constellations is also unlikely. See Sweatman, Martin and Tsikritis, Dimitrios, "Decoding Göbekli Tepe with Archaeoastronomy: What does the Fox Say?" *Mediterranean*

surely not yet yielded up all of its mysteries. I walked around the site and was unsatisfied, so turned back. The minibus honked its horn, but I turned my back on it, hunched my shoulders, and accelerated away from it. I wandered again around the site, fully respecting the posted boundaries,[32] and then left. Three young Turkish men who had also ignored the minibus were walking back the two kilometers to the car park, and I walked with them.

On the way back to the hotel, I asked Saleh to turn left at the sign to Göktepe to examine the suspicious mound I had seen on the way here. At first he resisted, as we had agreed on a fixed price for the excursion and I was demanding something extra, but I reassured him that I would compensate him proportionately and he turned onto the dirt track. A couple of kilometers from the road, we parked at the base of the tumulus and I scrambled up to the top. It was covered with potsherds. To my untrained eye it looked Neolithic, like Çatalhöyük but much smaller. From the summit I saw all of the village children running towards my parked taxi, such an arrival surely a rare event in these parts, and I scrambled back down. I greeted them all, made my way through them to the car and we left. After my return home to France I searched for information on Göktepe but found nearly nothing. I inquired of Professor Hodder of Stanford, director of the Çatalhöyük excavations, with whom I have had a brief and sometimes comical correspondence, but he did not know of the site. I also communicated with Mr. Jens Notroff of the German Archaeological Institute, a researcher at Göbekli Tepe who knows of the Göktepe site, and he confirmed that the period from which it dates is unknown, with no excavations conducted. He also said that his team had no interest in conducting excavations on the site. In cases like this one, I find the organization of academic archaeology to be sub-optimally risk-averse.[33] Here is a probable settlement mound

Archaeology and Archaeometry, Volume 17, No 1 (2017), pp. 233-50.

32. Often, boundaries at historical or archaeological sites are set to prevent visitors from endangering themselves. These I disregard. At Göbekli Tepe, violating the boundaries could result in damage to the artifacts, which I would never risk.

33. I mean "risk-averse" in the sense of choosing one site and excavating it in-depth for an entire career, rather than taking a chance at broadening the scope of research by attempting to

nearby a religious site with no settlement. Would it not be worthwhile to conduct at least an exploratory excavation to see if the two are from the same period?

On the drive back to Urfa, Saleh suggested that we could also visit Harran. I was curious, looked up Harran, and found out that it is an ancient Assyrian city literally on the border with Syria (a part of Syria controlled by Islamic State), so I politely declined and Saleh drove me back to the hotel. Enough adventure for one day! When he dropped me off I arranged for him to come the next morning to drive me to the airport. Then for the remainder of the afternoon I wrote at the covered terrace of a coffee house near the hotel while it rained around me. I then packed, had dinner, and wrote more. Finally I prepared my room for sleep, and slept, though not better than the previous night.

FEBRUARY 22, 2016

I woke up early, or rather I did not really wake up because I hardly slept. The Hassan Padişa Mosque, across the park from my new "better" room, was throwing a party. It started at roughly midnight, waking me up. And it continued all night long. There was chanting, almost singing, loud and with many voices, punctuated by Qur'an recitations, some of them beautiful, played over the loudspeaker for the benefit of all of the city. This was from midnight until 5:00 AM, probably in honor of a *Mawlid* (the birthday of a Sufi saint) or a folk religious festival. In Cairo I had attended some of these, including that of Sayyida Zainab, with more than a million people. I would have done so here as well but for the strong presence of Islamic State in Urfa and my desire to avoid unnecessary danger.

Saleh arrived on time at 6:00 AM. Though his taxi was slow and quite dusty, I valued his benevolence above all else. I had planned to give my knife to one of the doormen of the hotel, polite, helpful, and of a military demeanor, but he was not there at this early hour. So, arriving at the airport, I gave it to Saleh, saying, "This is a gift for you."

---

understand other nearby sites and the relationships among such sites. I think the administrative permission processes imposed by governments contribute to this risk aversion, but it leaves obvious questions disappointingly unanswered.

He was visibly happy, and thanked me, touching his heart and shaking my hand. I entered the airport and forgot to mentally "switch gears," speaking Arabic to the security guards as I presented my French identity card. They must have thought, "Bearded French guy speaking Arabic = TERRORIST," and they subjected me to an invasive search. Of my belongings. As I sat waiting for the flight, a fellow passenger resembling a younger version of Osama bin Laden, complete with Afghan dress, bushy black beard, and piercing eyes, passed through without being questioned or looked askance upon. I hoped he was not on my flight and mentioned him in a text message to my family. Then, twenty minutes later, I texted them again, "Osama just boarded Pegasus Air. I am on Turkish Airlines. So it is OK." And with that the trip is done.

6

THE BLACK SEA COAST

I AM ABOUT TO LAND IN ISTANBUL AFTER AN UNEVENTFUL FLIGHT. A strange calm has descended on me. I am not in a rush, am not stressed. My journey has begun, whether the plane to Trabzon is on time, late, or canceled. Whether I go there or elsewhere, no matter. The uncertainties of life become more apparent in travel, and for me easier to accept. Twelve hours ago I was home, in my habitual surroundings, days laid out before me like a stepladder to climb slowly, every rung known. Now I am free. Nothing is imposed on me but what I choose. There are no habitual actions to accomplish but those most basic to daily life.

The journey was long. I waited, bored, in Istanbul airport. I drew the short straw when it came to my seat in the plane to Trabzon. An old, fat, and (I discovered later) smelly Turkish man was in my assigned window seat, and refused to move when I asked him, so I called the flight attendant and she ordered him to move. It did occur to me, in deference to his age and my status as a foreigner, to offer him my seat, but wedging myself between him on one side and a younger fat man in the aisle seat seemed an unpleasant fate, so I didn't. I noted that the second fat man, also a Turk, didn't offer his aisle seat to his older compatriot either.

The arrival at Trabzon airport was pleasing, as the plane journey was an accelerated inverse of the land trip I would now make back to Istanbul, half of it over the land I would explore and the other half over the Black Sea. Landing, I saw a number of dry bulk cargo ships at anchor and one oil tanker steaming north-west. Trabzon seemed new and ugly from the sky, an impression later largely confirmed on the ground. Each time I begin a trip I am faced with a clean slate, a blank canvas, a pure mountain slope of powder with no ski tracks down it yet. Now begins the choosing of the path. The hotel driver was waiting for me at the airport, and everything went smoothly. I checked into the hotel, a large, modern, business hotel, and immediately made inquiries about onward transportation. Sumela Monastery is closed for renovations, as I had heard. And the receptionists seemed doubtful about finding a driver to take me to Cape Jason and Amasya. But I know that I will find one.

I went to my room, unpacked in a minute, washed, and went out to wander in the night. I had changed some money at the hotel and so kept my eyes open for a knife shop. I only walked for around an hour, seeing people relaxing in the Atatürk Park after breaking their Ramadan fast.[1] I heard three different groups of people speaking Arabic, at least one of which was a family from the Arabian Gulf. I also saw signs in Arabic, which surprised me in northern Turkey, but it seems that many middle-class Gulf families take holidays in and near Trabzon in the summer. Then, on the way back to the hotel, by chance there was a knife shop. I entered, considered carefully the various options, and purchased my *biçak* from the bearded young man tending the shop. Then I went back to the hotel for dinner, as I felt like having a beer, and during Ramadan I prefer not to do so in a public venue.

JUNE 14, 2016

Last night I was again musing about the emotional states I go through while traveling. Of course, these are quite volatile, full of peaks and valleys, but the more I consider the question the more it seems that I show greater stability alone than in the company of other people, at least insofar as the lows are concerned. I can feel bad alone, but to feel truly awful I generally require the participation of other people, my family

---

1. During Ramadan, observant Muslims fast from sunup to sundown. In June this can be quite daunting, as it means going without food and water from approximately 5:00 AM to 8:00 PM while the summer heat reaches well above 85°F (30°C).

usually. I have a good family (the one my wife and I raised, not the one in which I was raised, which is part of the problem), but sometimes when I am with them I feel so sad, impotent, and close to despair. I never feel that way to the same degree when I am alone. Naturally I also feel great love and joy with my family, more than when I am alone.

Not wanting to eat in front of people fasting, I ate breakfast in my room, and now I will go out to begin my exploration of this place, Trabzon. Marco Polo passed through here on his way home after a quarter-century of travels. He was only granted permission to leave the Mongol court of Kubla Khan in order to deliver a young bride to her groom in a far-off province of Persia. The journey took two years, and after fulfilling his charge he continued on to the Kingdom of Trabzon (which, at the time, was a Christian kingdom tributary of the Ilkhan Mongols) and then home to Europe.[2] I wandered in the bazaar. More stuff I do not want. Due to the summer season, my whole equipment now weighs only six kilos instead of seven. It was above 85°F (30°C) today, very hot. Generally I avoid wearing short-sleeved shirts in Muslim countries, but here many men seem to do so, and so did I. I entered the Çarşi Mosque, saluting a man at the entrance as I removed my shoes. It was cool inside but aesthetically uninteresting. I then took a taxi to the Hagia Sophia mosque and museum. This was a Byzantine church at its founding in the thirteenth century, but was converted to a mosque after Mehmet the Conqueror took Trabzon. Other travelers have mentioned this building, including the Turk Evliya Çelebi in 1648 and the Frenchman Pitton de Tournefort in 1701.[3] The frescoes under the western vaulted entrance have been gravely damaged by vandals, but are still beautiful. Colors vibrant but visages defaced. Earlier pagan temple, to church, to mosque. What next? The waves of history submerging each other. I am tired of history. I entered the mosque proper and was shooed away by an ornery old crone whom I greeted with "Peace be with you," a greeting which remained unanswered (it is very impolite of a Muslim not to reply to this greeting). Then I noticed the carpet

---

2. Polo, pp. 66-7.

3. These dates are according to the sign at the site.

cleaning machine near the doorway through which I had entered, and the cool, refreshing feeling of wet carpet soaking through my socks.

I went out and walked around the exterior of the building, noticing a few foreign visitors as well as a group of local high-school students. The group was occupying the area under the vaulted ceiling with the frescoes, which I wanted to admire again before leaving, so I sat under the northern portico and read until they left. I looked again at the frescoes, then decided to head to the main road to flag a taxi. This mosque is one of the main sites of interest in Trabzon. The city is a backwater, and I will leave it tomorrow. On my way out of the mosque grounds, out of curiosity I went to the end of a small esplanade overlooking the highway and the sea. Below me a pleasant surprise, hundreds of bright orange tiger lilies and further off, reflecting their colors in artificial fluorescent splendor, the bright plastic colors of a giant tubular jungle gym at a children's playground. The driver of the first taxi I took would not tell me the price to go to Böztepe, nor did he use his taxi meter, so I was annoyed and thought he was trying to cheat me. I said nothing, however, and when he dropped me at a taxi stand and refused any payment, I felt relieved and wished him a Blessed Ramadan. It is amazing how a small act of kindness by a stranger can improve one's psychic state. The second taxi, from the taxi stand, took me to Böztepe, a park on a high prominence above the city, which in ancient times was the site of temples and monasteries. Now it is a vantage point for people to picnic and enjoy the breeze and the view of the port below, and of the sea.

The taxi driver had mentioned a nearby mosque when he dropped me off, and had waved vaguely eastward, and after having walked through the park I turned in that direction. I passed an active military zone, with a barbed wire fence and guards armed with Heckler & Koch G-3 assault rifles, and further on I found the Ahi Evren Dede tomb and mosque. Ahi Evren was a Muslim missionary to Trabzon in the thirteenth century, and was killed by the Mongols. This tomb in Trabzon may not even be his.[4] It was surrounded by a cemetery,

---

4. https://en.wikipedia.org/wiki/Ahi_Evren. The Turkish Wikipedia page contains much more information.

which I contemplated. I looked through a small window at the tomb. The mosque was peaceful, with two men praying, and above the door was the Quranic inscription: "Enter it in peace and security." Q 15:46. I did so and sat for some time there, deciphering Arabic inscriptions and meditating silently. I then started to walk back to town, but abandoned the idea due to the heat, waved down a *dolmuş*,[5] and jumped in with the other passengers. The rest of the afternoon I spent reading, writing, and, especially, planning upcoming travels. I found a driver to take me to Sumela Monastery and to Ordu tomorrow, and his friend, named Mustafa, has invited me for tea tonight after *iftar*.[6] I will go.

I decided to take the *iftar* meal with other people, as is the custom here during Ramadan. I wandered, and selected first one, then another, restaurant, only to be turned away because they were full and were too fancy to seat me at the same table with strangers. I reduced my culinary objective and approached a popular restaurant, where they sat me with two Turks, who did not know each other. We hardly spoke, even the two of them, but exchanged greetings while waiting for the cannon to sound and the call to prayer to echo from the minarets, signaling the end of the daily fast. Prior to this, each man busied himself pouring a glass of water, staring at it, arranging the various dishes in front of him, and, for me at least, trying to decide by which dish I would begin. The waiters were slow to bring me water, and one of the men sitting across from me insisted several times, and when they brought a bottle which had not been chilled I could feel that his sense of fairness towards the stranger had been slighted and he demanded cold water on my behalf, which the waiter brought. I thanked him for this attention. We ate our meal quickly, and each of us left separately. The problem was that the meal was light and I was still hungry. On the way back to the hotel was a sort of Scylla and Charybdis of American Consumerism, McDonalds on the right and Burger King on the left. I was tempted, but passed through this

---

5. A *dolmuş* is a sort of collective taxi, usually a minibus, a very economical and fairly efficient mode of transportation in Turkey. They run on pre-determined routes but are not restricted by pre-determined stopping places.

6. *Iftar* is the meal which breaks the Ramadan fast at sunset. A cannon is sounded to mark the moment, and then the evening prayer is called.

strait and ate a chicken *shwarma* sandwich at a local fast food outlet. Then I returned to the hotel to meet Mustafa.

Mustafa works at the local Karadeniz Technical University (*Karadeniz* means "Black Sea") and in his spare time is a partner in a local travel agency, which is how I found him while looking for a driver to take me to Sumela and points west. He invited me to visit the university campus, vast and pleasant, with fewer students than usual since examinations are underway and some have finished already. We then went for a drink at the university's social club overlooking the sea. This was also vast, with the sort of cold and impersonal architectural feeling which prevailed in communist architecture some years ago. Our conversation revolved mostly around politics. Like many educated Turks with whom I have spoken, Mustafa is terribly dissatisfied with the direction in which Turkey is heading: towards autocracy. He gave several examples of this, some from his personal life, such as a group of teachers, including some of his friends, who had been arrested and accused of belonging to the Gulenist[7] movement (one of them was the mother of a month-old baby, imprisoned and separated from her baby). Others were reported in the international news, including the mass arrests of journalists for reporting on important events (such as the Turkish intelligence services providing weapons to jihadist rebels in Syria). Mustafa considers Erdoğan a criminal worthy of prosecution in The Hague. I related an interesting anecdote recounted to me by a friend who met Erdoğan years ago. When asked about democracy, he said "Democracy is like the Metro—you get off at the stop you want." It seems that he is getting off now.

The political situation in Turkey is complex. A month after my visit, there was an attempted military coup against President Erdoğan and his government. In Turkey's recent past, the military has acted as the guarantor of the secular order established by Atatürk, and has periodically taken power by force from elected governments. This

---

7. Fethullah Gülen is a Muslim cleric, former ally of Erdoğan's AKP, and now an opponent. He lives in exile in the US, and has been blamed by Erdoğan for organizing the coup attempt against him in the summer of 2016, though there is no evidence of this. The movement towards autocracy discussed by Mustafa thus started before the coup of July, 2016.

time, however, the coup failed. Hundreds of people were killed, mostly defending the legitimately elected government. Despite his autocratic impulses, Erdoğan has the genuine support and trust of a large section of the population, perhaps the majority. But his reaction to the coup, under a legal state of emergency, effectively removed whatever pretense Turkey had to being governed by the rule of law. Some 40,000 people were imprisoned without due process, and 120,000 others summarily dismissed from their jobs in various branches of the government.[8] Press outlets were closed, companies nationalized, and laws changed to favor autocratic decision making. I think Mustafa was probably caught up in these purges as well. Democracy and the rule of law are trees whose roots grow slowly. To be strong enough to withstand even minor storms requires centuries. When reading history, it is shocking how quickly such institutions can be undermined then toppled, how short is the road to serfdom.

JUNE 15, 2016

I woke this morning, had a very early breakfast, checked out, and met Mustafa and Yusuf, the driver, at 9:00 AM. I had decided to fast for the day as would an observant Muslim, to see how it feels not to drink anything for an entire day in the summer heat. I have gone a day or two without eating on numerous occasions, but have never gone without water for a full day. Yusuf was an older man, in his sixties, with kind eyes and a beard. He was pious, speaking no English, but had lived for ten years in Madina (the location of the tomb of the Prophet Muhammad, in Saudi Arabia) and spoke good Arabic. We took our leave of Mustafa and headed out of the city towards the south. Immediately my spirits started to lift. It still works. The very act of traveling, of moving, changes my inner state. We drove towards Sumela, and Yusuf commented on various points of interest as we passed. First, hazelnuts growing in trees. Then something I did not understand, *kivi*. Then figs. When he said

---

8. Reuters. "Victims of Turkey Purges Fear Heavier Crackdown after Referendum", *The New York Times*. April 13, 2017.

"figs" (*tin* in Arabic), I quoted to him the *ayat* from the Qur'an: "By the fig and the olive, and by Mount Sinai" (Q 95:1-2) and he replied with the next verse, "And by this safe country," and continued, saying, "Safe country, like Trabzon. You will never have any troubles here." And we continued on our way.

We reached the turning to Sumela, and slowly ascended a winding mountain road along a river, steeper and steeper, and deeper into a remote and forbidding valley. I knew that the monastery was closed for extensive renovations, but hoped to be able to see it from the outside, nestled into the cliff face like the homes of the Pueblo Indians at Mesa Verde. Sumela Monastery was founded in the late fourth century CE during the reign of the Byzantine Emperor Theodosius. It reached its apogee during the Kingdom of Trabzon in the thirteenth and fourteenth centuries, the time when Marco Polo passed through Trabzon, and Ibn Battuta traveled nearby. The monastic activity at Sumela continued unabated through the early twentieth century, but ceased after the Greek population of the Ottoman provinces which became Turkey was expelled shortly after the end of World War I and the fall of the Ottoman Empire, thus ending a period of more than 2,000 years during which Hellenistic civilization and later Greek Christian civilization flourished in these lands.

What could have led the founding monks to choose a location for their monastery so remote from the rest of humanity? Defense could be one reason, but at that time the region was under the control of Christian Byzantium, so the defensive requirements must have been limited. I believe what motivated them was the monastic ideal itself, the wish to live apart from the world. Many Christian monasteries are in places so remote as to give one pause. The monastery of St. Catherine, in the Sinai, also originally from the fourth century CE, is high in remote mountains. I saw there a moderately large room full, floor-to-ceiling, of human skulls, the skulls of monks who died there over the centuries, contributing their labor, their devotion, in some cases their ideas to the monastic life, and then at the end, some decades after their deaths, their bones to that ossuary.[9] Islam does not seem to have this monastic impulse, of

---

9. Places like St. Catherine's have limited space within their walled enclosures, and the ground

communal life apart from the world. Sufis have orders, but they generally are founded within existing worldly communities, and individual Sufis who have repudiated the world generally wander alone, sons of the road. Buddhism, on the other hand, has a very powerful monastic urge: witness the great monasteries of Tibet, among others. Sven Hedin, illustrious early twentieth-century explorer of Central Asia and single-handed filler-in of blank white spaces on maps, writes of a Tibetan monk walled inside a cave for life by his own volition in Linga Gompa:

> The hermit who dwelled therein bore the honorary title of Lama Rinpoche. He was thought to be a man of about forty. He meditated and dreamt of Nirvana...Every morning a bowl of tsamba, and perhaps a small pat of butter, were shoved in to him. He got water from a spring that bubbled in the interior of the cave. Every morning, the empty bowl was withdrawn and refilled. Every sixth day, he got a pinch of tea, and twice a month a few sticks, which he could ignite with a fire-steel...Should the immured man speak to the serving brother, he would sacrifice all credit for his years of solitary meditation. If the serving brother found the bowl untouched when he pulled it out, he understood that the recluse was either ill or dead. He would then push the bowl back again and walk away in dejection. If the bowl remained untouched the following day, and altogether for six days, the cave was broken open; for then it was safe to assume that the recluse had died...

> I could hardly tear myself away from the place. In there, only a few feet away from me, was a man, possessed of will-power compared to which all else became insignificant. He had renounced the world; he was already dead; he belonged to

---

is stony and inhospitable, making the creation of an extensive cemetery impossible. Bodies were thus buried and allowed to decompose, then the skeletons removed to the ossuary, or charnel house, to make room for the next generation. In the Zoroastrian regions of Iran and the Caucasus and also in Tibet, both stony desert regions, the solution of "sky burial" (allowing carrion birds to devour corpses) served a similar purpose. In 1985 in Azerbaijan I saw the location of such burials, a "Tower of Silence," and in Tibet in 1987 as well.

eternity. The soldier going toward inevitable death is a hero; but he does it once. The Lama Rinpoche's physical life persisted through decades, and his sufferings lasted until death liberated him. He had an unquenchable longing for death.

The Lama Rinpoche fascinated me irresistibly. Long afterwards, I would think of him of nights; and even today, though eighteen years have passed, I often wonder if he is still alive in his cave. Even if I had had the power and the permission, I would not for the life of me have liberated him and led him out into the sunshine. In the presence of such great will-power and holiness, I felt like an unworthy sinner and a coward.[10]

This monastic urge, to be apart from the world, to purify existence down to its very simplest essence, is thus innate in some part of humanity. There is no mystery why the founders of Sumela chose their remote location on the face of a cliff—to be alone.

I walked from where Yusuf parked the car slowly towards the path leading to the monastery. When I was about to embark on the footpath, a guard stopped me. I was the only visitor that day, others having surely judged that visiting a closed monastery was not worth the trip, and there were only a few workmen laboring near the path. I asked Yusuf to translate from Arabic to Turkish so that I could communicate with the guard, which he did. But all of my entreaties were rebuffed. Then I asked Yusuf to tell the guard that I had given a gift to an Egyptian guarding the Great Pyramid of Giza in order to climb to the top of it on New Year's Eve 1990. At this, I saw the guard's eyes light up, and I deliberately reached into my pocket and slowly began to take out my handkerchief. The guard watched intently, wondering what I was going to extract from my pocket. I waited for him to make an offer. I sensed that Yusuf, upright and pious man as he was, did not approve of my tacit attempt to suborn the guard, and I think the guard could also feel

---

10. Hedin, Sven, *My Life as an Explorer*. New York: Boni and Liveright, 1925, pp. 445–7. The last sentence quoted is astounding, as in all of my voluminous readings of exploration and travel, Sven Hedin is one of the most courageous men I have ever encountered.

Yusuf's moral reproach, so no offer came. I was not about to commit a criminal offense by openly attempting to bribe a government official. It was much easier in Egypt. So I climbed the Great Pyramid but was reduced to seeing Sumela Monastery from a distance. I have missed my only chance to enter it, as I will never return here again. Strange regrets, those places I have approached in my travels but not touched.

We came down the valley from Sumela, pausing at a trout farm employing the chill waters of the mountain river. The owner caught a couple of nice brook trout with a net to show me, and I saw a rainbow trout, not as fortunate as his fellows, belly-up on the surface of the pool. We then turned southward, going higher into the mountains. From the sweltering heat on the coast we had reached, at around 1,300 meters altitude, a very comfortable temperature, much easier for fasting. The vegetation here was still lush, reminding me of the Pennsylvanian mountains of my youth, with both conifers and deciduous trees. There were snow-capped mountains in the distance and patches of snow remaining on the northern slopes of closer mountains. Past these mountains was the high Anatolian plateau and cities such as Erzincan, source of fine cottons in Marco Polo's day, and Erzerum,[11] where I had been at the end of my 1987 trip to Turkey. As we were driving, Yusuf returned to the subject of the mysterious *kivi*, which I still couldn't understand. I looked it up in my Turkish dictionary but found nothing. Then Yusuf stopped the car near a field planted with small trees, went to one of the trees and showed me a kiwi fruit. I understood. I ought to have grasped the *w* to *v* transformation, as it is a simple linguistic phenomenon. We passed through a long tunnel cut through a mountain, and I had the distinct impression that both the geology and the climate were different on the far side. The rock was more yellow and red, and the climate much drier. Soon afterwards, a big piece of a truck tire was blocking a lane of the road, and Yusuf stopped to remove it. I commended his good deed.

We had been driving for a number of hours now, and Yusuf decided to stop at the town of Kürtün to pray. I had requested that we take this

---

11. Erzurum has its etymology in the Arabic words *Ardh al-Rum*, "land of the Romans."

mountain road rather than go back to Trabzon and drive along the coast (which would have been faster), so I was happy to give Yusuf a rest before continuing our journey. As he was in the mosque it started to rain, and then to pour. I took shelter as best I could against a building housing a wood-working shop, and seeing me there the workers invited me in and set down a wooden box for me to sit. Yusuf finished his prayers, picked me up, and we continued on our way, over a mountain pass which was both preceded and succeeded by lakes holding water for hydroelectric generation. The lake before the pass appeared pristine, but that on the far side was a disgusting trash bin of plastic bottles and other debris floating on the surface. I would not want to eat fish farmed in such water, but farmed they were nonetheless. In another hour and a half we were back to the busy coastal highway on our way to Ordu. I could tell that Yusuf was tired, as was I, so I remained alert to help him look out for traffic. I had a dull throbbing headache from not having drunk anything all day, and the temperature was now back above 85°F (30°C). We almost had an accident, but thankfully avoided it. Arriving in Ordu, I took leave of Yusuf, wishing him a safe trip home, found my quarters, broke my fast at sunset with the other people in the hotel (all Turks), then took a glass of whisky to my room and watched part of the France-Albania Euro 2016 football match being played in Marseille, near my home. Then I slept.

JUNE 16, 2016

I am in my room in Ordu now, the sun shining on the evergreens and the wind roiling gently the surface of the sea before my window. Last night there was a storm but now it is calm. I woke up this morning at around 4:30 AM. I had decided to fast this full day again but had not set my alarm. Sunrise is at 5:00 AM, and so from that time on until 8:00 PM I would neither eat nor drink, as I did yesterday. Ordinarily, fasting Muslims eat a large meal before sunrise and then go back to sleep, but I didn't feel like getting up in the night to eat, nor even like eating the "emergency" Clif Bar that my son had given me, instead drinking some water and going back to sleep, waking at 9:00 AM. I proceeded to read and make my immediate plans for onward travel, reserving a hotel in Amasya with a man who spoke only a few words of English. I did this by using my Turkish dictionary and speaking very slowly. I went down to the front desk and the receptionist, Pinar, called back the hotel in Amasya at my request to make sure I had not made a reservation for twenty people or a reservation three months from now. The reservation was correct. I also checked that my laundry had been done overnight.

At 11:00 AM, as planned, a taxi came to take me to Cape Jason (Yason). According to Greek mythology, the hero Jason was heir to the throne of Thessaly, and his uncle reigned during Jason's minority. Instead of passing the kingdom on to Jason upon his adulthood, his uncle asked Jason to go and recover the Golden Fleece from the kingdom of Colchis at the eastern end of the Black Sea. Jason assembled a group of heroes, the Argonauts, to undertake this quest.[12] Legend has it that Jason and his Argonauts stopped at a flat and relatively hospitable (compared to the rest of the coastline) promontory near here, offering sacrifice before continuing on their quest. The place is hence known as Cape Jason. This legend is what motivated my coming here. The drive from Ordu to Cape Jason is approximately thirty-five kilometers along the coast, on a road which was a major transport axis until a three-kilometer tunnel was dug a few years ago under the mountainous promontory, eliminating the need to follow the coast. The ride was uninteresting, though there were ruined buildings right on the beachfront, which I found unusual. When we arrived at the Cape, I walked around the nineteenth-century Greek church, which is said to have been built on the site of an older structure, perhaps even an ancient Greek temple. The interior of the church was sober but unremarkable, though not so its site, on a headland jutting into the sea, alone. I continued further out onto the Cape to where its rocky skeleton thrusts forward into the sea. I hopped from rock to rock looking to reach the end, the end of the earth. I have always loved such places. I stood my ground on the last rock of the promontory for a long moment as the waves came in, then returned as I had come, but again looked back. Maybe the Argonauts spied this flat haven from

---

12. Bulfinch, Thomas, *Mythology*. New York: Thomas Crowell, 1970, pp. 129-31.

afar and saw the sunlight play on the rocks and waves just as it does today. And then offered thanks, and made wishes for the success of their quest. What of my quest? It is shrouded in fog now, and I move blindly. Sometimes ideas come to me, like that of Musa Dagh, but when they do not I blaze my own trail. I do not want to leave this place. Each place seen and passed is one step closer to death. Over the rocks and the sea, the sun blooms louder now.

We returned to Ordu by the modern highway with its tunnel, saving twenty kilometers. I read, wrote, and rested, the dull throb of thirst aching in my head. I do not have trouble refraining from eating for a day or two, but abstaining from drinking is much more difficult, especially in this heat. Right now, with two more hours to go until *maghrib*,[13] I can attest that thirst is an unpleasant feeling, a sort of dull pulsing tension in the body, foremost in the head, which does not go away or recede even when one's attention is elsewhere. I think I could continue until tomorrow morning without drinking, but wouldn't sleep well, and after that I imagine my physical abilities would begin to decline. After yesterday and today I will have experienced Ramadan fasting in a modestly difficult set of circumstances: long summer days, hot weather, and a moderate level of physical activity. Clearly this bears no comparison whatsoever to the conditions borne by people who work outside in desert heat all day, nor with what such a fast would have meant in sixth-century Arabia when Islam was first revealed. But at least I know what the people around me here are feeling when they sit down to *iftar* in the evening, and I can share their feeling of joy at that moment. Shortly before sunset I went out to walk the promenade along the Euxine Sea.[14] Children splashing in the waves, families relaxing, lovers kissing on park benches. An unusual sight in a Muslim country. Walking towards the setting sun, towards the distant mountains and

---

13. Muslim prayers are undertaken five times per day. *Fajr* is the dawn prayer, *dhuhr* the noon prayer, *'asr* the afternoon prayer, *maghrib* the evening prayer, and *'isha* the night-time prayer.

14. The ancient Greeks called the Black Sea *Euxinos Pontos*, or "hospitable sea." Why they settled on this name seems uncertain, as the Black Sea is notoriously treacherous. Jean de Chardin, a seventeenth-century French traveler who wrote *Voyage de Paris à Isfahan*, when he visited this sea, mentioned that Turkish sea captains of the time told him that of 1,500 ships on the Black Sea at any given time, roughly 100 were lost each year.

coastline I had visited this morning. Two young girls fanning an unseen fire, preparing kebabs for *iftar*. Picnic tables waiting, people relaxing on blankets. Then across the road a large and harmonious contemporary building: a theater and library complex. This particular place could compare favorably with many a European beachfront resort, though most of the city itself is dusty and drab. I arrived at the end of the promenade and turned back.

I had reserved *iftar* at a restaurant with a pleasant outdoor terrace. In Islamic law, people traveling are exempted from fasting during Ramadan, though they must make up the days they miss at other times during the year. I think this rule shouldn't be applicable nowadays. In the early days of Islam, traveling implied dire physical hardship and a significant risk of death. It suffices to read sections of Doughty's *Travels in Arabia Deserta* to get an inkling of the extreme duress of primitive desert travel.[15] In modern times, however, almost all travel is far easier than normal daily life in the Prophet's time. Many modern Muslims experience no difficulty whatsoever fasting during Ramadan—they simply invert their diurnal cycle completely and sleep all day while taking meals at night. Somehow I do not think this was the intention. We humans need to be reminded of our mortality, our dependence, our insignificance, now more than ever. Modern people tend to lack humility before nature. A fast walk up a long steep hill, a hot day without water, an hour in a small boat in rough weather. Such experiences give us the proper perspective of our place in the universe. *Iftar* was a joy, something to give thanks for, when usually I would just take water and food for granted. I said, "*bismillah al-rahman al-rahim*" ("In the name of God, the Compassionate, the Merciful") before breaking my fast. I did as the Prophet had done, and started the meal with an odd number of dates, drank the wonderful chilled lemonade, but then proceeded to

---

15. Doughty, Charles M., *Travels in Arabia Deserta*. New York: Dover Publications, 1979. Doughty was the foremost desert traveler and explorer of Arabia. T.E. Lawrence ("Lawrence of Arabia") in his introduction to Doughty's work, had this to say: "It is not comfortable to have to write about *Arabia Deserta*. I have studied it for ten years, and have grown to consider it a book not like other books, but something particular, a bible of its kind. To turn around now and reckon its merits and demerits seems absurd. I do not think that any traveller in Arabia before or since Mr. Doughty has qualified himself to praise the book—much less to blame it."

stuff myself like an adolescent boy, so wound up with a stomach ache at the end of the meal.

JUNE 17, 2016

I awoke this morning having slept for almost ten hours. I had breakfast, checked out, and bade farewell to Pinar, the attentive receptionist who helped me. Mehmet, the driver, was on time and his car was new and clean. I wasn't fasting today, but out of courtesy I refrained from eating or drinking during our trip, as I generally do not eat or drink in the presence of people fasting, except in the privacy of a hotel as I did at breakfast. I asked Mehmet to go south by a smaller road rather than taking the highway in that direction from Samsun. I offered him additional payment for this, and after checking with his company he agreed. At Ünye, just before turning south, a strange billboard caught my eye: on the left, some people with a laden donkey struggling along a mountain track, and on the right, a modern road with cars. Elderly people must still remember the earlier situation, as even I remember the rudimentary infrastructure which existed in Turkey in 1987.

We turned south at Ünye, and the wonderful scenery and near total absence of traffic validated this choice. The mountainous topography here is less abrupt than it is directly south of Trabzon, more open and a little less verdant. And as we wound our way higher, the aridity increased, becoming a hybrid between the coastal and the Anatolian continental climates. As is my wont on certain occasions, I began to recite poetry to myself as I watched the scenery flow by. I know a number of poems by heart, though sometimes it takes me several passes through to reconstruct a poem in my mind. This time I recited Tennyson's "Ulysses," a marvelous poem which is all the more remarkable in that it captures perfectly the feeling of an aging and accomplished man who wants more from his life, but Tennyson wrote it when he was only twenty-four, after the death of a friend. How could such a young man have known this feeling?

The lights begin to twinkle from the rocks:
The long day wanes: the slow moon climbs: the deep
Moans round with many voices. Come, my friends,
'Tis not too late to seek a newer world.
Push off, and sitting well in order smite
The sounding furrows; for my purpose holds
To sail beyond the sunset, and the baths
Of all the western stars, until I die.

Sometimes I have trouble, especially at the beginning of an undertaking, seeing the value of what I am doing. This applies not only to travel or writing, but to other intellectual pursuits and to physical activities such as rock climbing. Why should I study ancient Arabic texts? My progress is slow, and with the same effort I put into Arabic I could have mastered three or four European languages. Why should I try to improve at climbing? I started late in life, and my accomplishments will always remain limited. Why should I travel and write this book? Does the writing make the travel more enjoyable, or is it merely an excuse? The common link among these diverse activities is the pursuit of transcendence.

I need to feel that my life is heroic. Heroic not in any grand epic sense, but in a personal sense, relative to my own abilities and personhood. There can be heroism in an ordinary activity, in an ordinary life. A couple of years ago, my wife Hélène visited her parents. Hélène's mother was dying, and her father, almost ninety, was in failing health. It was still dark outside when Hélène had to take a train very early in the morning, yet despite his physical infirmity her father got up unbidden to walk his daughter to the station, saying, when she expressed worry, "Don't you worry about me. I'll find my way back." Shortly afterwards, struggling up a snow slope after ten hours of high-altitude climbing, I felt inspired by the heroism of his gesture, and recognized that it represented a greater effort than the one I was making. This recognition of heroism in ordinary life is what makes modern literature so powerful. Heroism is not only for kings and mythological heroes. It is for all of us. We see this clearly in Joyce's *Ulysses*, in Tolstoy's *The Death of Ivan Ilych*, and in Kurosawa's film *Ikiru* ("To Live"), which Tolstoy at least partly inspired. Kurosawa's dying bureaucrat is no less a hero than the knights of Arthurian legend when he knowingly devotes the few remaining months of his life to overcoming administrative obstacles and realizing a playground for neighborhood children. His courage is both moral and physical when he refuses to back down and simply smiles at the violent thugs who threaten him. He has nothing to lose, having consecrated himself entirely to his goal, and appears bemused that gangsters expect him to be afraid of them. This is not a different type of heroism from that of Lancelot, or of Enkidu and Gilgamesh, it is one and the same thing. Once we realize this, we can give ourselves fully to our pursuits, those we choose, but likewise those which are imposed upon us by our lives.

After working myself into this frenzy of ideas and emotion, I returned to the scenery. I thought I saw an old woman carrying a large axe. I dismissed this as an incongruous possibility. But then I saw another one. Perhaps old women bear the responsibility for cutting firewood in these parts. It would be easy to feel Homeric if you are felling trees as an old lady. We crossed a vaguely defined mountain pass and descended the other side towards Niksar, where we turned west on a perfect highway. A throwback to the road trips of my youth through the American West. A ribbon of highway. This was the very first time in Turkey that I wished I had my own (fast) car! My euphoric mood was troubled later when I saw a brown sign marked "*Horoztepesı.*" In Turkey, brown signs denote sites of cultural interest, and *tepe*, from which *tepesı* is formed, means "hill," as in "tell" or archaeological site. But before I could activate mobile data on my phone and learn that Horoztepe was an ancient Hatti and then Hittite settlement, we had gone too far and I could tell that Mehmet was impatient to begin the long return journey to arrive home in time to break fast with his family. So I didn't ask him to go back, which made me feel guilty for having missed a site. I later learned, however, that Horoztepe had been covered with a tobacco farm for a number of years despite its protected archaeological status, and only in 2015 were new excavations begun, so I do not think I missed much. We arrived in Amasya, and I liked the town from the first. I said goodbye to

Mehmet and settled into my lodgings. The receptionist asked me what my job was, and for the first time in my life I replied, "I am a writer."

After a short time spent organizing my affairs and making plans for onward travel in two days, I went out to wander round the town. Amasya is much cleaner, more attractive, and richer in cultural artifacts than Trabzon, though the latter is more than twice as populous. There is a whole neighborhood of traditional Ottoman houses in Amasya, and I am staying in a room of one such house, with the windowed balcony directly above the river. There are many significant Islamic monuments here, which I will explore tomorrow. And the municipality even has a sense of humor. Along the southern riverbank is a life-sized bronze statue of an Ottoman soldier, bearded, girded with scimitar and turban, stoic of mien, taking a "selfie" with his smart-phone. I had a single initial goal in my wandering, to find the tourist office and get some information pamphlets and a map. I asked a dozen people, including a policeman, and made a game of following their instructions precisely. In slightly over an hour I reached my illusory destination. Illusory because the employees there informed me that they had neither information pamphlets nor map to give me. In Turkish, to say there is not something one names the thing and follows it by *yok*. "*Harita yok*" ("There is no map"), "*Danişma yok*" ("There is no information"). So what was there? A museum of mannequins of Ottoman Sultans, which, for lack of anything else to do, I looked around. This museum was dedicated to the Ottoman Governors of Amasya province, seven of whom ascended to the throne as Sultans of the Ottoman Empire. The museum (and illusory tourist office) was in a well-restored Ottoman house. The high point of the visit was the *Ayat al-Kursi* done in beautiful Arabic calligraphy, which I recited aloud, to the astonishment of the cleaning lady.

Leaving this place, I found myself at the base of the long staircase leading to the tombs of the Pontic Kings,[16] carved in the cliff above the town. Looking up, they seemed empty of visitors, so I climbed the (many) stairs, going first to the tombs on the west side of the cliff face.

---

16 The Kingdom of Pontus was a Persian kingdom from the third to the first century BCE, whose capital was here at Amasya. It was later conquered and incorporated into the Roman Republic.

The monumental tombs were hollowed out of the limestone. A gate had been inadvertently left unlocked, and I went behind one tomb in a space cut six to eight meters deep into the cliff face. The highest tomb on this side was reached by following an ascendant gallery carved in the face of the cliff. The limestone (not like the poor quality rock in the mountains east of here to Sumela) had a crack leading partway up to the large tomb opening. Others had attempted it before, as witnessed by the stone polished smooth and entirely bereft of holds, slippery like wax. I tried to climb it, but it was exposed to a bad landing, so I gave up. I next went to the tombs on the east side. I mantled up onto a ledge[17] to look into one, but there was nothing there. I read in the information pamphlet given to me with my ticket that a Seljuk Sultan had recovered treasure from these tombs, which would mean that they had gone unmolested by grave robbers for 1,500 years. I find this highly doubtful, as they were not exactly discreet, giant carved arches on the cliff face, nor were they so hard to reach, even before the tourism infrastructure was installed. I sat for a while looking over the city, heard the afternoon call to prayer and slowly descended. I had reserved *iftar* at the hotel restaurant, and after resting and reading I enjoyed the feeling of fellowship with the other people, hearing the cannon shot and then the call to prayer announcing the sunset and breaking the fast with them. I sat and wrote for quite a time after dinner, then retired.

JUNE 18, 2016

Last night after I had prepared for bed, the night-time call to prayer echoed from the Bayezid Mosque just across the river from my room. This ethereal call transported me back to Cairo so many years ago, when I would lie awake at night and wonder on what alien planet I was, surrounded by such otherworldly sounds. Or, watching at sunset the flocks of pigeons circling over the ruinous tenth-century buildings of Fatimid Cairo, summoned home to roost by competing pigeon owners

---

17. "To mantle" is a climbing term meaning to pull oneself up to a horizontal ledge and rise onto it using only the ledge itself for handholds.

from the surrounding rooftops, and hearing this same call echoing down the centuries. I remember thinking then that after the last jet plane had faded from human memory, this call would echo still. In Cairo also, there was an old, poor, blind man, a *hafiz*,[18] who had learned the Qur'an by heart and would recite it at evening time sitting outside on the pavement. Many times I sat near him on the curb in the dirty Cairene street and listened to him recite. The first verses of the Qur'an revealed to the Prophet were an instruction to recite: "Recite, in the name of thy Lord, who created!" Q 96:1. The old man would silently cup his hands behind his ears before reciting, straining to hear those words pronounced by God as they were the first time, so that he might recite them truly. Each time after listening I would feel blessed and give him alms, and salute him verbally so that he came to know me. When I left Cairo after two years I never saw him again, but I can sometimes hear his voice when another reciter gives voice to God's words as the old blind man did.

Having decided to cease my experiment with fasting after two full days, I went to breakfast in the hotel restaurant. All of the curtains were drawn, as if some secret society were meeting there that morning. And around a dozen Turkish patrons (not hotel guests, of which I was the only one during my stay) were violating their fast and eating a normal breakfast. I joined them, all of us bound by the joint presumption of secret wrongdoing. I suppose that customers relaxing in the parlor of a nineteenth-century bordello must have shared a similar feeling. After breakfast I set out to visit the Islamic monuments of Amasya, first the Museum of Medical History, since it was furthest away and the day would become hotter as it progressed. Walking there I passed busts of several Ottoman Sultans and of the ancient geographer Strabo, born here. The museum building was a hospital built in the thirteenth century during the Ilkhan period (the Ilkhans were Mongol invaders who ruled certain regions of Anatolia and converted to Islam). Apparently this facility was one of the first to use music and the sound of water to treat mentally ill patients. The building was in the form of a madrasa,

---

18. A *hafiz* is a person who has committed the Qur'an to memory.

a rectangular open courtyard with rooms on three sides (it is entered from the fourth). There were displays of various surgical implements with old illustrations demonstrating their use, as well as a summary of various medical theories of the day concerning "humors" and the treatments adapted to each one based on Aristotelian medicine, having been transmitted through Ibn Sina, Ibn Rushd, and other Muslim scientists.[19] Then as now, progress in medicine was largely a matter of trial and error.[20]

I left the medical museum and walked back the way I had come, to the Sultan Bayezid Mosque and madrasa complex, from the fifteenth century. I paid to enter the "Museum of Miniatures" and expected to see fine miniature illuminations or other works of art, only to feel cheated when confronted with a miniature scale model of Amasya in 1914. Who would pay to see that? I walked around it and left, offending the Turkish tour guide who was presenting it to the other visitors. She reproved me in Turkish, asking why I was leaving so quickly. This is now the fourth or fifth time people have spoken Turkish to me spontaneously in as many days. Perhaps the more I travel here the better I fit in, unconsciously adopting local mannerisms. The Bayezid Mosque, at least, was not a disappointment. It was grand and airy, though its Quranic inscriptions were sparse. At the *mihrab* was a set of two "prayer wheels," and a young fellow went up and turned the one on the right side. I have never seen this in a mosque before. They resemble Buddhist prayer wheels like those at the Jokhang Temple in Lhasa (Tibet) or other Tibetan Buddhist temples. Something brought here by the Ilkhan Mongols?

As I left the mosque, a whiff of a wondrous fragrance was carried to me on the air. My head turned towards it, wondering from whence

19. Much of the knowledge of Antiquity was first transmitted back to Europe through Arabic, having been translated from ancient Greek or Latin into Arabic (and sometimes also Hebrew, by Jewish scholars such as Maimonides) and then from Arabic back into Latin in the late Middle Ages. Much of this activity took place in Andalusia and Sicily. Ibn Sina was known to the Latin Middle Ages as Avicenna, and Ibn Rushd as Averroes.

20. In modern clinical trials, complex statistics demonstrate the efficacy, or lack of such, of a drug or device. Its mechanisms of action are often unknown, and even if known, are not as important as a precise measure of efficacy. For modern surgery, we know better what we are aiming for, but nonetheless we choose among competing procedures by their statistical results, which is to say by a sophisticated form of trial and error.

it emanated. I saw a beautiful dark-haired woman. The scent was her perfume, and it was positively intoxicating. On my way to Gök Mosque (Blue Sky Mosque, so named for its azure tilework) I passed some fourteenth-century tombs filled with rubbish and rubble. The mosque itself was an anti-climax. Hardly a trace of blue remaining, and the whole interior, lit like a third-world police station with ugly neon lights, smelled like dirty laundry. The last site I planned to visit was the Amasya Museum. As soon as I entered a young and overzealous guard seemed to put me under special surveillance, following just behind me as if he suspected me of trying to make off with the exhibits. The museum contained pottery, coinage, and other artifacts from the Bronze Age (Hittite), the Hellenistic Period, and the Romans. There were hoards of coins from Alexander the Great's time, and others. But the most remarkable artifact was a statuette of Teshup, the Hittite storm god who wears a conical hat like a dunce's cap. The temple at Yazılıkaya (near Hattuşa) which I saw is dedicated to him and to his consort Hepat, and both are represented there. There was also a map showing over 100 archaeological mounds in Amasya province alone. Turkey has eighty-one provinces, so that gives an idea of the wealth of archaeological sites in the country. Upstairs was an uninspiring recent ethnographic collection as well as some Ilkhan/Seljuk fourteenth-century mummies. Their skin was like ruptured black plate armor tented over the jagged bones. The lubricious posture, skeletal legs splayed wide, of the Sultan's concubine gave no hint of the pleasure he surely found between them. Nothing is left. Nothing survives but the blank stare of the raven-black mummified child. Nevermore.

My excursion finished, returning to the hotel I bought a small bottle of whisky to drink in the privacy of my room over the rest of the trip, not wanting to offend Ramadan sensibilities by ordering alcoholic drinks in public. And on my way I saw a man afflicted, truly afflicted, begging. He may have had leprosy, as part of the flesh of his face was eaten away and he had lost control of one of his eyes. With the other he looked at me, and I said, "Peace be with you," and gave him alms. In 1987, after leaving Turkey, I had traveled to Pakistan. On the second day there in a town near the famous cemetery at Makli Hill, I was eating a piece of chicken in a poor restaurant of an even poorer quarter, and a leper passed me in the dirt track in front of the restaurant. He raised his hands to beg, and his fingers were but stumps. The orbs of his eyeballs were visible, denuded of flesh, eaten away by disease. I was young, twenty-two, and knew of misfortune and disease, but not in such an immediate manner. The experience turned me inside out. Of course I gave him alms, but for a week I kept seeing his ravaged and decaying face before me, and repeated to myself, "There, but for the grace of God, go I."[21] I can still see his face now.

JUNE 19, 2016

I awoke this morning rested and ready to depart for Sinop. Yesterday was a full day, but what does not show through in this journal is that most of it was actually spent reading, writing, and reflecting. Travelers vary in this respect, but when I travel at least a third of my waking time is spent immobile, especially when the heat becomes severe, as it is now. Two impressions remain with me from yesterday—the perfume of the dark-haired woman and the leper's face. But I will hold to her image and to the intoxication of her scent. When given the choice, I choose the positive, the animal axiom of affirmation of life. I noticed in the news that yesterday a group of fans of the rock group Radiohead was attacked by Islamists in Istanbul. They had gathered at a music store to listen to the group's new album, *A Moon Shaped Pool*, and the Islamists destroyed property, physically assaulted some of the fans, and threatened to kill them. Islamists, particularly the most extremist elements among them, have the upper hand in the intellectual civil war tearing Islam apart, and seem likely to widen the gap between themselves and the modernists.

I checked out from the hotel, and Özal, the taxi driver, was early. I asked him in my limited Turkish whether the contemporary building high on the hillside facing the Pontic tombs was a hotel, and he confirmed that it was. Otherwise, the ride was boring. The mountains further east

21. This phrase, whose origin I did not know in 1987 nor even now until looking it up, is attributed to John Bradford, a sixteenth-century English martyr who was burned at the stake. https://en.wikipedia.org/wiki/John_Bradford

had given way to hills here, and instead of the clear climate demarcation between humid verdant coast and Anatolian continental inland, the whole of the trip was something in between. Indeed, the only remarkable aspect of the drive was that we were stopped three times by police at checkpoints. I may have been stopped once or twice in all of my prior trips combined, but nothing like today. There was a recent bombing in Mardin, part of the ongoing civil war with the Kurds rekindled by President Erdoğan to help him win the new elections he called last November after having obtained an unsatisfactory result five months earlier. It worked. I also read that Turkish border guards killed eleven Syrian civilians trying to cross into Turkey. So Angela Merkel and the EU have successfully outsourced the murder of refugees to Turkey in exchange for money and visa-free travel to the EU for Turks. Worse things have happened, but I am surprised that Europeans do not see their own hypocrisy. That said, if Egypt or another large country collapses, Europe will be faced with a stark choice: accept enormous rogue waves of migration and the ensuing collapse of European society, or repel the migration by force and abandon the moral principles we pretend to espouse.

Along the way, I saw an enormous bird's nest on top of the dome of a mosque, and a coastline scarred by benighted development. As we approached Sinop, this receded and the coastline became beautiful, almost Mediterranean in aspect. We arrived in Sinop after three and a half hours, and I checked in to the hotel I had chosen, unpacked, then went out and wandered by the sea, walking to the end of the pier to feel the strong sea breeze, the pleasure of the small sailboats manoeuvring before me. This was the port from which Robert Ballard worked on his research expeditions on the prehistoric coastline of the Black Sea. In 2000, on an expedition sponsored by the National Geographic Society, Ballard created a sensation when he discovered a prehistoric coastline under the present Black Sea, and claimed that this was evidence of a prehistoric great flood, recorded in the legend of Atlantis and the story of Noah's Ark.[22] According to this hypothesis, first published in

---

22. Sea level is approximately 120 m higher now than it was at the end of the last Ice Age, with the progression being relatively linear from 18,000 BCE to 8000 BCE, so the Black Sea could have had an ancient coastline even if the flood hypothesis is untrue.

1997 by Walter Pitman and William Ryan, the Black Sea, which was a freshwater lake, and the Mediterranean, a saltwater sea, were separated by land in prehistoric times, and this land was breached, leading to a sustained and violent flow of salt water from the Mediterranean into the Black Sea. An underwater canyon predicted by geologists as a result of such a flood movement was actually found. This flood hypothesis has been the subject of academic controversy,[23] but one element which is sure is that the lower reaches of the Black Sea are oxygen-starved, leading to unusual preservation of ancient wood from shipwrecks. This is thought to be because the heavy salt water sank below the fresh water, which acted as a cap and prevented oxygen exchange between the layers of water. Recently many well-preserved ancient shipwrecks have been found by Ballard and others.[24] I personally find the idea of a true ancient flood as the origin of the various flood legends to be very intellectually attractive, and the most recent compendium of the research on this subject supports this hypothesis, with the flood thought to have occurred at roughly 7300 BCE.[25]

After watching the sea and the sailboats, I went back to my room and took a nap, as the heat was overbearing. To my surprise, I slept for two hours. Then I read for another hour until the heat of the day was well past and went out to walk again. I followed the city walls heading south, then, without having a reason to do so, followed a group of young Turkish men who passed through a low doorway in the city walls and walked uphill (west). I realized that the high wall to my left was that of the Sinop Fortress Prison, which I had intended to see. There were sections of Byzantine, or Roman, columns which had been reused in this wall by the Seljuk masons in the thirteenth century. Apparently the fortress had initially been built in the seventh century

---

23. The Wikipedia entry on this subject has fairly complete academic citations: https://en.wikipedia.org/wiki/Black_Sea_deluge_hypothesis

24. Broad, William, "We Couldn't Believe our Eyes: A Lost World of Shipwrecks is Found," *The New York Times*. November 11, 2016.

25. Yanchilina, A., Ryan, W. *et al*, "Compilation of geophysical, geochronological, and geochemical evidence indicates a rapid Mediterranean-derived submergence of the Black Sea's shelf and subsequent substantial salinification in the early Holocene." *Marine Geology,* Issue 383 (2017), pp. 14-34.

BCE, when Sinop was founded as a colony of the city of Miletus (near Priene, on the western Mediterranean south of Izmir, so around 1,100 kilometers by land, and more by sea, from here). I wonder why the colonists found no closer location to their liking. The fortress began to be used as a dungeon in Seljuk times and continued as a prison until 1997. At the ticket office the employee informed me that only an hour remained before closing time, but I still entered. Horror. The thick walls, the iron doors, the large common cells, with no one knows how many violent criminals crammed in together along with the "writers and poets" who were put there to silence them, according to the poor English of the tourist information panel near the dungeon. The prison was enormous and I was determined to explore all of it. One section had wailing plaintive music playing in a dank cell, along with quotations on the wall by Sabahattin Ali, imprisoned here for criticizing Atatürk in 1931, and then murdered, seemingly with government complicity, some years later while attempting to escape from Turkey.[26] Then the solitary confinement cells, around one and a half meters square, dark, the only opening a slot in the steel door. And far around the elongated exterior courtyards, the women's prison, where I imagined I could hear the screams of those raped by the guards, and of the babies born into this hell. From here a high steel gate surmounted by barbed wire, except at the rightmost extremity. Past this gate I saw the way out to the other parts of the prison I had not yet seen and so scaled it to save five minutes of retracing my steps. I could make out from a model of the prison what remained to be seen, then opened a closed door, prompting a guard to question me. I said, "*Lütfen dakika*," "A minute, please," and he deferred, allowing me to go inside. More of the same. And then, last, I read the text next to the dungeon. Summit of horror, it stated that until 1960 there was no record kept of the people imprisoned here, and thus no one knew who they were, who entered, who was released, who died and was buried in secrecy. In "The Grand Inquisitor" chapter of

---

26. The Turkish government refused Ali a passport, so he attempted to leave the country illegally. His writings have recently undergone a renaissance. See Arango, Tim, "A Forgotten Novel Unites Turkish Readers in Troubled Times," *The New York Times*, February 26, 2017. The novel is *Madonna in a Fur Coat*.

Dostoyevsky's *The Brothers Karamazov*, Ivan cites a work called "The Wanderings of Our Lady in Hell"[27]:

> There is, for example, one little monastery poem (from the Greek, of course)...with scenes of a boldness not inferior to Dante's. The Mother of God visits hell and the Archangel Michael guides her through the torments. She sees sinners and their sufferings. Among them, by the way, there is a most amusing class of sinners in a burning lake: some of them sink so far down into the lake that they can no longer come up again, and "these God forgets"—an expression of extraordinary depth and force. And so the Mother of God, shocked and weeping, falls before the throne of God and asks pardon for everyone in hell, everyone she has seen there, without distinction.

In this prison here in Sinop, where I stand now, until 1960, there was no list of the prisoners. And these God forgets.

JUNE 20, 2016

I am sitting in my room with a glass of the whisky I bought in Amasya, recording today's events. I slept relatively well and woke early. I went up to breakfast, alone, with a wonderful view of the port, the sea, and the mountains of the coast. While I was eating cheese and olives, a large seagull began slowly and deliberately tapping its beak on the pane of glass between the breakfast room and the adjoining balcony, wondering at the solidity of this invisible barrier. It continued to do this on and off throughout my breakfast, returning to the pane of glass as if it were an insoluble moral quandary. I was overtaken by a feeling of sadness as I served myself watermelon, bread, and fine raspberry jam for the second (sweet) part of my breakfast. I have liked raspberries since I was a young child. My Nana would always give them to me, fresh berries in summer

---

27. Dostoyevsky, Fyodor (Translated by Richard Pevear and Larissa Volokhonsky), *The Brothers Karamazov*. New York: Farrar, Strauss, and Giroux, 1990, pp. 246-7. The religious work he cites is apparently an apocryphal Byzantine text translated into Old Slavonic (footnote 3, p. 247).

and frozen ones in winter. And homemade jam. Time has passed; my Nana is gone; and I am no longer young, but I still like them. I am sad.

I set out to see more of Sinop. It is truly a pleasant town, both geographically and culturally. Most of the local women dress in a manner Westerners would consider moderately conservative but close to "normal": blouses; below-the-knee skirts or dresses; trousers. The atmosphere is not oppressive, the people simple and friendly. I went first to the city walls overlooking the port. Either the Hittites or the settlers from Miletus who colonized Sinop were the first to build these fortifications. They were extensive, protecting the entirety of the peninsula's narrow isthmus, but now most are in ruins. The walls offered a grand view of the port and the sea. The stone they are made with is of generally poor quality, as I found out more pointedly later. It was extremely hot today. Only 82–85°F (28–30°C) on the thermometer, but the humidity-laden air made it feel hotter, and my merino wool T-shirt ended the day with white salt formations from my sweat making a strange design on the fabric. My next destination was the mosque of Ala'eddin Kaykubad mentioned in previous chapters. The conquests of this Seljuk ruler reached to the northern confines of Anatolia, right here in Sinop, and he built this mosque to celebrate them. There were inscriptions over two of the entrances to the mosque, but to read them I would have had to stand in the middle of the busy street. So I will presume, based on prior experience, that our friend Ala'eddin did not neglect to water the tree of his ego on this edifice as well. The interior of the mosque was unremarkable, but the courtyard and large funerary hall were calm and restful. Ibn Battuta visited Sinop around 1333 and spoke highly of this mosque. Strangely, he was suspected by the local population of being a Shi'ite Muslim. The locals were Hanafi Muslims, whereas Ibn Battuta was a Maliki, whose prayer rites differ slightly from those of the Hanafis.[28] As a test, the locals made a present of a rabbit to Ibn Battuta and his companions (the Shi'a do not eat rabbits),

---

28. In Sunni Islam, there are four schools of Islamic law: Hanafi; Maliki; Shafi'i; and Hanbali, each named after its founder. For the most part they are distributed geographically, each predominant in a certain area, though in some places several schools coexist. Shi'ite Islam, largely concentrated in and near Iran, has its own legal schools and doctrines.

which they promptly ate, lifting the doubts of their hosts.[29] Ibn Battuta also related an interesting anecdote about Ghazi Chelebi, the ruler of Sinop from just before the time he passed through:

> Ghazi Chelebi was a brave and heroic man. God had granted him a particular ability to stay long under water, and to swim strongly. He often went aboard naval vessels to combat the Byzantine Navy. When the confrontation occurred, and the men were occupied with making battle, he would swim underwater, an iron implement in hand, and pierce the enemy ships. The enemy sailors did not know what was happening to them until their ship was sinking... He was of unequalled merit, but it is said that he consumed hashish excessively, and died because of it. One day he went out hunting, an activity he loved, and was following a gazelle, which ran into a forest. Ghazi Chelebi spurred on his horse, but a tree was in his way and hit his head, breaking it, and he died.[30]

Just west of the mosque was the Pervane Madrasa, which has been given over to coffee houses and tourist shops. It was pleasant but vapid.

Having exhausted the main historical sites of Sinop and annoyed by the midday heat, I started to feel fidgety and bored. I walked to the statue of Diogenes the Cynic, a Greek philosopher born here in the late fifth century BCE, but it was an utter disappointment, bearing a certain kinship to the animal statuary sold in K-Mart that certain people in America use to decorate their lawns. It was situated in a place resembling a cross between a vacant lot and a dump, near another section of the ancient city wall. I crossed the street, determined to do *something*, and followed the example of a small child clambering on another section of the city wall. I chose a vertical section around five or six meters high and started to climb it. Not long afterwards a brick-sized chunk of rotten rock simply came off in my hand. I pushed off

---

29. Harb, p. 332.

30. *Ibid*, p. 331. Author's translation.

and landed on my feet, as this event was not unexpected, even more annoyed than before. I went to a cleaner section of the wall and tested the rock. Better. I climbed to a small arched window, passed through it and traversed around five meters on very small holds around four meters above the ground with an inauspicious landing zone below, so I didn't want to fall. I concentrated and made the necessary movements, feeling relieved of my boredom and annoyance. Then I noticed that my three-dimensional wanderings had unintentionally landed me inside the grounds of the Sinop Fortress Prison. Already here, I might as well look around. All of the windows of all of the buildings were crisscrossed with iron bars. I climbed a short distance on the stonework of one of the buildings and pulled on the iron bars to test their solidity. They were solid, so I repeated the manoeuvre and raised my feet onto the windowsill while holding the bars and leaning back. My reward for this audacity was a clear view into a relatively large common cell, like those I had seen yesterday except that this one was in a section of the prison not open to the public, and was not empty. It contained a collection of junk: a rough wooden table, garden tools, buckets, basins. It looked like a groundskeeper's storage room. Except that when I looked more carefully, on the wooden table was a metal basin filled with jumbled bones, crowned by a human skull looking crookedly toward me. There were human femur bones, among others. Perhaps the gardener had been digging to plant a new tree and found this poor soul's remains where the guards had buried him after one beating too many. One of those whom God forgot. Satisfied at my discovery, I returned by a circuitous route to the hotel and read.

After reading and resting, my boredom returned. The room phone rang, and it was Muhib, one of the hotel owners. Yesterday he had kindly offered to show me around the Sinop Peninsula by car, and now he was making good on his offer. I was very happy and went down quickly to meet him in the lobby. Muhib was around my age, ran the hotel and a local real estate and construction company, and was a bachelor. We drove along the eastern coast to the end of the peninsula, then walked further to a promontory several hundred meters above the sea with a marvelous view. On the western side were cliffs, then green hillsides, then a dark lapis blue bay, darker than the turquoise of the Mediterranean. We drove back along the western side, through the town and further west, past the small airport to Hamsilos Fjord, a very beautiful spot which was surprisingly unspoiled. We talked a fair amount during our tour and I gave him my card and said to contact me if he came to France. I read more in the afternoon about the geology and hydrological history of the Black Sea. Before dinner I walked for another hour, looked for and found (with the help of some passers-by) the Balatlar Church (a ruined seventh-century Byzantine church), then had dinner and wrote. I will sleep early tonight, as tomorrow will be a long trip following the coast to Amasra.

JUNE 21, 2016

The temperature today was well over 85°F (30°C), yet now I sit outside in Amasra shrouded in cloud from the sea and chilly despite the wool sweater I wear. I woke early this morning at 6:30 AM instead of 7:00 AM when my alarm had been set. As I always do while traveling, I checked my phone when I awoke. My two children, both students in Boston, had each baked an apple pie, my son an American apple pie (with the apples cut up inside and covered with a top layer of pastry crust), and my daughter a French apple pie (with the apples cut into thin slices and elegantly layered without a top layer of crust). They were planning to meet to share both pies, half and half, and this warmed my heart. Regardless of how my wife and I feel in our own lives, knowing that we have raised two good children gives us a sense of fulfillment and meaning. When I got out of bed, despite the apple pies, I felt groggy and in a bad mood, knowing that I had a six- to eight-hour ride before me. I showered, ate breakfast (the window-tapping seagull returned), and left.

The taxi was driven by Hakan and his father, whom he introduced to me as "Baba." Muhib had vouched for them as conscientious men and good drivers. The first part, at least, was true. The beginning of the drive was a succession of one-horse towns interspersed with a few larger ones. The scenery was pleasant but nothing more. The road was decent for this initial part of today's trip, and it was possible to make sixty kilometers an hour on average. Some sections were really fine, whereas others had been damaged by landslides of the gray unstable dirt which forms these hillsides, or by rock fall. And then there were the small red arrow signs by the right-hand side of the road. At first I did not pay them much notice, but as I looked more carefully I realized that they marked spots where the supporting earth had been eroded from beneath the road surface, leaving nothing but a thin layer of asphalt, clearly not enough to support a car or even a person. Erosion works faster where water runs quickly on steeper terrain, so some of these "erosion traps" were located in places where, if the car went too close to the edge, it would fall through the road surface and literally be pitched sideways off the side of a cliff or into a steep ravine, probably not stopping until it hit the sea a couple of hundred meters below. After Inebolu, roughly the midpoint of the journey, the mountains became steeper and rockier, and there were more of these red arrow warning signs. Our speed decreased to less than forty kilometers per hour for around two hours. While I have traveled on more terrifying roads than this (parts of the Karakoram Highway in Pakistan, the track south from Kashgar into the Kunlun Mountains, and the road from Lhasa to Kathmandu all come to mind), those were all a very long time ago when I was braver and more serene. I have become more anxious in middle age, and when Hakan started sending text messages from his phone while driving I became even more ill-at-ease, especially when he did so while rounding one of the hundreds of sharp bends in the road right into the path of an oncoming red truck. I made a disapproving sound and gesture and Baba in the back seat agreed with me; Hakan put his phone away. The bad thing about traveling along a coastline in one direction is that you either get the good side or the bad side, and you get it for the whole trip. We had the bad side, meaning the outside of every turn, and any collision would have pushed us off the road and probably down the mountainside.

The most stressful section of the ride ended after Cide, and our speed increased to around sixty kilometers per hour. The Cide region is the site of the eponymous Cide Archaeological Project, surveying the ancient inhabitation of the area by attempting to systematically measure the prevalence of potsherds and other archaeological artifacts, and then determine their chronological origin.[31] It is a difficult region for archaeology because the luxuriant vegetation covers and obscures everything, more so than would happen in a Mediterranean or Anatolian climate. The road continued to improve, and at Gideros I noticed a natural port enclosed in an almost perfect circle, with only 40 or 50 of 360 degrees open to the sea. I am certain that the Milesian maritime settlers who settled Sinop in the seventh century BCE would have used this location as a waypoint, and I wonder if there been any excavations here. We finally arrived. I was thankful for our safe arrival and noticed on the way an eagle watching over us like the angel in *Godspeed*,[32] as they sometimes do when I run in the mountains near my home.

The hotel in Amasra is a dump. I tried to pick a good one but I think there are none here. Not only is the room small and shabby, but the TV in the neighboring room sounds as if it were in mine. I look forward to tomorrow, having just reserved a room in a supposedly nice hotel in an authentic Ottoman house in Safranbolu. Perhaps it will be like the hotel I stayed at in Antalya, which was also situated in a restored Ottoman house. Given my lack of enthusiasm for my room, I didn't wait long to go out. I followed Amasra's high city wall to the west at a distance imposed by the properties which abutted directly against it. I saw steps leading up and followed them. The walls were a mixture of well-cut stone blocks and re-used stone from prior constructions. At the top of the steps, I found myself in front of the Fatih Mosque, a ninth-century Byzantine church converted to a mosque in 1460 by Mehmet the Conqueror. A sign in English stated that the tradition of beginning the Friday sermon by drawing a sword had been preserved until the present. Islamic State was right to ridicule those who say that Islam is a religion of peace.[33] Islam makes a serious attempt at a just ordering of life, but sees itself as a universal faith legitimately spread by force. In its foundational texts, Christianity does not see itself this

---

31. B. During, author of a previously-cited book on the prehistory of Anatolia, directs this project.

32. A woodcut print by the artist Rockwell Kent, mentioned in the August 26, 1987 entry above.

33. *Dabiq*, Issue 7, pp. 20-24.

way, but in practice it has done exactly the same thing or worse (witness the genocidal "conversion" of the Americas). This place still has the feeling of a church, perhaps due to an unconscious assessment of its architecture on my part.

I left and while looking around the grounds heard music from a stringed instrument, not a guitar. I saw two boys sitting on a balcony nearby, playing. Or rather one was playing and the other listening. I quietly walked, unseen, to a park bench near them but out of their sight, and held court there among a dozen stray cats in varying states of physical decrepitude while listening to the music. The cats tolerated my presence among them, though I think it annoyed some of them. After a few songs I walked east in the old streets, saluting the young musicians with a nod as I passed through their field of vision. I found the old chapel, also ninth-century Byzantine, but it was locked and I looked in through the windows. The Ottoman Empire was truly a multi-ethnic and multi-faith polity. Modern Turkey has replaced this with a mono-ethnic and mono-faith alternative. The minority groups not effectively exterminated (as were the Armenians and Assyrians) were subjected to pogroms and expelled (mainly the Greeks, who had been in Asia Minor from the very origins of Greek civilization in the second millennium BCE through to the twentieth century). The only significant minority group left, the Kurds, is too large to expel or exterminate, yet Turkey forbids them from using their own language and is now engaged in violent civil war in which the Turkish army has reduced some of its own cities to rubble. The Kurdish south-east is a live war zone, far more dangerous than the borderlands of Syria. Tank shells do not discriminate between savvy travelers and greenhorns and cannot judge a man based on his knowledge or diplomacy. It is the only region of Turkey I will not have explored for this book, though I did pass through some of it in 1987.

I returned from my walk, which extended to the northern peninsula over the Kemere Bridge and then along the seacoast. I took *iftar* in a restaurant near the hotel at a table with Muhammet, a young Turkish mining engineer working for a company developing a coal mine near here. He said the local people opposed the coal mine but the government supported it, and the government is likely to win. I told him that a nuclear power station was planned at Sinop, which Muhib had mentioned to me yesterday. Muhammet knew of it and said that the local people also opposed that, but that again the government would prevail. He was slightly anxious, from what he said, because he was thirty and not yet married. We spoke for around an hour after dinner, exchanged contact details, then went each separately to watch the Turkish team play in the Euro 2016 football tournament back at home in France. Turkey won.

JUNE 22, 2016

I awoke after a poor night's sleep in my shabby hotel room and went to breakfast. For the first time on this trip, and perhaps the second or third time in all of the months I have spent in Turkey, the waitress was obnoxious. When I asked for coffee, she said "*Yok*" in a loud, raucous, and insistent voice. This reminded me of being in Kashgar, in north-western China on my way to Tibet, pointing to an item I wanted on a shelf, and receiving the repeated answer "*Mayo,*" meaning the same, namely "there is not any (of what you want)." In Kashgar I was actually pointing to the thing I wanted, so "*Mayo*" was a lie, but here in Turkey there may not have been any coffee. Not to be daunted by a rude waitress, I insisted, raising my voice to match her offensive tone, and so she sent the other waitress to buy some instant coffee at the store downstairs, which she brought to me two minutes later. I packed my things, paid the hotel, and left with the taxi the hotel had organized for me. The driver was named Ekrem and I wasted no time in negotiating tomorrow's trip to Istanbul with him. We drove through a river valley being prepared for a hydroelectric dam, then continued on over a gentle mountain pass at 1,030 meters in altitude and arrived in Safranbolu. As we were driving I wondered to myself, of all the things I could have done, why had I chosen this?

The hotel in Safranbolu really was beautiful, refreshing after the aesthetic doldrums I had recently endured. An authentic old Ottoman house, with others like it nearby forming one hotel, its restored woodwork was immaculate, the cushioned benches around the windows of my high wind-ventilated room inviting relaxation. All that was missing were the harem girls. I read and relaxed in the heat of the day, then went out to walk in the old town. Safranbolu is a UNESCO World Heritage site thanks to its Ottoman architecture, and is indeed an excellent example of the style. I looked at a small mosque in the old quarter, but didn't enter. There was a larger one nearby and I went inside to escape the still sweltering heat. There were six or seven old men present, and I sat on the side under its lost moonshine dome. One of the old men was kneeling before the *mihrab*, swaying gently side to side in silent contemplation. I left the mosque and went to Cinci Han, a seventeenth-century caravanserai. It reminded me of the Çukurhan in Ankara, the first hotel of my first trip in 2014, though Cinci Han has been left in a more authentic state, with a rectangular open courtyard and rooms all around on two levels. I walked back to the hotel in the heat, and sat in the sombre, cool reception area. I read Rumi on the spiritual search being the only "adult" pursuit, and wondered about my own. I then went to my room and meditated, falling into a deep non-slumber for an hour. I awoke in a trance-like state, knowing nothing, where I was, what I was doing there, why I had come. I wanted to stay in this state, but forced myself to rise and went back to Cinci Han for *iftar*, my hotel's restaurant being closed today. In fact, traveling during Ramadan has seen me often the only customer in the hotels I have frequented. Likewise, most sights are nearly empty of visitors. So it has had its benefits though they are outweighed by the abstinence from alcohol with meals. The *iftar* meal was good, and those I shared it with were all large Turkish families. I was the only traveler.

JUNE 23, 2016

I awoke with the light streaming through the windows and into my mind, a million bright ambassadors of morning. "By the glorious morning light, and by the night when it is still, thy Lord hath not forsaken thee, nor is He displeased." Q 93:1-3.

I felt refreshed, rested, and newly grounded in my life, the doubts of last night having evaporated without trace. The hows and whys of such inner changes are beyond my ken. I can only accept them. I had breakfast, served by two young women, one of them utterly beautiful. Now I will leave for Istanbul and then home. I packed, paid, and went out to meet Ekrem. His brother Ferhat had accompanied him, as the journey was long. The first part of the trip was pretty, an empty highway through Anatolian hills and forest. But once we neared the Sea of Marmara, the environment became an industrial wasteland like the parts of New Jersey blighted by oil refineries, and traffic became heavy. To make matters worse, a warning light flashed on the dashboard. We stopped to check it at a service station, but it required the attention of a specialized mechanic and the station attendant simply shrugged. I kept my fingers crossed that it would hold up until our arrival. A heavy industrial stench preceded Istanbul by fifty kilometers and the traffic was awful. Finally we made it into the city and navigated to Sultanahmet. I walked the last 500 meters to avoid the complicated streets around the monuments. I visited another (former) prison, more recent than that of Sinop, and likewise the temporary home of Sabahattin Ali shortly before his death. It was also home to Nazim Hikmet, a great Turkish poet, and to a taxi driver who etched his name in a marble pillar, still visible.[34] The trip is at an end, and I need to rest.

> Our revels now are ended. These our actors,
> As I foretold you, were all spirits and
> Are melted into air, into thin air:
> And, like the baseless fabric of this vision,
> The cloud-capp'd towers, the gorgeous palaces,
> The solemn temples, the great globe itself,
> Yea, all which it inherit, shall dissolve
> And, like this insubstantial pageant faded,
> Leave not a rack behind. We are such stuff
> As dreams are made on, and our little life
> Is rounded with a sleep.[35]

---

34. *A History of Sultanahmet Prison*. Four Seasons Hotel Istanbul at Sultanahmet.

35. Shakespeare, William. *The Tempest*, Act 4, Scene 1.

As a troubling epilogue, after a restful few days in Istanbul, I went to the airport to fly home. Remembering the large crowd of people at the first of two security checkpoints at Atatürk Airport, I dreaded going there and was determined to pass through as fast as possible. I felt that this was the single most dangerous point of the trip, as a suicide bomber could pack a suitcase with forty kilos of explosives and wait in line next to me. I was vigilant, choosing the shortest line and watching the people around me and the entrance. Alert for the smell of rosewater.[36] But such a risk is simply not possible to manage. Two days later, Islamic State terrorists attacked this airport at this very place, killing forty-five people and wounding over 200. I was lucky.

---

36. Would-be suicide bombers often cut their hair, trim their beards, wash themselves very carefully, and perfume themselves with rosewater to prepare for their entry into the hereafter.

7

TWO BATTLEFIELDS:
ILION AND GALLIPOLI

I am calm and rested now. I am looking out of the window of my room onto the sea, plied by container ships overloaded like the multi-colored Lego constructions of a megalomaniac child. I flew here, to Izmir, yesterday from Geneva. Already at the airport my cares fell away, like scales from the eyes of a blind man cured. Everything is in order, nothing to retain me. My wife and children are together in Boston, while I am here. The first flight, to Istanbul, was uneventful but late. Arriving in the terminal, I saw a gigantic queue at immigration so went to the business class priority line, donned an aura of calm authority, and explained to the guard that I would miss my connection if he didn't let me through. He agreed to my request and I passed through immigration quickly, saving at least half an hour. Leaving the secure part of the airport, I ran the gauntlet of Arrivals, walking as fast as I could to avoid lingering in the part of the airport attacked by Islamic State just after my last trip.

The flight to Izmir was fine. I arrived at the hotel and checked in. At first I planned to have dinner, but after meditating I was very tired, so ate a snack, brushed my teeth, and slept ten hours until this morning. When I woke up I was well-rested but ill-at-ease. There is always a transition phase between sedentary life and travel whose leitmotif is

"What am I doing here?" As I write this, twelve hours after awakening, this phase seems to have passed, but this morning it disoriented me. I opened the window blinds to see the magnificent sea, new kaleidoscopic colored container ships replacing those of yesterday. Then I showered. The wall facing the open shower was dark reflective glass, in which I could see my reflection. A mythical Achilles stared back at me, conical helmet of shampooed hair, naked musculature enhanced by the steam in the air, standing easy, ready to do battle. I wish women saw me the way I looked in that reflection!

I left the hotel to wander south parallel to the waterfront. I had two practical errands to run, changing money and acquiring a knife for the trip, and I intended to do both in the Kemeraltı Bazaar, a maze of streets with a few architectural monuments scattered among them. I went into an angling shop, quite impressive in the selection of fishing equipment on offer, but the selection of knives was not up to the same standard. I continued to Konak Meydanı, with an ornate but ugly clock tower built in 1901 for Sultan Abdulhamit. Next to it was the diminutive spire of the minaret of Konak Mosque, a tiny eighteenth-century building decorated with friezes of blue Ottoman tilework. Above the doorway was the Arabic inscription of a well-known *hadith*, "Prayer is the pillar of religion." I admired this small jewel of a mosque and crossed the square to enter the bazaar.

I wandered over an hour, finding one bureau de change whose rate did not entice me, and no knife sellers. I saw no foreigners. I was about to swallow my pride and ask someone in my broken Turkish, when a man accosted me politely in the street asking where I was from and what I was looking for. We spoke in his broken French until he took me to a woman who spoke excellent French. I explained to her what I needed, and the man kindly took me to a store where I bought a knife from a young Kurdish man who spoke basic Arabic. I then acceded to my benefactor's request to visit his shop, a large, well-kept premises full of high-quality leather goods. I felt sorry for him, as business was obviously extremely slow. He said it had been a bad year. After wishing him well, I continued wandering, my mental state fluctuating from clarity and calm to curiosity and disquiet. Twice I thought a man was following me, but I was mistaken both times. I passed another mosque, almost hidden among the shoes, cooking pots, and underwear being sold in the shops, the Kemeraltı Mosque. Above its door was inscribed the *Ayat al-Kursi*, my good luck charm, which for years I have carried hand-written in my wallet. So I entered the unremarkable courtyard and small mosque, empty but welcoming. I leaned over to look in, too lazy to remove my shoes, then left the courtyard and followed a brown sign to the Agora, the second or third location of ancient Smyrna, supposedly founded by Alexander the Great. The site was quite large, perhaps two hectares or more, and I nearly circumnavigated it because I unluckily chose the wrong direction to start: on a road, then a path, then a rubbish-strewn hillside, following the high steel barrier protecting the historical site from the squalid neighborhood surrounding it. I finally arrived at the entrance, paid for my ticket and entered. To the left was a large terebinth tree, the source of turpentine, which had been noted by Evliya Çelebi in the seventeenth century when he passed through here. One of the information panels stated that Smyrna was mentioned in ancient Hittite texts as "Tismurna." Hattuşa is roughly ten hours from here by car. The ancients managed to cover very large distances despite their limited means of transportation. This city was apparently a rival of Ephesus and Pergamon in its time, but its ruins, though extensive, are relatively uninteresting.

I left the Agora and set a course for the hotel. On the way I passed another money-changing office. The bid-ask spread was 0.6 per cent, meaning that the rate offered was only 0.3 per cent above the real interbank rate. This was an anonymous cash transaction, so ordinarily one would expect higher transaction costs, but here they were less than a quarter of what I pay using a large international bank at home. I happily changed money and having accomplished this, my second errand, and visited a significant part of old Izmir, I returned to the hotel. I examined various sources of information in order to decide what to do in the coming days. The Izmir tourism office map given to me by the hotel indicated two Neolithic archaeological sites in the region, and I resolved to try to see them. I found the contact details of Professor Zafer Derin, of Ege University, and sent him an email. Professor Derin had published a large number of articles and books on the archaeology of the Neolithic period near Izmir, and is a foremost authority on the subject. I was happily surprised when he replied very quickly and offered to guide me around Yeşilova, one of the sites, this afternoon.

I spent two hours researching the next stages of the trip, an activity which started to feel suspiciously like work, then left for Yeşilova. The taxi driver had absolutely no idea how to get there, it apparently not being a common destination, and took me on an hour-long tour of the less salubrious districts of Izmir. Finally we found the related site of Yassitepe, which narrowly missed being buried under a shopping mall, and a man working on the excavations there knew Professor Derin and explained to the driver how to get to Yeşilova. Really the driver should have known given that the municipality of Izmir had put up a large building there to house the archaeological laboratories and excavation museum. When we finally arrived I told the guard I was there to see Professor Derin, and was escorted to him. I introduced myself, saying that I was not an archaeologist but had a long-standing interest in archaeology and had visited many sites. Professor Derin was a man roughly my age, early-fifties perhaps, with a graying beard, like mine when I let it grow. He was very welcoming and first showed me the work being done by his team of roughly a dozen Ege University archaeologists and graduate students, classifying pottery, chipped stone tools and other finds from the site. They seemed a cheerful lot, both men and women, working together. Professor Derin then showed me around the building financed by the municipal government of Izmir (not by Turkey's national government). For a moderately small archaeological site, the building was extremely impressive. Aside from housing archaeological laboratories, there are exhibits for local families and children to visit and be introduced to archaeology, including a special area for children to excavate and also to prepare their own pottery using techniques from the Neolithic. I have never seen this idea anywhere else, and think it is an excellent way to introduce the younger generation to the study of archaeology.

The site of Yeşilova is not overly impressive in itself. It is not a large tell like Çatalhöyük because, as Professor Derin explained, the town site was at the intersection of two streams and was regularly washed away by flooding, so the successive generations did not physically build on each other and leave a large mound. The site was inhabited from roughly 6500 BCE (Pre-Pottery Neolithic) through to 3000 BCE (Early Bronze Age). The Neolithic structures had stone foundations, mud walls, and probably wooden thatched roofs. They seemed a good deal simpler than those at Çatalhöyük. Life must have been rudimentary, with not many inhabitants and fulfillment of basic needs the primary objective. In such a context, Göbekli Tepe, from 3,000 years earlier, a civilization able to spare the resources to create a monumental temple complex, seems positively alien, as if it had come from outer space.[1] The visit with Professor Derin lasted for an hour and a half, and on the way out I thanked him for his generosity. He called my attention to a quotation inscribed near the entrance of the building:

> 8,500 years ago, when mankind first settled here, this was an empty land. The city behind you, the highway passing by, the wall in front of you … there was nothing; nothing but raw nature, the fertile land, the streams and blue skies. Yet the settlers were not that different. They had a social life, though not the same as ours. Like us they lived and worked together to make a community. Just beyond this wall, lay their village, their humble huts, their "home." It was so long ago and all is now deep beneath a changing land. Before you cross to the other side, close your eyes briefly and think of nothing but the earth on which you stand, the air you breathe and the wind blowing around you. If you listen, you may hear their muted voices across thousands of years as they welcome you into their home.

I returned to the hotel and continued planning the rest of the trip, making plans for tomorrow and for my next destination, Bergama (ancient Pergamon), then showered to clean the dust and exhaust fumes

---

1. This is a joke. I am not one of the group of writers of far-fetched fantasies who suggest such things as solutions to quandaries raised by research. I do suggest that all possible logical explanations be explored, including, in the case of Göbekli Tepe, that sedentary civilization existed roughly 2,000 years earlier than previously thought.

from my body. The vision of Achilles from my morning shower did not reappear. I went down and had dinner, and have been writing here looking out over the sea.

OCTOBER 8, 2016

It is evening again. Today was a long day. I forgot to bring my notebook and am writing this on the back of a restaurant placemat. Sometimes when I am alone in a crowd of people I feel one with them, part of their lives, and other times my presence among them redoubles my solitude. This evening is the former. I walked along the seafront, with the sea and setting sun on my left. Thousands of Izmiris were walking too, some with me, some against. So many of them were young! A country can be young. I have studied and worked in economics for many years, but I still do not know where the impetus comes from to create, the "animal spirits" put forward by Keynes. A good part of it must come from youth. Youth is necessary but not sufficient, as the example of several other countries shows, young but stagnant. Here, the people are young and vibrant, building things, writing songs, traveling their country and the world. The single most important thing a country can do is harness and channel the energy of its youth, provide them opportunities to create. If they do not have such opportunities, darker ones will present themselves.

I passed many restaurants and cafés, then sat down at one, called by the plaintive voice and guitar of a lone musician. I am here now, and will recount my day. When I awoke this morning, the "What am I doing here?" feeling, unwelcome as it was, had returned. I showered, had breakfast, quite good at this hotel, and met Ibrahim, who had driven me from the airport on my arrival and would drive me again today. I sensed a certain dismay on his part as I explained in broken Turkish where I wanted him to take me, and he sensed an element of "wild goose chase" in my requests, as I had an exact address only for one of the destinations I hoped to visit. I love a good wild goose chase, in which I attempt to find something which may or may not be feasible to find, and which, in some cases may not even exist.

Our first objective was Ulucak Höyük, another Neolithic site from the same period as Yeşilova, around 6500 BCE. All we had to go on was the poor-quality map from the tourist office which had not helped at all yesterday when looking for Yeşilova. To make matters worse, Ulucak was further from town. We stopped several times and by a combination of modern technology and asking at least six passersby we finally found the site. It was closed and it seemed no one was there. The gate had nasty spikes on it, but I climbed over it while Ibrahim looked on curiously. I wasn't there long, calling out loudly "*Al-Salam 'aleikum*" when I saw that there was a guardhouse on the site. No one came out. Ulucak is also in a valley, but a hilly valley, and is not, like Yeşilova, in a river bottom. The excavations thus go much deeper, around eight meters below ground level, not having been washed away by repeated flooding. The construction seems similar to Yeşilova, and according to Professor Derin there are many similarities, though I do not know if the inhabitants of the two sites traded with each other. Presumably an analysis of the pottery types and other artifacts from the two sites might have answered this question in the academic research. I wonder if the bravest young men of Ulucak ran the twenty kilometers to check out the girls in Yeşilova, and vice-versa. I cannot imagine that they did not. We are now as we were then.

I climbed back over the fence and we decided to head straight to Sardis, and stop in Manisa on the return journey. Clouds were threatening rain, and later came through on their threat. This region is beautiful. Fertile plains encircled by gentle mountains. Fig trees and olives, as in the Qur'an. After half an hour, we arrived at ancient Sardis. There is an entire website devoted to archaeological expeditions to Sardis, which have continued from 1910 up until the present, so for more than a century, under the direction of various universities, with Princeton and Harvard playing major roles.[2] Sardis was the capital of ancient Lydia. It was here that people first learned to refine gold and silver, to separate the two elements and make pure coinage from them. The name of Croesus, king here in the sixth century BCE, became synonymous with limitless

2. www.sardisexpedition.org

wealth. Another King of Sardis, King Candaules, gave his name to the sexual practice of Candaulism, in which a man deliberately exposes his wife to other men. This cost King Candaules his throne and his life. We went first to the Temple of Artemis. No one there. The site was excavated over a century ago in the earliest stages of the Sardis expedition. Artemis: sister of Apollo, the Huntress, she of the arrows. Her temple is still impressive. Massive columns, most fallen but several still erect. Unlike the swampy disappointment of her temple near Ephesus. Ancient Greek divinities were male and female, and female divinities had female priestesses. Much less patriarchal than the subsequent monotheistic (all male?) religions. Why do I like history, and especially archaeology, so much? To look into our origins, that which makes us human.

I learned here that ancient Greek monumental structures were often curved, with the foundation base higher in the center of each side than on the two ends. I wandered around the temple and entered a small Byzantine church built up against its outer wall, much later. The wooden door creaked and slammed, trapping me into the Middle Ages and out of ancient Sardis. I managed to open the door and after asking for and receiving a glass of water from the young woman at the ticket booth, Ibrahim and I left. We stopped at another part of Sardis (which is a huge site, covering several square kilometers all-told), which included an area for smelting gold and silver for Croesus. We then continued on to the gymnasium area. I started with the (ancient) latrines. The curved spaces over which the patrons could sit demonstrated that physical proximity to other people while defecating was not as problematic as it would be now. Their thighs would have touched, except in the case of very small individuals. I am not a timid person, but feeling my neighbor's thigh pressing against mine as I dropped a turd into the water channel below would not be my cup of tea. The Roman gymnasium, a bath and exercise complex, was vaguely reminiscent of Ephesus. The construction was of stone and brick, and on a flat area near the Temple of Artemis I had just seen workmen preparing mud bricks. The attendant had told me they were for restoration work, undoubtedly for this part of the site. There were some beautiful decorative mosaic friezes on the floor of the fourth-century synagogue, and other handsome designs inlaid in cut marble on the walls.

Built up against the gymnasium walls were ancient shops and restaurants. And across the (modern) road were ruins whose vestiges extended nearly one kilometer to the east, though most were hidden under olive groves and orchards. Apparently there were a theater and a stadium here.

We departed for Manisa, and I spied the tomb mounds of the Lydian kings in the distance, once filled with riches, the metals they had refined. These tumuli are among the largest in the world. That of Alyattes is 65 meters high and 355 meter in diameter. It was described by Herodotus, who saw it in the fifth century BCE shortly after its construction, and also saw *stelae* giving details of those who built it:

> But there is one building to be seen there which is much the greatest of all, except those of Egypt and Babylon. In Lydia is the tomb of Alyattes, the father of Croesus, the base of which is made of great stones and the rest of it of mounded earth. It was built by the men of the market and the craftsmen and the prostitutes. There survived until my time five corner-stones set on the top of the tomb, and in these was cut the record of the work done by each group: and measurement showed that the prostitutes' share of the work was the greatest.

The women of ancient Lydia were, it seems, not to be outdone by their men when it came to strange sexual practices. Herodotus continues:

> All the daughters of the common people of Lydia ply the trade of prostitutes, to collect dowries, until they can get themselves husbands; and they themselves offer themselves in marriage.[3]

Modern expeditions actually discovered and excavated tunnels built by tomb raiders intent on robbing the buried treasures from these tumuli over 2,000 years ago. Tunneling under an area the size of eighteen football fields with Iron Age technology was surely an arduous and dangerous activity. Its ancient practitioners were, however, generally successful, as

---

3. Herodotus, *The Histories*. 1.93.

few Lydian tombs were found intact by modern archaeologists. There are over 100 other tombs in the same area. Given that these are not open to be visited, I opted not to get closer to them and as such only saw them from afar. I bitterly regretted this decision after having read more about them in a series of documents by the archaeologists who excavated Sardis in the early part of the twentieth century. I often feel that no matter what I do, or how hard I try, life slips through my fingers. When my children visit, I am with them and give them my full attention, but then they are gone and I ask myself, "How did I miss it? Where did these moments go?" Will I feel this way about my whole life when I am old? And here I was, a few kilometers from this wondrous field of ancient tomb mounds, only to have stood on top of one of them and contemplated kingdoms past, as I contemplated the New Year of 1991 from the top of the Great Pyramid at midnight, but I missed it, and it is gone.

The land between Sardis and Manisa is rich and fertile, a valley overlooked by brooding mountains catching the clouds and sending raindrops. As we approached Manisa I changed to the left hand side of the car to look out of the window at the cliffs above for the statue of the Anatolian mother goddess Cybele, thought to have been carved into one of the cliff faces high above in the late second millennium BCE by the Hittites. Interestingly, Cybele, who was worshipped through Roman times, was often depicted accompanied by felines. She may have her origins in a statuette from Çatalhöyük, dated to the sixth millennium BCE, which represents a seated female figure with each of her hands on a leopard's head. We drove up and down the road several times, gazing at the mountainside, but couldn't see her. So we stopped. In town we asked several people, who had no idea what we were talking about. I asked Ibrahim to go back to a place outside town where the mountain showed enough bare vertical rock for a carving. Here, at a children's playground and café rest stop, a man we asked said it was up in the mountains above. I walked through the playground and finally saw the carving from afar. Getting to it was tricky. At first, there was almost no path, just rubbish and toilet paper strewn on the ground in a wooded glen. But I went through this latrine area and found a footpath, then a larger one, and then a barbed wire fence with a hole in it. I knew I was getting closer, steadily gaining altitude. I jogged, as Ibrahim was waiting below but especially because it had been raining intermittently and I was worried that coming back down in a rainstorm could be dangerously slippery. The final sections were steep and somewhat exposed, but when I rounded a large block of stone and saw Cybele's statue, around six meters high (seated), I was happy. There is something satisfying about accomplishing this sort of miniature quest that does me good. After touching the statue and reflecting, I jogged quickly back to the car, having been away for a little over half an hour. I thanked Ibrahim profusely, which he probably didn't understand, but I had been reluctant to climb up to the statue due to the lack of clear path and the possibility of rain, and his persistence had encouraged me.

We got back into the car and drove into the town of Manisa, ancient Magnesia, site of an important battle of the second century BCE in which the Romans defeated the Persians, starting to solidify their control over Asia Minor. There are very few extant ruins now. I went to the Manisa museum, which was unremarkable but for a fossilized footprint from 25,000 BCE found at Salihli-Cakallar Hill. More recently, Ibn Battuta left footprints in Manisa during his travels in the fourteenth century, when the region was under the control of the Seljuk Turks. He made interesting ethnographic observations about funeral rites:

> We traveled from that city to the city of Magnesia, arriving the day before Eid al-Adha[4]...Its Sultan was named Saru Khan. When we arrived in the city we found him at the tomb of his son, who had died several months earlier. He and the boy's mother spent the night of the Eid and the following morning at the tomb. The body of the young man had been mummified, and put in a wooden coffin covered with wrought iron. The coffin was suspended in the middle of an unroofed dome, in order that the odors of decay might escape, after which a roof was built on the dome and the coffin brought down to the floor, and covered

---

4. *Eid al-Adha*, the Feast of the Sacrifice, is one of the two holiest days of the Muslim calendar, and occurs at the end of *Hajj*, the pilgrimage to Mecca. The other is *Eid al-Fitr*, the breaking of the fast at the end of Ramadan.

with the clothes of the deceased. I have seen this custom among other kings as well. We saluted him in that place, prayed the Eid prayers with him and returned to our lodging.[5]

Next to the museum was a sixteenth-century Ottoman mosque built by Sultan Murad III. The mosque was designed by the illustrious architect Mimar Sinan, and his mastery was immediately evident. I went into the courtyard, but the entrance to the mosque itself was occupied by a group of several dozen Turkish women. I wondered whether I had mistakenly blundered upon the women's entrance to the mosque.[6] In a bizarre juxtaposition of genres, I spoke in Arabic to a solitary woman smoking a cigarette and wearing a black miniskirt, and asked her whether there was a different entrance I should use, and she understood, chuckled, and replied that I should use the entrance I had seen. I duly removed my shoes, made my way politely through the group of women and was alone in the mosque. The tilework was magnificent—deep, pure, blue. Above the *mihrab* was the *Ayat al-Kursi* in *thulth* calligraphy. Then another verse, which, in my humble opinion, gives the most concise theological view of God in Islam: "He neither begets nor was begotten, and there is none like unto Him." Q 112:3–4. These verses are often found in mosques. But there were also large medallions, equally spaced around the vault of the mosque, with large and beautiful letters. At first I struggled with the calligraphy, as working a verse into an oblong medallion necessarily renders it less legible, but then I realized that these too were the *Ayat al-Kursi*, broken up into segments and each fitted into a medallion. I read it aloud and was filled with a wave of emotion. Beautiful words have always done this to me. Sometimes when I run in the mountains near my home and reach the extremity of my endurance, I recite and am moved to tears by ubiquitous beauty.

---

5. Harb, p. 319. Author's translation.

6. In Turkey, most mosques have a women's section for prayer but not a women's entrance. In some more conservative countries there are both a separate prayer space and a separate entrance. There is a *hadith* of the Prophet which stipulates that women should not pray in front of men because the position used for prayer would give the men impure thoughts.

This morning I awoke, packed, and read. I settled the hotel bill and met Ibrahim at noon, the third day he has been my driver. Sunday, almost no traffic. We passed the Izmir container port quickly, yesterday having spent half an hour stuck in front of its gigantic inventory of variegated boxes, shipping containers from over the world. Some were marked CSA/CGM, from Marseille, where I had just been a week ago and admired from the sea this firm's new modern headquarters building designed by Zaha Hadid. The drive to Bergama was ugly at first. High-rise apartment blocks, all the same. Modern utilitarian architecture with no aesthetic meaning. I would truly prefer a Neolithic existence to life in a modern vertical pigeon coop, though the Neolithic life would surely be shorter: "I don't want comfort. I want God, I want poetry, I want real danger, I want freedom, I want goodness. I want sin."[7]

From Aliağa onwards innumerable olive groves covered the hills and the ugliness disappeared. There were a few cars and a few minibuses with the common (for minibuses) "*Allah Korusun*" written on them ("God, protect us!"). We arrived in Bergama, crossed into the old quarter on the flank of the acropolis mountain and got totally lost in a very small area with streets barely wide enough for one car. Finally, a hospitable man on a scooter led us to the hotel, which took him ten minutes. I offered him some money but he declined and I shook his hand and told him he was *karim* ("generous, noble"). The hotel owners were a well-educated elderly couple. The husband, Iskender, spoke English and his wife, Mevhibe, French. It was more of a guesthouse than a hotel. I arranged my things, then set out to look at the town. The map given to me and explained by the hotel proprietors was from the town's tourism office. Somewhat unusual for this type of map, it was of excellent quality and very precise. I passed through the two main plazas of the town, the largest of which contains a statue of Galen, one of the founders of ancient medical science, born here in the second century CE. I noticed an unsavory personage who seemed to be following me. If he was following me, he was stupid in addition to

---

7. The character of John Savage in Aldous Huxley's *Brave New World* says these words.

being unsavory, since when I stopped, leaning on a wall, and looked at the map, he stopped in the middle of the pavement and stared at me. I resumed my walk and he continued to follow. Nearing the museum, my destination, I asked directions from two young men of honest demeanor, in poor Turkish. They told me that they were off-duty soldiers at the local military base, sent here from other parts of Turkey, and they walked me to the museum. The unsavory character disappeared.

I entered the museum gate, thinking the ticket booth was further on, but a voice called me back and I realized I had passed it. I stooped to look through the window, and was rewarded with the bright, smiling face of a young woman. The museum was small but contained some interesting pieces. In the ethnographic section, I was surprised that the traditional dress of Turkmen nomad women resembled that of Tibetan nomad women I had seen years before. There was also a statue of a Greek youth, a *kouros*, which struck me as being strongly influenced by Egyptian art. Sometimes, as in this case, a perceptive traveler can notice similarities in artistic styles or technical details which are borne out by further academic research. There were some ancient coins, one of which, of gold or electrum (an ancient mixture of gold and silver, before the two could be easily separated by smelting), from the second or third century BCE, had developed a sublime patina of colors over the centuries. I used to collect coins as a child, and still enjoy looking at them. After completing the museum visit, I bade farewell to the young woman at the ticket booth and entered the city again.

I located the road leading to the Asclepion, an ancient hospital complex a few kilometers from town, and confirmed this information with a man sitting on a tractor in the road, waiting for I know not what. I then visited the Kurşunlu Mosque, a quaint fifteenth-century building of utterly no interest from the inside. I followed the accurate tourist office map to the Red Basilica, a Roman and Byzantine religious complex built in the second century CE and dedicated to the worship of Egyptian deities. The Apostle John, in the Book of Revelations, writes of Pergamon as the seat of Satan:

And to the angel of the church in Pergamos write; These things saith he which hath the sharp sword with two edges; I know thy works, and where thou dwellest, even where Satan's seat is: and thou holdest fast my name, and hast not denied my faith, even in those days wherein Antipas was my faithful martyr, who was slain among you, where Satan dwelleth.[8]

That seat was probably right here. I thought I could detect a scent of sulfur. The buildings were large and in poor repair, under renovation and with large pieces of brick wall falling off onto whatever lay below. Fortunately, the entire construction site was open, and it was even possible to safely scale some of the scaffolding for a better view. There was a Turkish tour group there, following their guide like sheep. I went to the opposite end of the site from them and was alone inside the massive unroofed building. I snatched a pomegranate from a tree growing within the ruinous ancient hall, climbed to a nice seat and ate the fruit of Hades while crows cawed around me. I left, bought bottled water and biscuits, and walked back toward the hotel. The exhaust fumes in the streets are noxious, and the city is filthy. Civilization seems to have taken a step back here in the past 1,500 years from the "most illustrious city of Asia Minor"[9] to a dirty backwater. There is even a stream running through the middle of town, separating the Acropolis and old town from the new city, and serving the dual function of garbage dump and open sewer, with all of the odors this implies. After arriving at the hotel I read on the terrace, meditated, and went out for dinner in a lousy restaurant with worse service. Then I slept.

OCTOBER 10, 2016

I awoke early and came out of my room to write on the terrace. A man on a rooftop below was feeding his pigeons, just as I had seen in

---

8. *King James Bible*. Revelations, 2:12-17.

9. Pliny the Elder, *The Natural History*. Book V, Chapter 33. In Pliny's time, the first century CE, the population of Pergamon was around 150,000. That is 50% more than its present population. I wonder what it looked like then. Was it as filthy? Was the stream used as a sewer and dump? There are numerous examples of ancient cities demonstrating a much higher level of civilization than the present-day hovels surrounding them, availability of "modern" technologies notwithstanding.

Fatimid[10] Cairo twenty-five years before. I will now go to the Acropolis of Pergamon. I left the guesthouse and followed Iskender's instructions to the cable car up to the Acropolis. I asked directions from one man on my way and fended off an aggressive dog. When I arrived on the main road and saw the cable car station below and ramparts above, I decided to walk up, the ramparts seemingly quite close. There were several small trails up to the walls above, but they were steep and, more importantly, I would miss the ticket booth if I took one of them, and did not want the guards to think that I was trying to cheat the Turkish government of its legitimate museum fee. So I kept walking on the road. Round about the time I had decided I should have taken the cable car, a young man on a scooter spontaneously stopped for me and motioned to hop on behind him. With the lake below, a tumbledown Roman aqueduct in the distance, wind in my hair and gentle sun on my face, the ride up was exhilarating. At the top I thanked my benefactor, bought my ticket, and entered ancient Pergamon.

I visited the various temples, first that of Athena, ruined, then that of the Roman Emperor Trajan (second century CE). In ancient Greece and Rome emperors were, or could be, considered divinities. The gulf between gods and men was thus at least partly bridgeable, with heroes such as the great Achilles begotten by intercourse between gods or goddesses and humans. One need only read Homer to see the proximity of gods and men, and their likeness in almost every respect. Trajan's temple had been partially restored. The German archaeology and engineering team did exceptional work here, following the practice of "anastylosis," which means restoring only those elements of the ancient ruin for which identifiable parts are present, and for which the relative positions of such parts can be deduced. It makes for an authentic experience of antiquity in which the viewer sees the present reality, ravaged by time, in the form of blocks and column sections scattered on the ground, juxtaposed with the past reality in the form of parts of buildings which have been quite fully reconstructed exactly as they had been. This scholarly restoration style is far superior to, for example, that

---

10. The tenth-century Fatimid dynasty built many architectural wonders in the old part of Cairo.

used by Arthur Evans at Knossos (in Crete), which gives an impression of having been slapped together with wishful thinking and reinforced concrete.

The most remarkable aspect of the Pergamon Acropolis was the level of skill and knowledge of structural engineering demonstrated by the Romans. The esplanade of the Temple of Trajan was supported by a series of vaulted arches beneath it totaling roughly twenty-five meters in height from the sloped mountainside to the paving stones of the beautiful esplanade. Everything was designed at one time, as explained in the excellent signage left by the German restoration team. And, most marvelous of all, for this entire visit of the upper Acropolis of Pergamon, I was utterly alone for two hours. I have experienced many archaeological sites in my travels, and the feeling is completely different when one is alone among the vestiges. I spent three whole days alone in the ancient city of Mohenjo-Daro[11] in Pakistan in silent communion with the past. And so it was here this morning. Finally, a Turkish family arrived to rupture my solitude, and later a few more people. I saw the Arsenal, in which 900 rounds of spherical stone shot were found in thirteen different calibers. I presume that these were launched by catapult. Accurate ranging must have been very difficult, but not so difficult as to render such weapons useless, or they would not have been made. I wanted to go down to the huge theater of Pergamon, but could not find the access tunnel mentioned in the tourist brochure, so I climbed down a section of wall and a steep slope. No one with vertigo nor anyone severely out of shape could have attended a performance in this theater, as the steps to reach it were too steep, like an Alpine red ski slope in declivity, perhaps a twenty-five- or thirty-degree angle.

Coming down from the theater by a path, I went through a jumble of ruins and climbed up to the emplacement of the famed Pergamon Altar, looted by the Germans who excavated it in the nineteenth century and moved the entire monument to Berlin. I thought to go and see it

---

11. Mohenjo-Daro is still the most amazing archaeological site I have ever witnessed. One gets the strong feeling of walking in the ruins of a modern city, the buildings lined up flush along the street, underground sewers, municipal rubbish collection. Mohenjo-Daro was part of the Indus River Civilization, from 2500 BCE, which covered an area of 600 by 800 km and had standard weights and measures and an as-yet-undeciphered system of writing.

this winter, but then learned that it is being renovated and is closed to the public for several years, so even that is not possible. I sat in this spot for a while, then returned to the top of the theater and found the tunnel I had missed before. Leaving the museum area, I decided to walk all the way down through the successive areas of ruins below the Acropolis, but as I began my descent, two sleek, black forms, immobile and serpentine, barred my path and startled me. I tossed pebbles at this intertwined living Caduceus, hoping the snakes would leave the path, but one of them remained unperturbed while his companion slithered slowly away. Giving the serpent a wide berth, I inspected more temples on the way down as well as a remarkable building with well-preserved and beautiful mosaics. Several monumental gymnasia remained, where men, adolescents, and boys had separate training areas. Further down the hill, I saw a barbed wire fence and the intersection of the main road with the road back to the guesthouse, but I was under no illusion that anyone would be there to let me out and I had no wish to walk back up to the top, a good forty-five-minute hike. I saw a gate above which the barbed wire had not been strung, and made for it. I climbed it and returned.

I rested for the middle of the day, sheltered from the heat, and wrote. Now I will go to the Asclepion, named after the Greek god of medicine. I walked quickly through the town so as to have sufficient time to see everything before dusk. Leaving the town, the uphill road to the Asclepion passes through a poor and dirty neighborhood. I am alert. On my right, an infernal vision. A young and beautiful black horse tethered to a ruined refrigerator, grazing in a field of trash. More litter than dried grass. Bucephalus in Hell. I walked further. On the left, first an army barracks, tanks lined up ready for war, then the entrance to the Asclepion. I entered and was alone again, walking along the sacred road to the healing god's temple. I paused to reflect at the gate. Heal me. Heal my wife. Heal my family. I walked around the treatment building, through the tunnel whose use remains unknown. Running water from the sacred spring. Automatic gunfire from the base nearby, my hollow footfalls and the ringing echo of a stone slab's wobbling percussion. Washed thrice at the sacred spring and drank. Here two of Asclepius' daughters, Hygeia and Panacea, labored, healing the sick or easing their passage onwards with kindness and beauty. When I am dying I wish to be cared for by a woman, to look into her face and remember life before I die. These two have given their names to medicine, have become the names of what they did. "I am become a name."

This is one of the places in the world where the science and art of medicine was developed. Did we build on what they learned here? This is a complex question, the history of science. To pose initial boundaries, first, it is obvious that we benefit from the discoveries and developed knowledge of our predecessors. Otherwise we would still be eating berries and grubs and living in caves. The question is hence of the continuity of this transmission process rather than its existence, and the extent to which it reaches into the distant past. Without presuming to possess sufficient knowledge of this subject, it appears that the transmission of knowledge is definitely discontinuous. What was known in the second century CE, when Galen was here, was lost, not transmitted. Medieval Europe knew less of medicine and science in general than was known in Hellenistic times. Then, parts of it, those parts written down in texts, were rediscovered, translated, some of them from Greek into Arabic and Hebrew and then into Latin. They then perhaps built the foundation for the Renaissance, a full thousand years after being forgotten. Or perhaps they only provided the impetus to research. So the knowledge-transmission process seems to have been discontinuous both temporally and geographically.

I left the Asclepion near dusk, walking slowly, knowing already that I had missed something but not yet knowing what it was. I always miss something, a stone unturned, a door unopened, behind which lie the secrets of the world, which would ease my suffering and explain it all to me. And yet I left. I passed the demonic pasture, Bucephalus still dragging his refrigerator. Going down the hill towards town I became uneasy. There were many young men of aggressive demeanor doing tricks on scooters, arguing, horsing around. And looking at me. "*Al-Salam 'aleikum*" offered but no response given. No one else here to whom I might appeal if trouble ensued. I moved carefully, staying close to the wall on my right side, alert. Three young women walked toward me from the group. I repressed the urge to look at them, staring straight ahead, giving no reason to take offense. Relief as I passed without incident and re-entered the city. I was still walking quickly, yet a man passed me, tall and thickly built, asymmetrical in his gait, jacket too small and trousers too large, but seeming well-to-do. He saved me from a beggar woman, who engaged him in conversation, and I passed him in turn. I arrived at the hotel, read, and prepared to go for dinner.

Iskender and Mevhibe, the owners of the guesthouse, had kindly invited me to go to Ayvalık, sixty kilometers away, and dine at a restaurant owned by their son, who had studied in Boston. After the mediocre food and poor service of last night I happily accepted their invitation. A Canadian couple who had stayed here several times before and arrived this afternoon was also invited. We left, Iskender driving his well-kept old Mercedes. The Canadian woman sat next to me and did not stop talking for the hour it took to get to Ayvalık. She was pleasant, but I was overwhelmed by her constant chatter. Her husband, also a nice person, was largely silent, probably thankful to have me occupy his wife's conversational attention. We arrived in Ayvalık and walked through the cobblestone streets of the old Greek quarter to the restaurant. Mevhibe's family was moved in the infamous population transfers of the early twentieth century from Salonika (Thessaloniki in present-day Greece) to Ayvalık. And many Greeks were forced to leave Ayvalık and go to Thrace. The town's well-built stone buildings in the Greek style attest to their having been here. We arrived at the restaurant, formerly a storage depot for olive oil from the myriad olive trees of this region. With modern décor, stone and white stucco, vaulted ceiling, and colorful modern paintings on the walls, the restaurant had a very enjoyable atmosphere. Cem, Mevhibe and Iskender's son, had studied for eight years in Boston, then lived in Istanbul and now had just opened this restaurant after closing a similar one in Bergama due to lack of business. He was nearly forty. Iskender left the table several times to take long phone calls, and when I asked he explained that he was negotiating to purchase a building here to open a second hotel for his son. I told Iskender that he strongly reminded me of my own grandfather, who worked into his eighties. Iskender lifted his glass of wine and toasted my grandfather. They had the same name: "Iskender" is Turkish, and Arabic, for "Alexander," my grandfather's name. Iskender then asked if I knew why people clinked glasses when drinking wine, and I replied, "because they didn't trust each other, and poured wine from one glass into the other, in case it was poisoned." He agreed that this was the historical origin of the custom but added that the spiritual one was that wine touches all of the senses: taste, smell, touch, sight, but that the clinking of the glasses provides an extra auditory impression. I concur with him, though the voices of companions, well-known or newly met, with whom we raise a glass and drink a toast, also touch the hearing sense. We finished our excellent meal; I thanked my hosts and we drove back to Bergama. Mevhibe remained attentive the whole way, watching the traffic and making sure her husband noticed everything. At first I watched from the back, ready to help, but as the Canadian woman was trying my patience with her incessant speaking I feigned sleep, and in feigning was overtaken by it.

OCTOBER 11, 2016

I took my breakfast alone, paid the hotel bill, and bade farewell to Mevhibe and Iskender as well as to the Canadians, who came out of their room as I was leaving. The taxi driver, Ali, seemed trustworthy and I gave him a small list of the places I wanted to visit on the way to Assos, our final destination for today. First on the list was Yiğmatepe, a tumulus of the Attalid Kings of Pergamon, on the outskirts of Bergama town. The first tomb mound we saw was Maltepe, of the same dynasty. I climbed it, thoroughly impressed by the permanence of such a monument, though it could be mistaken for a large hill by the uninitiated, with trees and shrubs growing on it. It boggles the mind to imagine the work it took to build a mound 180 meters in diameter by 28 meters high (Maltepe), or 158 meters in diameter and 35 meters high in the case of Yiğmatepe (and double these dimensions for the larger tumuli of the Lydian kings at Sardis). Did they not have anything better to do? Aesthetics were surely not a primary consideration, for a mound is a mound. Presumably this work was not done willingly by all participants.

After time spent walking up and around these two tumuli, and thus assuaging my regret at not having done the same at those near Sardis, we took to the road. We passed Ayvalık, of last night's excellent dinner, and continued north. I saw Mount Ida, a military radar dome on the summit. This is where Hera seduced Zeus and caused his somnolence so that other gods could intervene on behalf of the Achaians in the Trojan War, as recounted in *The Iliad*. According to Homer, when Zeus sees his wife, who has dolled herself up to seduce him, coming to him on Mount Ida, he launches into a soliloquy listing other females, divine and mortal, with whom he has enjoyed carnal relations and tells her that he had never desired any of them as much as he now desires her![12] A mortal husband might have difficulty taking such liberties. This mountain was also the site of the Judgement of Paris, a divine "beauty contest" in which the mortal Paris (of Troy) was asked to choose the most beautiful among three goddesses, Aphrodite, Athena, and Hera, and was offered differing enticements by each. Clearly such a choice for a mortal man is a no-win situation, but Paris chose, perhaps unwisely, Aphrodite, and her promise of the love of Helen, the most beautiful mortal woman in the world but also the wife of Menelaus of Sparta. Aphrodite honors her promise and Paris brings Helen to Troy, causing an oath of mutual assistance to be invoked and launching the Achaian invasion of Troy. Tempted by Mount Ida's historical and mythological importance, I had considered climbing it, but when I made serious inquiries I found out that, first, it had become the site of a military base, as witnessed by the large radar domes on its summit, and, second, it could only be visited with a hired guide. There is a road all the way to the summit, and though I do not mind using the services of a guide when they are really necessary, I have an aversion to being "guided" up a road that I could drive up in a car. So I abandoned the idea of viewing the ringing plains of windy Troy from Mount Ida.

We continued on our way, looking for and finding with some difficulty Antandros, a Roman settlement. I walked silently through an olive grove to reach it, moving slowly and making myself invisible

12. Homer, *The Iliad*. Book 14, lines 312-28.

to the nearby workers, hopped the barrier, and wandered over the site completely unnoticed. I then descended to where the archaeologists and assistants were at work and introduced myself. My spell of invisibility having succeeded, they were surprised to see me even though I had been there for fifteen minutes, mostly in full view. The young archaeologist in charge was welcoming and polite and took me around what I had already seen alone, adding some interesting detail. If I had anticipated his welcome I would have announced my presence straight away. To my untrained eye, it seems that there is excellent archaeological work being done by Turks in Turkey, but that they do not receive the recognition they deserve due to weak English language skills. The international academic community does not read Turkish. The main attraction of the site was a fifth-century CE Roman villa, with well-preserved floor mosaics as well as a fresco on the wall of one room. I thanked the young man for the visit, returned to Ali in the car, and we went on our way.

The next stop was the village of Adatepe and an ancient altar of Zeus nearby. These sights, as well as Antandros, had been recommended to me by the owner of the guesthouse I would stay in at Assos. There were no signs for Adatepe on the road, but at the last second as we were entering a construction zone I saw a brown sign for "Zeus Altar" and Ali backed up to make the turn. We followed the winding road up the mountain, arriving at a spot to park with a green gate and a path. Nearby was the quaint little village, old stone buildings, no modern apartment blocks, Adatepe. It was harmonious, and I have not seen many places like it here. I followed the path for around a kilometer, wondering where it led and why it was so long, until I arrived at a glen. Strange bushes bore thousands upon thousands of white ribbons, inexplicable and strange. Approaching, I saw that they were pieces of plastic shopping bags, knotted deliberately onto the twigs of the bushes. It felt positively diabolical, an object of pollution deliberately affixed to trees and bushes. It also reminded me of my first Christmas away from home, 1984 in Amsterdam, at the Melkweg, a room full of Christmas trees suspended upside-down from the ceiling. On the far side of this glen was the Altar of Zeus. I climbed the steps, intending to spill a libation of water to the god and thinking that in this day and age he might appreciate even such a meager offering, not receiving so many thigh-pieces of fatted oxen. But arriving on top of the altar I surprised a young Turkish couple, probably making out. I saluted them and asked what the bizarre ornamentation of the trees below meant, and the young man answered *"dilek, istek"*—"wish, desire." So people make wishes and tie these pieces of plastic to the tree branches. An ignoble material for a noble gesture. As I was returning to the car I realized I had forgotten the libation to Zeus and promised to make one of wine in the evening.

We drove on towards Assos along an unspoilt coastline. Campsites and small simple dwellings were in evidence but no industrial tourist blocks such as those near Antalya or Bodrum. I like this place. Arriving, I paid Ali and shook his hand, and a young man from the guesthouse took my small backpack to assist me. I went to my room after meeting Ece and her family, the owners, unpacked my things, and read. The weather was stormy and I opened windows and door to get fresh air, playing tag with a stubborn cat intent on taking up residence with me. It took a glass of water to dissuade him. After a couple of hours, I walked up to the top of the mountain to see the Temple of Athena. What a place for a temple...On the mountaintop, looking over the sea, a wild panorama! Sun and wind and clouds. I can see the island of Lesbos. Gray-eyed goddess, grant me wisdom! What am I running from? I sat for a long time, looking down at the ancient city, feeling the wind on my face, contemplating life, nature, the past. I have no answers. When I was young I thought I would know more when I was older, and would be wise then. But like the imprudent swimmer who strikes out for an island he sees in the distance and thinks close by, now in middle age I look again to the goal and see it no closer than before. Alas it is too far, and I will never attain it. Long I lingered there, meditating upon the goddess, she whom I would choose if granted Paris' choice, and then I walked down. I stopped in the empty, forlorn village at the only open inn and drank a beer in the cold wind and warm sun intermittently passing through the clouds, then went back to the guesthouse. And now I sit in this same inn, utterly alone, surrounded by the wrack of darkness and the wind outside, an empty bottle of wine, one young man who made my dinner and served me, almost drunk, and having poured the promised libation to Zeus upon the ground. To struggle back now up the Sisyphean hill to my bed, again alone, burdened by the solitude I love so much, exceeded in strength by my own desire and unable to honor my own intention.

OCTOBER 12, 2016

I awoke with a headache. I had ordered a bottle of wine and drank what was not poured out in dedication to Zeus. Not up to the level of the wines I drink at home, but an honorable effort, it was from Suvla, one of the Gallipoli battlefields, where the Allied army suffered the worst casualties in one of the most ill-advised episodes of an ill-advised invasion. One wonders at the *terroir*'s content in ferrous human blood, brass from shell casings, and lead from bullets. I washed and then had an excellent Turkish breakfast prepared by Ece. Then read, at one stretch, a book about the archaeology of this region, the southern Troad,[13] by the archaeologist who directs the excavations at Assos,[14] and left by car for Chryse (modern Gülpinar) with Ibrahim, the driver recommended by Ece. The most interesting information gathered from my reading: under the sacred road leading north from Chryse, site of the Apollo Smintheus temple, to Alexandria Troas, a Chalcolithic site from 5000 BCE was discovered. So there were settlements at Chryse long before the present temple was built in the third century BCE, and there may very well have been a settlement here at the time of the Trojan War, roughly from the fourteenth to twelfth century BCE.

In the late nineteenth century, when Heinrich Schliemann discovered the ruins of Troy thanks to a close reading of *The Iliad* and other ancient texts, the help of another scholar, Frank Calvert, and the knowledge of local legends, there were few corroborating historical sources about the Trojan War, and the scholarship of the day did not know to what extent the Homeric epics were historically true. Nowadays, with many more

---

13. "Troad" means the region of Troy.

14. Arslan, Nurettin and Böhlendorf-Arslan, Beate, *Assos – Living in the Rocks (An Archaeological Guide)*. Turkey: Homer Publishing, 2010.

historical sources, especially those of the Hittites, having been read and analyzed, we have a much clearer idea. Ancient Greek historians themselves, working in the fourth or fifth centuries BCE, placed the war for Troy between the fourteenth and twelfth centuries BCE (whereas the Homeric epics were not written down until the eighth or ninth centuries BCE, so four or five centuries after the events occurred).[15] The physical archaeological evidence now known matches this timespan, as do Hittite texts which refer to the city of Wilusa (Ilion, after which *The Iliad* was named) being attacked by the Ahhiyawa, apparently the Hittite rendering of the Greeks' word for themselves, Achaians. According to this interpretation, which is solidly supported by the evidence, Ilion was a Hittite vassal state,[16] which would explain the astounding list of foreign warriors participating in the defense of Troy, as these warriors were also from other Anatolian Hittite vassal states (one such warrior was Sarpedon of Lycia, killed by Achilles' companion Patroclus, but there are dozens of others, mentioned by name in the Homeric text). The archaeological evidence itself points to a possible devastating war at Troy from Troy VI or Troy VIIa, roughly spanning the period mentioned.[17]

Arriving at the site of the Apollo Smintheus[18] temple in Chryse, I walked slowly around, looking at the monumental temple, partially reconstructed, then the other structures, mostly of later construction.

---

15. The temporal disjunction between the actual events of the Trojan War and the time when these were recorded can be noticed by someone interested in military techniques through the descriptions of the use of Bronze Age weaponry in *The Iliad*. The text was written down during the Iron Age, long after the Trojan War happened, and Homer seems not to know how Bronze Age chariot warfare was conducted: in *The Iliad*, the warriors ride up to the enemy in their chariots, dismount, and fight on foot, whereas it is fairly clear now that chariots were used for mounted combat, not simply as a form of transportation.

16. It is not known for certain which language the Trojans spoke at the time of the Homeric epics, but Calvert Watkins, Professor of Indo-European Linguistics at Harvard, asserted that the language spoken was Luwian, an ancient Indo-European language.

17. Ancient Troy is not one city. It is a succession of cities built upon each other, dating from the early Bronze Age in 3000 BCE all the way through Roman times. The archaeological layers have been denoted by Roman numerals, and those most likely to be contemporaneous with the Trojan War are Troy VI and Troy VIIa, though Troy VIIa particularly seems to have been destroyed by war. Note that this historical paragraph is largely based upon the introduction to Richmond Lattimore's translation of *The Iliad* by Richard P. Martin of Stanford University.

18. Apollo Smintheus means "Apollo of the Mice."

I washed my hands in cool spring water pouring from an old clay pipe in a subterranean chamber. Perhaps the beautiful Chryseis drank from this same font, she whom her father, priest of Apollo, saved from the depredations of the Achaians. This story from *The Iliad* motivated me to come here.[19] There were pomegranates growing everywhere. Pomegranates, along with raspberries, were my favorite fruit as a child, and I picked a magnificent specimen from a tree, the archetype of a pomegranate: deep red berries and crisp acidity. There was a gallery of champions, with dozens of inscribed bases for statues, both wrestlers and victors at *pankration*, a sort of ancient MMA (mixed martial arts) incorporating wrestling and boxing. But only the bases were here. Where had the statues of the champions gone? Only the inscriptions of their names and accomplishments remain. There was a square room enclosed by iron bars that contained, I think, a mosaic, which had been covered by a textile and then by gravel to protect it. There was also seemingly a Latin inscription here, though I did not see it. Of the hundreds of inscriptions I have seen in Turkey at Roman sites, virtually all were in Greek, not Latin, including edicts from Roman emperors. I can read simple Latin, but in Greek I get no further than the alphabet and basic pronunciation.

Ibrahim was waiting for me when I came out of the site, and we drove south down the magnificent wild coastline towards Babakale. One hillside was blighted by tourist development, the rest pure. We arrived and I went to the Ottoman fortress while Ibrahim drank tea. It was empty. This is the westernmost point of Turkey. I have been at both extremities of this country. I climbed the lighthouse on the fort and gazed out over the Aegean, closed my eyes, and listened to the surf, then gazed a little longer. We headed back to Assos, Ibrahim at times driving too fast for my taste, especially when we passed through villages. In Bektaş, a small village on the road, I thought I spotted some sections of ancient columns but did not ask to stop. Before returning to the hotel

---

19. Homer, *The Iliad*. Book 1. Chryseis was taken as a "war bride" (i.e. slave girl) by Agamemnon, but in answer to her father's prayers, Apollo visited plagues upon the Achaians, prompting them to return Chryseis to her father. Agamemnon, in his arrogance, then demanded Briseis, the war bride of Achilles, in replacement, thus humiliating the latter and causing him to withhold his invincible strength from battle, leading to many of the events depicted in *The Iliad*.

we went to the harbor of Assos. Nothing to see but empty restaurants in clean stone buildings, probably built by former Greek inhabitants. I went out on the pier as far as I could to look up to the promontory with the Temple of Athena far above. I had seen this port from there yesterday. We also stopped at the theater on the way back up, a fine sight like others, except made of andesite instead of limestone or marble. This particular type of stone, and its flesh-dissolving properties, are at the origin of the word *sarcophagus*, meaning "flesh-eating." According to Pliny the Elder, a dead body left in a sarcophagus of this stone will be fully consumed in forty days.[20] I wonder whether a person who sat in this theater and watched the whole Oedipus cycle played in sequence for six or eight hours would find his ass starting to dissolve.

Ibrahim took me back to the guesthouse, and I read intensely for two hours and planned out the rest of this trip for an hour more. Reading and planning vastly enhance the appreciation and value of my travels. Before leaving home, I had read the chapters on Gallipoli from Professor Eugene Rogan's excellent book, *The Fall of the Ottomans*, mentioned earlier. Coincidentally, I had also re-read T.S. Eliot's poetry and noticed that he had dedicated one of his books to "Jean Verdenal, 1889–1915, mort aux Dardanelles."[21] I looked up Verdenal, which I had not done before, and learned that he was Eliot's friend, and that he had died aged twenty-five, along with more than 130,000 other young men, in a stupid, useless series of battles that gained absolutely nothing for the Allied aggressors (Britain and France and their colonial dependencies). I resolved to try to find out where Jean Verdenal had died and wrote to Professor Rogan, who replied almost immediately, informing me that he died at Seddulbahir on Cape Helles on May 2, 1915. I decided to go there and pay my respects to him.

When the sun was lower in the sky and the day's heat had subsided, I went out again. I found the restaurant recommended by Ece. A cheerful, round lady told me it would be open in the evening. Then I walked by a circuitous, clandestine path up to Athena's temple to watch the sunset.

---

20. Pliny the Elder, *Natural History*. Book XXXVI, Chapter 27.

21. Eliot, T.S., *Prufrock and other Observations*. New York: Knopf, 1920.

The site had officially closed at 5:00 PM, but several Turkish couples were there. I was the only romantically challenged lover present. One of the Turkish couples spoke to me in Turkish, and I replied in Turkish, "I do not understand Turkish." Duygu and Bilge were working on a travel blog and I took a few photos of them for their blog and we talked for a while. Then they left and I returned to my contemplation of the sunset from the Temple of Athena. At sunset I came down. I didn't want to walk down in the growing darkness the path by which I had come up in daylight and instead went to the ticket booth. I had checked yesterday when leaving and knew I could climb the gate. This time, however, I noticed a security camera covering it, which I hadn't seen yesterday, so I moved directly under the camera and climbed over with my back facing it the entire time, then walked back to the restaurant. The last embers of sunset were glowing in the western hearth as I arrived.

OCTOBER 13, 2016

I woke early, bathed before breakfast, and packed my backpack. I ate quickly while talking with Ece about travel. We went down to meet the driver. It was not Ibrahim from yesterday, but instead his father Yusuf. I assumed, correctly, that being an older man, Yusuf would not be given to driving at excessive speeds. We drove first to Alexandria Troas, on the coast north of here by forty-five minutes. The ruins of the ancient baths were interesting, arched stonework still surmounting the rubble in the middle of the forest. I climbed on top of a wall to spot other ruins in the surrounding area and started walking to these after exploring those close at hand. At one point I jumped as I surprised a large snake, the third of this trip. I had never seen snakes in Turkey previously. On the way to the ruins, the plowed earth of an olive grove I crossed contained roughly one potsherd for every three stones. Returning to the car, I crossed the road and looked at the Nymphaeum, climbing on top of a well-preserved part of it that was built with finely cut stone ashlar masonry. We then drove nearly a kilometer to the forum ruins. The city was huge, several kilometers square. I saw the first Latin inscription of the trip, despite all of these places having been under Roman rule, but it was only a fragment. The forum area had been fully excavated. There was a well, and when I tossed a pebble into it the time it took to splash indicated a depth of at least ten meters. After walking around 800 meters south and finding further unexcavated ruins, we drove to the coast, another few hundred meters, and I walked to the ancient port. St. Paul sailed from here to begin proselytizing in Europe, having been asked to do so in a vision.[22] The basin of the ancient port had been silted in, and now it resembles a sandy salt flat surrounded by raised banks facing the sea.

Leaving Alexandria Troas, we drove on the smooth modern road to Çanakkale, taking a short detour to see the entrance to Troy and its surrounding area in order to get an idea of the lay of the land for tomorrow's visits. Arriving in Çanakkale, I was overwhelmed by the presence of so many young people in this university town. I decided immediately that I would spend two nights here. I am sick of solitude now. I had not reserved any hotel but had researched two possibilities. I looked at both of them, and one was clearly superior, offering a view over the port and the strait separating Europe from Asia. I took a room with this view. I then sat at a café and drank a beer, looking at the Gallipoli war monument across the strait, with an image of a Turkish soldier in white against the dark hillside and the words, "Stop, wayfarer, the ground you tread once witnessed the end of an era."[23] I took a taxi to the Archaeology Museum. I told the driver where I wanted to go in Turkish and then he started making conversation, so I told him, also in Turkish, that I cannot speak Turkish. He laughed. It is possible to get the pronunciation of certain phrases accurate enough to pass for a native speaker yet know very little more of a language. The museum was a disappointment. The exhibits, as might be expected in a smaller museum, were not of major importance, but ninety percent of the informational texts were in Turkish only. One gravestone read, "Farewell, Paresia, daughter of Parthenias." It was from the second

---

22. "And they passing by Mysia came down to Troas. And a vision appeared to Paul in the night; there stood a man of Macedonia, and prayed him, saying, Come over unto Macedonia and help us." *King James Bible*. Acts of the Apostles 16:8-9.

23. These lines are from a poem by Necmettin Onan. Translation from a tourist office brochure.

century BCE. Generations pass, one to another, like leaves falling from trees after their season, and nothing is permanent:

> High-hearted son of Tydeus, why ask of my generation? As is the generation of leaves, so is that of humanity. The wind scatters the leaves on the ground, but the live timber burgeons with leaves again in the season of spring returning. So one generation of men will grow while another dies.[24]

I left after patiently taking in all of the exhibits. On the main road there were no taxis, but a bus driver allowed me on his vehicle even though I had no electronic payment card and he was not equipped to take cash. The bus was full of students. I asked a young man if the bus went to the port (near my hotel) and he said it did. A while later, a kind young woman told me that she would get off at the stop nearest the port so I could follow her. I kept my eye on this spontaneous benefactress and made (very) small conversation with her using the Turkish dictionary on my phone and my ability to conjugate verbs in the present tense. When we got off the bus she shook my hand, and said carefully, in English, "Nice meeting you."

I walked along the seafront to the site of the silly wooden horse donated by the makers of the film *Troy*, which starred Brad Pitt as Achilles. Since I have now seen the wooden horse on the Troy site itself, this version on the waterfront is at least less silly since it is not made from modern board lumber like its Troy counterpart. This one looks slightly more convincing as something that might have been made in pre-modern times. On the way back to the hotel, I stopped in a centenary exhibit about Gallipoli. I had difficulty holding back tears. There were multimedia images and quotations from Atatürk and others: "We buried an entire university in Anafartalar." Gallipoli was an honorable and necessary victory for the Turks. They were attacked by the British and French at a vital point, and had to defend themselves from utter subjugation and ruin. For the attackers it was an absolutely

---

24. Homer, *The Iliad*. (Book VI, p. 175, Lines 145-9).

colossal mistake, a useless waste of human life. I lie becalmed, having seen and felt too much these past days. I need to rest, and eat and drink among people.

OCTOBER 14, 2016

I spent a bad night. I had dinner in a good fish restaurant and for some unknown reason I had stomach cramps and slept badly. I had none of the symptoms of food poisoning. Perhaps I am just worn out. I resolved to take it easy tomorrow. But today I will visit Troy. I decided to give my digestive system a rest and consume only water until dinner. I researched, and attempted to make sense of, the numerous tumuli found on the plain of Troy. I achieved only partial success at this task since in fact no one knows the site of the tumulus where Achilles was buried, nor the identities of any of the other personages entombed in the various tumuli (barring one Roman-era tumulus). I did, though, manage to gain a basic idea of the geography around Troy, the plains with the twin rivers, the Skamander and the Simois. Baudelaire, in his great poem "Le Cygne," writes about Andromache, Hector's wife, augmenting the flow of the Simois with her tears at her heroic husband's death before being taken as a slave. Taking this classical symbol of irrevocable loss, Baudelaire builds on its foundation one of the greatest modern poems.

At 9:00 AM I met Idris, the taxi driver organized by the hotel. He was a soft-spoken elderly gentleman, and he told me later that his son worked at the hotel. I explained where I wanted to go, first to Kumkale, site of a French diversionary attack at the start of the Gallipoli campaign, then on a wild goose chase looking for Achilles' tomb, and last to visit the Troy archaeological site. I also reassured him that if our outing took longer than half a day I would pay him more than the amount initially agreed. Past Troy, we crossed both rivers and turned south near the mouth of the Hellespont, a military area as it has effectively been for thousands of years. Troy was, it seems, an important commercial center because ships heading towards the Black Sea had to stop and wait here for fair winds, infrequent in an easterly direction. The road we drove on was terrible, but this allowed more time to scan the horizon for symmetrical hills, almost always tumuli on a flat landscape, either tomb mounds or ancient cities. Bingo! A small one on the left. Through later research, I identified it tentatively as Kumtepe, around twenty meters in diameter and eight meters high. I ran to the top and almost fell into the vertical pit dug deep into the mound with a horizontal shaft running off from it. This was surely not Achilles' tomb; not large enough, nor very visible from the Hellespont, even before the delta of the two rivers had filled with alluvium to form the present coastline. Homer gives this precise indication of the location of Achilles' tomb in *The Odyssey*:

> "Around them then, we, the chosen host of the Argive spearmen, piled up a grave mound that was both great and perfect, on a jutting promontory there by the wide Hellespont, so that it can be seen afar from out on the water by men now alive and those to be born in the future."[25]

There is an excellent discussion of the textual and physical considerations regarding Achilles' tomb published by Harvard's Center for Hellenic Studies, which helped me a great deal even though I am not sure I agree on its tentative selection of the most likely tumulus for the tomb.[26] We continued south towards the village of Yenıköy. I caught sight of a mound too steep and too symmetrical to be a natural hill, far off on the right towards the sea, but Idris said it was not a tumulus. He listed the five tumuli he knew near Troy, though in reality there are many more. But we passed on, asking directions in the town from a group of farmers in a coffee house. South of Yenıköy we reached a beach near the ancient city of Achilleon, named after Achilles, but the road was impassable after that point. I saw a regular and large hill to the east of the track and set out for it jogging. This was Sivri Tepe, the mound thought to be Achilles' tomb by the ancients, although its status

---

25. Homer, Richmond Lattimore, translator, *The Odyssey*. New York: Harper & Row, 1967. Book XXIV, lines 80-84.

26. Burgess, Jonathan, "Tumuli of Achilles", in *Classics@3, The Homerizon; Conceptual Interrogations in Homeric Studies*. Cambridge: Harvard University.

is now considered uncertain. It was high enough and could surely be seen from the sea, even though it was quite far from the Hellespont. The site of Achilleon was visible from the top of the mound. According to Arrian, Alexander the Great laid a wreath here to honor Achilles, a hero he saw himself resembling.[27]

I wasn't satisfied. The mound we had passed on our way south was too regular and too close to the sea to be ignored. Surely it could be the one! It is strange how inside us is a resistance to changing our plans, to recognizing that we were wrong and going back on our initial decision. But I know myself, and knew I would be forever unsatisfied if I did not go back. I asked Idris to retrace our tracks to allow me to walk to this tell and climb it, and promised I would remunerate him for his extra time. We drove back northwards, parked, and I walked briskly around a kilometer, across a field, through a hedge, then another field. The mound was large, not as large as those of the Lydian Kings or at Pergamon, but perhaps twenty-five meters high and 100 meters across at the base. It was certainly man-made, situated in the middle of a flat field. And none of the other tumuli could have been seen nearly as well as this one from the sea. I paid my respects to the great Achilles, and to Patroclus, as Achilles' will was to be buried in one grave with his friend. Like generations of travelers before me all the way back to Alexander the Great, I will never know whether I chose the right tumulus or not,[28] but such a homage is spiritual, and Achilles as much an ideal as an historical figure.

This was the chosen end of my wild goose chase. Further research showed this tumulus to be Kesik Tepe (the Demetrius Tumulus) on the Sigeion ridge. We turned back south to go to Troy by completing a loop around it, and to the east I noticed another very obvious tumulus. This one was more recent, Roman, built by the Emperor Caracalla for his freedman Festus in the second century CE. It is now called Üvecik Tepe. Thinking so much about the Trojan War, I looked at the local people

---

27. Arrian, p. 67.

28. Even the academic research on this subject is not conclusive. No one knows for sure where Achilles' tomb is located.

here in the villages we passed through. Surely, without the shadow of a doubt, some of these people are direct descendants of the citizens of Priam's city.

We reached the entrance to the Troy site. It is very well-organized, though no map is provided with the entrance ticket. I had taken the time to copy a detailed archaeological map into my phone and was able to navigate easily. It should be noted that this was only the second "normal" visit to an archaeological site in many years. "Normal" meaning that, with one exception, I stayed within the official boundaries because there were a number of other visitors (all Turks) and I did not want to cause offense. The Troy site is quite large, with much archaeological work remaining to be done, though the present state of the main areas permits a good understanding of the city's layout except where the site is bisected by Schliemann's huge and destructive exploratory trench. Aside from its literary interest, this site is remarkable mainly because of the span of time over which it was inhabited, namely from around 2920 BCE through to the fifth century CE, nearly 3,500 years. Successive cities were built on top of each other at Troy, and as a result it takes some study and imagination to see the site as it must have been in the Trojan War (most likely Troy VII, twelfth or thirteenth century BCE and seemingly destroyed by war). I walked along the ancient ramparts, imagining the great Achilles dragging Hector's broken body behind his chariot in front of the terrified Trojan civilians. And in the citadel, the orgy of destruction which followed the Trojan defeat. The epic events which happened here in this small place formed the collective imagination of all of Western civilization for 2,500 years.

In our time, Troy is overrun with cute, small, brown, Trojan squirrels, cavorting among the ruins. I wonder if their ancestors nibbled the acorns of the great oak tree at the Scaean gate.[29] Afar, due west, like a small pyramid, is the tumulus where I was this morning, wavering in the heat from the bright sun like a pennant on a battlefield.

---

29. Hector came to the Scaean gate, one of the gates of Troy, where there was a large oak tree, and many Trojan wives and children ran to him there to ask news of their husbands and fathers. Homer, *The Iliad*. Book VI, Lines 237–40.

OCTOBER 15, 2016

This morning I read and relaxed as planned, having felt somewhat burned out from the intensity of recent days. I went down to breakfast and sat next to a group of Iranian visitors, a young man named Mujtaba, studying English in Istanbul, and two of his brothers and their wives, on their way to spend a few days on the island of Bozcada. Iranians are quite isolated from the rest of the world due to their country's status, more or less as a pariah state. The opportunities for someone born there and someone born in a wealthy country of Europe or America are very different. Mujtaba is the same age as my own son. He told me that there is a great openness to Europeans and Americans in Iran these days. Perhaps it would be a subject for a future travel book. I would like to live there and study Persian for six months, and then travel through the whole country.

I finished breakfast and packed my things, checked out, and walked to the ferry dock in Çanakkale. I sat in the front of the ferry. I like to face the elements, and always have, on the promontory facing the storm. Several other people came to sit near me, but the wind was strong and chilly and none stayed for lack of warmer clothing. What I was wearing was warm enough and I stayed. Paranoid as I am, I found myself wondering whether one should attempt to leave a listing, sinking ship on the side that sinks first or, on the contrary, stay on the side which remains out of the water longest. Pondering this, I concluded that the greatest risk of immediate death in such a shipwreck was probably from blunt trauma rather than drowning, at least for a passenger on deck. None of these intellectual speculations were put to the test, thankfully.

I arrived in Eceabat and wandered around the port town for a while before approaching the taxi stand. As I was nearing it, a man addressed me in English: "You must be Nicholas." In effect, I was the sole traveler here, and the man was Anil, whom the hotel had engaged to drive me around the Gallipoli battlefields tomorrow and then on to Edirne the following day. He drove me to the hotel and I occupied my quarters, a pleasant room with a large balcony looking onto the dominant ridge of the peninsula. I noticed a Turkish flag flying high on this ridge around five kilometers from the hotel, I thought, and asked the proprietress, who informed me that it was Chunuk Bair, the site of a decisive battle. After resting I decided to hike to the top of the ridge. She said it would take an hour. I set out on tracks through farmers' fields, then followed a path marked as that of the 57th Regiment, led by Atatürk at Chunuk Bair.[30] I felt like running and left the path, striking straight up the fall line of the mountain as fast as my heart would allow. I ran along a gully, perhaps the remnant of a communication trench, hopping across it when the terrain was better on the other side. I was at the edge of my endurance, running uphill too fast, and I thought of the poor youths whose short lives ended near here. I spoke yesterday with my son. Sometimes I am concerned about him, as any father would be. We are so fortunate. We in Western democracies have at least gained something in the last century. Unlike Lord Kitchener, whose troops executed hundreds of wounded and surrendering men at Omdurman,[31] and who was the primary decision-maker for the Allied catastrophe here at Gallipoli, our present leaders think twice before sacrificing the lives of 50,000 young men, playing war as a strategy game. This is a very recent development, of course, as in Vietnam we did exactly that. I am no historian, but it seems that in the modern era aggressive war has a poor record of benefits for those who initiate it. I would tentatively suggest that this is due to the industrial efficiency of modern weaponry in killing people, and the fact that the relevant technologies are widely distributed and easy to use, rendering ground combat, especially in cities, relatively equal despite widely disparate development levels between the adversaries. It may also be due to the refusal of the populations of Western democracies to countenance the deaths of our young men in combat for objectives that are often dubious. With these macabre thoughts in my mind and the iron taste

---

30. Mustafa Kemal, later Atatürk, led the 57th Regiment in the fighting here. He told them, "Men, I am not ordering you to attack. I am ordering you to die. In the time that it takes us to die, other forces and commanders can come and take our place." The men of the 57th obeyed, and were annihilated, Atatürk himself being saved from a deadly shrapnel wound by a pocket watch worn in his breast pocket. In honor of this regiment, there is no 57th Regiment in the Turkish military now.

31. Churchill, Winston, *The River War*. London: Longmans Green, 1899 (First Edition), Volume II, pp. 195–7. Churchill expunged the most critical aspects of his account of the Battle of Omdurman from the second edition of this work, clearly for political reasons.

of blood in my mouth, I kept running uphill. As if to confirm my path, two eagles soared overhead. I watched them circle twice and disappear.

I slowed to a walk as I reached a firebreak bulldozed through the forested hillside. I followed it to the main road. What I saw shocked me. Tour buses, at least two dozen of them, with signs reading "Municipality of Antalya" and "Municipality of Sinop." These cities are around twelve hours from here by bus. Not one bus with foreign tourists, only Turks. So the monuments I had hoped to see alone were swamped with at least a thousand people. I was the only one who got here on foot. I tolerated their presence for the time it took to read the inscriptions and pay my respects to the fallen, many here, then followed the line of trenches around the summit of the hill, where there was no one. This hilltop was taken and then lost by the New Zealand Expeditionary Force. Almost all of the 850 dead buried here are anonymous. Yet "their name liveth for evermore," according to the inscription. I sent a text message to a friend from New Zealand, inquiring if he had ancestors buried here, then sat alone and reflected.

After some time I decided to go down, as the sun was setting. I realized that I was disoriented. I had come from the south but could not easily follow the same path back since it went across country on no real trail. Clearly, descending on the wrong side of the ridge would be very tiring, and, the wisdom of experience dominating my innate impatience, I took the time to verify my bearings from my map and compass until I was certain which direction I should choose. I found the path marked as that of the 57th Regiment and followed it down. I was pleased when I reached the place where I had left this path, for now I knew my way back to the hotel for sure. I reached the hotel, showered, read, and had dinner. And here I sit, having eaten well and drunk half a bottle of Merlot from Suvla Bay.

OCTOBER 16, 2016

I slept very badly last night. It was windy and there were rustling noises on the terrace which woke me several times. I even looked outside to make sure no one was there. And a nearby dog frantically barked in the night until it was hoarse, its volume diminished to a cough. I visited Gallipoli today. This is not the first battlefield I have seen, but it has left me in a state of deep moral confusion, one I am unsure to be able to dig myself out of easily.

Initially conceived as a diversionary action to assist the Russian Empire by drawing Ottoman resources away from the eastern front, the attack on Gallipoli was supposed to be a purely naval engagement, from which Lord Kitchener assured his colleagues on the British War Council that they could simply "withdraw" if events turned against them.[32] The idea was for Allied (Britain and France) warships to force the Dardanelles straits and threaten Istanbul from the Sea of Marmara, where Russian ships would then join to assist them. The initial naval assault was a catastrophic failure, with a third of the Allied fleet lost in a day and over 1,000 men killed. Instead of reviewing their initial assumptions of weak and disorganized Ottoman resistance, Kitchener, Churchill,[33] and the Allies doubled down and decided to make a land invasion. This went badly as well, with almost none of the major objectives attained. After seven months of intense trench warfare, the Allies withdrew in total defeat. Of the 800,000 men who fought here, there were 400,000 casualties, roughly 44,000 Allied and 86,000 Ottoman deaths.[34] The Ottomans were fighting on their death ground, for survival, and they prevailed, but the Allies seem to have gained literally nothing for the blood and treasure spent, with the sole exception of having diverted Ottoman resources from other uses.

Bülent, my guide to the battlefields, and Anil, the taxi driver I met yesterday, were both courteous and attentive. After breakfast they met me at the hotel and we drove south towards Cape Helles, the extremity of the Gallipoli Peninsula, one of the two initial major landing sites of the Allied armies. Stopping and climbing to an observation platform at

---

32. Rogan, p. 132. My understanding of the Gallipoli Campaign is largely based on this excellent book. Of course, I solely bear the blame if this understanding is incomplete or incorrect.

33. As First Lord of the Admiralty, Churchill bore responsibility for the naval aspect of the debacle at Gallipoli, which stayed with him for the rest of his career.

34. There are many sources for Gallipoli campaign casualty figures, but I have used the New Zealand government figures, at https://nzhistory.govt.nz/media/interactive/gallipoli-casualties-country

the hill of Achi Baba, we surveyed the entire area. This high ground was one of the main early objectives of the Allied forces, but in nearly eight months they never even approached it despite three major attempts to do so. Having identified myself as French and requested to see the areas where the French forces had fought, we went first to the French cemetery, stopping on the way at the site of a battle. I wanted to visit the cemetery to pay my respects to Jean Verdenal, who died here, and to whom T.S. Eliot dedicated his first collection of poetry, *Prufrock and Other Observations*. In the book Eliot followed his dedication with an epigraph from Dante:

Or puoi la quantitate
Comprender dell' amor ch'a te mi scalda,
Quando dismento nostra vanitate,
Trattando l'ombre come cosa salda.

translated as: "Now canst thou comprehend the sum of the love that warms me to thee when I forget our vanity, treating the shades as if a solid thing."[35] Some months ago I had re-read much of Eliot's poetry, and found myself moved by this dedication. Jean Verdenal and Eliot had met when they lived at the same rooming house in Paris in 1910 while Eliot was still an undergraduate student at Harvard. Verdenal was a medical student who served as a medical officer in the Dardanelles campaign for less than a week before he was killed. The French involvement in this campaign included an initial diversionary attack on the other side of the strait, at Kumkale, where I was yesterday, and then fighting in the sector of Seddulbahir alongside British forces. According to French military records, Verdenal served bravely, spending a good deal of time rescuing wounded men in the water near the shore. He was killed by enemy fire on May 2, 1915 in this sector while helping a fallen comrade.[36]

---

35. Dante, *Purgatorio*. Canto XXI, lines 133-6. Translation by Charles Eliot Norton.

36. I thank Professor Eugene Rogan, author of *The Fall of the Ottomans*, mentioned above, for being so kind as to look up and send me information on Verdenal at my request while I was traveling with limited research resources, notably Verdenal's death certificate. Later I was also able to find information on Verdenal in the French military's online record of World War I soldiers.

The French cemetery was solemn. Black wrought iron crosses, with the tips cut and twisted into a primitive *fleur de lys*, a Roman symbol which was later used on the heraldic arms of French royalty. Each cross a life not fully lived. It was a well-kept cemetery, with several thousand individual graves. Those of non-Christian soldiers (North African and African colonial troops also served here) omitted the horizontal cross bar, a single, black, wrought iron spike in the ground bearing a name plate. I knew Verdenal had no individual grave here, having searched the French military database of fallen soldiers. His grave was one of four ossuaries at the front of the cemetery near the spire dedicated to Immortal France, *Ave Gallia Immortalis*, each containing the remains of 3,000 unidentified French soldiers (true to the separation of Church and State, there are no references to God in French military cemeteries). So roughly 15,000 men are buried or remembered here. Such figures are too abstract, at least for me. But when I know one young man's story, that of Jean Verdenal, and look at these twisted metal memories and realize that each of them represents a life, only then can I begin to seize the horror of it all, the meaninglessness. I wonder if one of these other tombs is that of the last brother-in-arms Verdenal died trying to save (or perhaps Verdenal succeeded, and that man did not fall here). Officers' tombs included also the date of death in addition to the name: "Lieutenant L'Hermitte, 4ème Génie Civile, 2 Mai 1915." Perhaps it was he. Or "Capitaine Théval, 4ème Zouaves, 2 Mai 1915." Or "Capitaine Ginde, 175ème Infanterie, 2 Mai 1915." May 2, 1915 was a busy harvest day upon those beaches and fields. "And what I want to know is, how do you like your blue-eyed boy, Mister Death."[37]

Leaving the French cemetery, we went to the Turkish Çanakkale Martyrs' Memorial above Morto Bay. Bülent explained that the foreign military authorities had sent forensic teams shortly after the war's end to find, catalog, and properly bury the bodies of their fallen soldiers. He said the Turkish soldiers were buried in unmarked graves wherever they fell, and no effort at all was made to keep track of them or to build monuments in their honor. Much more recently, as late as the

---

37. cummings, ee, "Buffalo Bill's Defunct". *Complete Poems 1904-1962*. New York: Liveright, p. 90. Reprinted with permission of W.W. Norton.

1960s, monuments were erected with lists of names and representative tombstones, but no actual graves. The whole peninsula is their grave. At this monument, one of the largest Turkish memorials, is a quotation from the Qur'an (in Turkish, so I had to look it up): "And say not of those who are slain in the way of God, 'They are dead.' Nay, they are living, but ye perceive it not." Q 2:154.

Of course, the question remains as to what is "the way of God." In the case at hand, defending their homeland from foreign invaders waging an aggressive war, the moral position of the Turks was definitely superior to that of the French and British (not that many people care about such questions). This monument comprises four high pillars with a heavy flat platform on top of them. Four pillars on which was raised a nation. That nation is still being solidified, as the busloads of Turks brought here at government expense from the far corners of the country attest.

We left the memorial and went to the landing sites: S Beach, Morto Bay, V Beach near Seddulbahir Fort, where the French contingent arrived and Verdenal died, and W Beach. These latter sites, especially V Beach, were terrifying to imagine. No cover on the beach. A fortress to the east and a line of cliffs to the west. Even the few Turkish troops present here were able to inflict massive casualties on the attacking army arriving by boat. I saw a photo of the *River Clyde*, a coal ship converted to troop carrier, discussed in Professor Rogan's book, its deck entirely covered with corpses stacked like logs on a lumber barge. These places remind me of the Normandy beaches but for two differences: first, the Normandy landings succeeded and were well planned by the Allied military authorities; and second, the moral objective of the Normandy invasions was to respond to aggression and was much more than the mere will to power of megalomaniac colonial empire builders. At W Beach, Anil the driver stooped to pick up something from the sand, smiled and tossed me a .303 Enfield cartridge case, surely fired by some British soldier in his moment of need. Catching it, I wondered what became of him. What can objects from the past represent to us? *Sunt lacrimae rerum et mentem mortalia tangunt.*[38] We also went to look at

---

38. Virgil. Aeneid. Book 1, Line 462. Loosely translated as "There are tears for things, and mortal things touch the mind."

the British Helles Memorial, a square base of stone around forty meters on a side, covered on three sides with names, names and more names—20,504 names of soldiers with no known graves, including those who perished on the many ships sunk during the campaign. From here we went to Alçitepe (the formerly Greek village of Krythia), initially taken in the first days by the British but immediately relinquished and never recaptured despite multiple efforts spanning months. There were Turkish visitors to Gallipoli having coffee, but no foreigners. I saw only one foreign family during all my time here. Bülent, Anil, and I had coffee and chatted.

We drove back up the peninsula to ANZAC Cove, the other major initial landing site. As its name indicates, it was here that the Australia New Zealand Army Corps disembarked and fought. I imagined these young men from their farms in the Australian wilds, sent here to die. For what? The outcome of these battles would not have affected them for good or for ill. We stopped first at the ANZAC commemorative site, where there were plaques on the wall and, looking up, a view of the impossibly steep terrain from which the Turkish defenders fired down on those who landed here. Quotations on the plaques from soldiers' letters home: "There is hell waiting here." And more touching: "I am prepared for death, and hope that God will have forgiven me all my sins." And finally Atatürk's famous message of friendship to the mothers of the fallen troops:

> Those heroes that shed their blood and lost their lives ... You are now lying in the soil of a friendly country. Therefore rest in peace. There is no difference between the Johnnies and the Mehmets to us where they lie side-by-side, here in this country of ours ... You, the mothers, who sent their sons from faraway countries, wipe away your tears; your sons are now lying in our bosom and are in peace. After having lost their lives on this land they have become our sons as well.

Then to Lone Pine, where, in the course of a few days in August 1915 several thousand men died in an area the size of a couple of football fields. One soldier wrote: "... the trench is so full of our dead that the only respect that we could show them was not to tread on their faces, the floor of the trench was just one carpet of them..." Pine trees. Empty graves with names and heart-rending inscriptions, filling the void. "Beloved son...our best we have given unto the Lord." Or, "He died for us." Or, quoting a poem: "Submissive still, would I reply, Thy will be done."[39] A large inscription on the dominating monument read, "To the Glory of God." I felt sick.

We came down from here after visiting the Nek, site of an utterly futile charge in which four successive waves of ANZAC soldiers were cut down by machinegun fire without causing a single Turkish casualty. Their officers were following orders without regard for the lives of their men.[40] This is the battle depicted in Peter Weir's film *Gallipoli*, in which the Australian Light Horse was annihilated. Australian official historian Charles Bean remarked, "The flower of the youth of Victoria and Western Australia fell in that attempt." And we continued on to Suvla Bay, last major landing site, where thousands more Allied soldiers fell during four days of August 1915, the British generals throwing yet more lives at a problem whose solution clearly lay beyond their means.[41] Scimitar Hill is in the distance, a Turkish flag flying. More cemeteries. I have had enough of this.

OCTOBER 17, 2016

At dinner last night I felt disoriented, thrown off balance by the scale of what I had seen at Gallipoli. I wanted to write about it but felt I could not without considering the moral implications of the facts I had learnt and the places I had seen. I felt that I could proceed no further without letting my ideas coagulate for a few days. I awoke this morning having slept better than the previous night, the hell-hound next door having granted me silence. After breakfast I packed, then met Anil for the drive to Edirne. It was windy and raining hard by the time we left. Rain and wind and waves on the strait. We passed the ancient Greco-Roman site of Sestos, home of Hero, the girl who loved Leander, who

---

39. This last line is a quotation from a poem by Charlotte Elliott (1789–1871), "Thy Will Be Done." The other inscriptions, I presume, were chosen by the families of the fallen soldiers.

40. Rogan, pp. 203–4.

41. *Ibid*, p. 206.

swam the Hellespont for her, and inspired Lord Byron to repeat this feat twenty centuries later. The shores are not so far apart here, and each year people swim it in commemoration, but not in October, and probably after shipping through the strait has been suspended for a few hours. I have seen enough ancient cities for this trip and it is not worth getting soaked to see one more of minor importance.

I enjoyed the ride and despite the outer weather the blue sky prevailed in my soul. We made fast progress amid light traffic, leaving behind the Sea of Marmara and arriving in fertile, rolling farmland. Sugar beets, wheat, barley, sunflowers. The smell of roasting sunflower seeds from an oil factory, nutty, warm, and rich. And two hawks circling overhead. We arrived in Edirne and found the hotel by asking directions from numerous bystanders, the first of whom was around ten kilometers out of town, a farmer who had never heard of the hotel, saying only "in the town." After checking in I felt a sort of inexplicable contentment, a mild euphoria that I had not felt for some time. Going out to explore the town, I looked at several of the mosques from the outside without going in. Civilization has clearly declined in Edirne, from Ottoman capital to provincial modern backwater. But the sources of its former glory are still here. In the grounds of the Selimiye Mosque I visited the Islamic Art Museum. A quotation by Mimar Sinan, the great Ottoman architect of the fifteenth and sixteenth centuries (he lived nearly a century):

As long as the world remains, wise people who see my work and my efforts will look at me with mercy, considering the seriousness of my effort, and remember me with prayers of goodness, I hope.

Refreshing humility in a great man.

OCTOBER 18, 2016

Dinner last night was poor, and breakfast this morning worse. Everything in the breakfast buffet was old, dried out, wrinkled, almost fossilized. I think we are two guests in a fifty-room hotel. After breakfast I went out again to wander around Edirne. It was bright and sunny but chilly, and

I had not chosen my clothing wisely and was cold. First I visited first the small Lari Mosque, from the sixteenth century. The outer courtyard had been glassed in, a nice modern touch. I found a McDonald's, where I planned to dine (wanting a change from Turkish food) and on the way saw a strange statue from a bygone era (the 1960s?): two life-sized couples dancing, women in high heels and sexy cocktail dresses. Few women here now would dress this way, at least not in public. I crossed Talaat Pasha Street, the Turkish equivalent of Hitlerstrasse in Vienna. (Oops, I forgot. Austria does not name streets after its own genocidal war criminal, but here they do.) Talaat Pasha was born in Edirne, a native son. I crossed the street, and saw Üç Şerifiye Mosque, with four minarets containing three balconies. Each of the minarets was different, all beautiful, one with a rounded spiral of red stone rising up it like a gigantic candy cane. The mosque is from the fifteenth century, but at the entrance were two green stone columns that I assumed are much older. The inner dome is magnificent, set on a hexagonal base, creating a huge and airy space that features stained glass, something I have rarely seen in mosques. Some Quranic inscriptions were faded with age, others in flowery script on tilework. I left and walked north, hoping to find the Sultan Bayezid II mosque and hospital complex. I passed a caravanserai, perhaps fifteenth-century, converted into a government building. The guards patiently tolerated my presence for a few minutes in the courtyard, though it was obviously not open to visitors. Then I realized that I had taken the wrong road, and ended up reaching the Bayezid II complex after around four kilometers of extra walking. A group of young men, students, set me on my way.

The Bayezid II complex was beautiful, standing alone in a field north of the city. It dates from the fifteenth century by the same Sultan Bayezid whose mosque and madrasa I had visited in Amasya (site of a memorable olfactory experience set down earlier). The mosque and part of the attendant buildings are now used by a university, with the hospital complex next door a museum. The grounds were silent and peaceful. I looked into the mosque but did not enter, as it was prayer time and I did not wish to disturb the faithful. I left the mosque area and went into the museum next door in the medieval hospital. Perhaps Bayezid II, while overseeing the construction of his mosque and madrasa in Amasya, had visited the hospital there, founded under the Seljuks in 1309, and got the idea for his own hospital complex here in Edirne. This one is more advanced, larger, and had a teaching faculty adjoining it. I admit to being surprised or even astounded at some of the medical procedures done here 600 years ago as described on the museum's signs. Inguinal hernia operations by a woman surgeon (!) complete with consent/release forms stipulating no recourse in the event of patient death. Elective breast-reduction surgery, for men, discussing how to remove the unsightly fat that can form "man boobs." Various gynaecological and obstetric interventions. And ear, nose, and throat procedures too disgusting to describe (they made me wince). I left, walking toward town, but managed to flag a taxi driven by a smelly and careless young man.

I had him drop me off at the Selimiye Mosque to look at it more carefully than I had done yesterday. From afar it showed off its splendor, dome upon dome cascading down like a waterfall dividing into different reflecting pools. The inside was also magnificent: vast open space under the dome, but too ornate in style for my taste. Quranic inscriptions abounded, too many to read, and mostly in a flowery and difficult script. And a Turkish tour group, loud and obnoxious, threatened to ruin it all, until they left. Patience is a virtue of which I have little, but more now than when I was younger. As I left I noticed a large (one hectare?) area of excavations in front of the mosque. Roman or Byzantine, I would guess. I briefly returned to my room, then went out again and came across a sixteenth-century marketplace, the same now as it was then but for the items on sale and the ubiquitous Turkish flags and photos of Atatürk. Twice I felt that men were following me and took evasive actions. Once I think I was correct and was not just being my usual paranoid self. I continued into the old neighborhood around the bazaar, but few original buildings remain. Being by now weary of Turkish food, I took refuge under the Golden Arches, exchanging smiles with three Turkish women who then sat near me and enlivened my meal with their presence. And on the way back to my room there was the acrid smell of coal smoke, which I actually find pleasant if not too strong, and which wafts in now through my slightly open window as I write and prepare to sleep.

OCTOBER 19, 2016

The taxi this morning was unpleasant and the driver stinky and uncouth. We drove through open rolling farmland, growing less fertile as we approached Istanbul. I had toyed with the idea of taking a bus since this time there was nothing I wanted to visit between the endpoints of the trip, but decided against it due to official warnings of potential terrorist attacks against transport hubs such as bus stations. The driver kept trying to make conversation and, annoyingly, persisted even after my limited Turkish was exhausted, and I had no desire to make the effort with my dictionary to converse with him. He tested my patience, but I passed the test and remained polite. I have not been rude to anyone during my recent travels in Turkey (during my 1987 trip I am not sure if this was the case). At one point we passed a small but conspicuous tumulus in a farmer's field near the road. What great hero lies sleeping beneath the sunflowers? Arriving in Istanbul, we took several wrong turns and an involuntary diversion along small streets through a wealthy and handsome district built on a steep hillside, then arrived at the hotel.

OCTOBER 20, 2016

I am in a nice hotel in Istanbul and just had a carefree night's sleep, not waking at every strange noise, ready to jump out the window of my room. I felt I needed to see the Sultanahmet area again, as this will be my last visit to Turkey for some time. I first took a taxi to Süleymaniye, Mimar Sinan's most famous mosque, though he himself preferred Selimiye in Edirne. Noise, traffic, and exhaust fumes. A short visit to Sinan's tomb, then Süleymaniye. Sultan Suleiman the Magnificent, who ordered the mosque to be built, was born in Trabzon in 1484. His tomb is in the grounds of the mosque, as is that of his wife, Hürrem Sultan (Roxelana). Suleiman broke with tradition by marrying Roxelana, one of his harem girls, and she bore Selim, who succeeded Suleiman as Sultan of the Ottoman Empire. Sultan Suleiman was also a poet, and expressed his love for Roxelana in a poem which was quoted at their common grave. Visiting the mosque itself was unpleasant due to the omnipresent and obnoxious guards, who forced female visitors, already modestly dressed, to don ridiculous additional garb. Their attitude was insulting to foreign women and made me wonder whether this mosque had become a hotbed of extremist Islam, as I had never before seen this behavior in a Turkish mosque. The interior is huge and magnificent and the domes cascade like those of Selimiye, but it is even larger and more impressive. When I left I wandered to the Bayezid Mosque, then went through the bazaar, thoroughly empty of tourists, and bought some *lokum* (Turkish delight) to bring home. Aiming for Sultanahmet, I passed through a street of luxury shops combining top European brands with handmade silk carpets and pleasant cafés, crossed Pierre Loti Street, then arrived in Sultanahmet Square. Sultanahmet Mosque (widely known as the Blue Mosque), despite its magnificence, seems bulkier than Süleymaniye. Mimar Sinan's student, Sedefhar Mehmet Ağa, who designed it, perhaps did not attain the level of his teacher.

I inspected the tombs of several Ottoman Sultans at Hagia Sophia, together with those of their families, including multiple sons strangled to death to ease the conflicts of succession. It made me think of rats or male lions eating the young fathered by their predecessor with their current mate. Who said lions (or people) were noble? Four of the five tombs were beautifully decorated with blue *thulth* calligraphy on white tiles or vice-versa, adorned with various quotations from the Qur'an. On that of Sultan Selim the *Ayat al-Kursi* was followed by, "There is no compulsion in religion. The right way has been made clear from the wrong." Q 2:256. There is plenty of textual support for a moderate interpretation of Islam if only its proponents would stand up and argue for it. One tomb alone was ordinary, an unadorned broom cupboard for Sultans Mustafa and Ibrahim ("the Mad"), raised in the cages of Topkapi Palace when murdering royal sons to simplify succession had faded from fashion, leaving them psychologically scarred. They drew the short straw in life and also in their unadorned tomb.

Quitting the tombs, I walked around Sultanahmet. Tourist groups were blown up here recently and none are here now. The businesses are struggling. Everything is empty. Islamic State hit their target. I wandered through an empty bazaar to the "Little Hagia Sophia," a Byzantine church built by Justinian and later converted into a mosque. One of the Quranic inscriptions caught my eye: "We have not sent thee [Prophet Mohammad] but as a mercy upon the two worlds." Q 21:107. Then onto the open plaza between Sultanahmet Mosque and Hagia Sophia, surely blessed with one of the greatest densities of architectural beauty on our earth. Here stands the spiral column of bronze melted by the victorious Greeks from Persian armor and shields in the fifth century BCE. More battles. Leonidas, and his Spartans at Thermopylae. Another last stand. "Stranger, go and tell the Spartans that here we lie, having obeyed their laws."[42] The fifteenth-century BCE obelisk brought here from Egypt by Theodosius, like the one taken to Place de la Concorde in Paris by Napoleon. The Museum of Turkish and Islamic Art replete with calligraphic marvels charting the development of the Arabic language and script, and a mistakenly labeled astrolabe supposedly from Seville in 650 CE with full diacritical markings in Arabic—when these did not yet exist in the language, and when Seville had not yet been conquered by the Arabs.[43] Museums make mistakes too.

Finally, looking for food in the tourist wilderness I sighted the venerable Pudding Shop, unchanged since 1987, with the same owner whose hand I shook. I sat down to a meal serenaded by the dueling *muezzins* of Sultanahmet Mosque and the Hagia Sophia, repeating the verses of the call to prayer in staggered camaraderie so that both could be heard in their haunting, luminescent beauty. Sultanahmet's *muezzin* has my vote, transporting me back to the years in Cairo when I first answered the call to that untravel'd world.

---

42. Epitaph on the Cenotaph of Thermopylae, recorded by Herodotus, written by the poet Simonides of Ceos, fifth century BCE.

43. The museum must have mistakenly labeled the date as a Roman date when it was a Hijri date, as 650 in the Hijri (Islamic) calendar corresponds well with the time period intended.

EPILOGUE AND FUTURE TRAVELS

When I conceived and developed the idea for this book, I saw two main uncertainties surrounding its outcome. The first was whether I could re-establish the transformational power of travel in my own life, and the second whether I would be able to attain powerful emotions through my experiences and communicate them in writing. I was relatively confident in a positive answer to the first uncertainty, since when I undertook exploratory travels in 2012 and 2013, and wrote a travel journal each time, I found myself quickly at home on the road as I had been in my youth, and once I returned to my real home I was rejuvenated and enriched by my journeys.

The second uncertainty was much more difficult for me to understand and resolve. Aiming for a goal so utterly different from anything I had done in my adult life intimidated me. I was unsure of even being able to *feel* the emotions I hoped to attain, much less to communicate them. But by a process of gradual introspection and letting slip the fetters of my mind, I finally unearthed a wellspring of emotion that almost overwhelmed me. Once unearthed, the emotions simply poured forth and my task became to refine their quality and channel them into my writing, "to recreate life out of life."

I am going away again, this time to Iceland. I have started reading Nansen's *Farthest North* and re-reading Shackleton's *South*. I wrote a full inventory of the equipment required for the trip, more complicated and technical than that which I brought to Turkey. Some of it is right now strewn over the floor of my study: sleeping bag; tent; bivy sack; boots; lightweight crampons for glacier walking. And though the goal of this trip is to clear my mind of the efforts of these past three years, of course I will also bring a paper notebook and a couple of pens.

ACKNOWLEDGMENTS

Many people have assisted me with my work on this book and the travels it recounts. I am profoundly grateful to all of them for their help, though of course I bear sole responsibility for any shortcomings or failures. Most fundamentally, I thank the people of Turkey for providing a hospitable and fascinating destination for my travels.

The following individuals provided assistance with specific parts of the book or stages of the journey. Professor Andreas Schachner, director of the Hattuşa excavations, patiently answered all of my questions about this site in a lengthy email correspondence. Professor Ian Hodder of Stanford, director of Çatalhöyük excavations, answered questions and made suggestions for further readings in the Neolithic history of Asia Minor. Dr. Tony Greenwood, director of the American Research Institute in Turkey, kindly advised me on some of the destinations I visited. Mr. Andrew Leathwood, headmaster of the Tarsus American College, hosted me for several days in Tarsus, and shared his experience of Turkey with me. Professor André Thess provided me with valuable information on visiting Musa Dagh. Mr. Jens Notroff, archaeologist at Göbekli Tepe, answered questions in our brief email correspondence. Professor Zafer Derin personally guided me around the Neolithic site of Yeşilova near Izmir and answered my questions. Professor Eugene Rogan generously answered my questions about Ottoman history, raised in reading his excellent book.

More generally, Professor Samir El-Bernoussi of the University of Nice, with whom I have studied Arabic for the past seven years, helped me with various of the Arabic texts translated here, as well as many others. Mr. Kevin Dolgin, friend and more experienced writer, suggested repeatedly in the past that I write a book, and then provided valuable comments on this one when I finally did. Mr. Jim Batty, whom I met on the site of Mohenjo-Daro in Pakistan in 1987, and who sewed the straps and drew the winged thumb on the canvas grain sack I used as a backpack from Hunza to Tibet and India, still a close friend, also read and commented fruitfully on the draft. Admiral Jim Stavridis was generous with his time, ideas, and assistance on my project. Professor

Andrew Hess of the Fletcher School, my doctoral thesis advisor, kindly read and commented on the manuscript. James Ferguson, publisher of Signal Books, commented on the text in an extremely precise and detailed manner, and greatly improved it. And, of course, I thank Hélène, my wife, for her critical reading and re-reading of the manuscript, and even more for her steadfast support in all I have done during more than thirty years of life together. Finally, I thank all those others, unnamed, who helped me on my way and extended their courtesy and hospitality to this "son of the road."

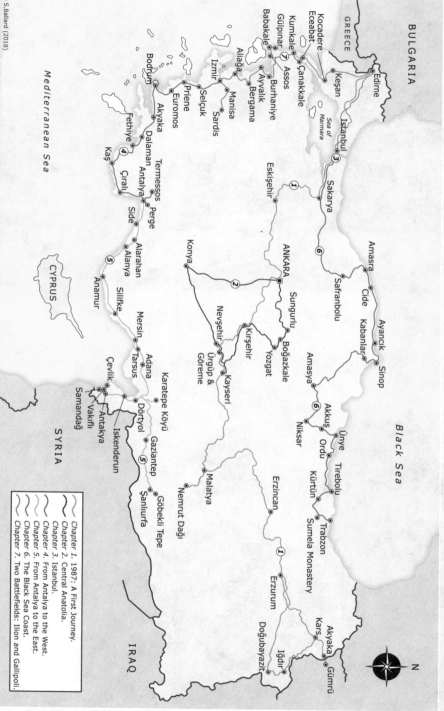

© S.Ballard (2018)

BULGARIA

GREECE

Mediterranean Sea

Sea of Marmara

CYPRUS

Black Sea

SYRIA

IRAQ

N

Edirne
Keşan
İstanbul
Kocadere
Eceabat
Kumkale
Gülpınar
Babakale
Bodrum
Burhaniye
Ayvalık
Bergama
Aliağa
İzmir
Manisa
Selçuk
Sardis
Euromos
Priene
Akyaka
Fethiye
Dalaman
Kaş
Çıralı
Antalya
Termessos
Perge
Side
Alarahan
Alanya
Anamur
Silifke
Mersin
Tarsus
Adana
Dörtyol
Karatepe Köyü
İskenderun
Çevlik
Vakıflı
Samandağ
Antakya
Gaziantep
Şanlıurfa
Göbekli Tepe
Nemrut Dağı
Malatya
Konya
Eskişehir
Sakarya
ANKARA
Sungurlu
Boğazkale
Yozgat
Nevşehir
Kırşehir
Ürgüp & Göreme
Kayseri
Safranbolu
Amasra
Cide
Kabanlar
Ayancık
Sinop
Amasya
Akkuş
Ordu
Niksar
Ünye
Tirebolu
Trabzon
Kürtün
Sümela Monastery
Erzincan
Erzurum
Kars
Akyaka
Gümrü
Iğdır
Doğubayazıt

Çanakkale
Assos

Chapter 1. 1987: A First Journey.
Chapter 2. Central Anatolia.
Chapter 3. Istanbul.
Chapter 4. From Antalya to the West.
Chapter 5. From Antalya to the East.
Chapter 6. The Black Sea Coast.
Chapter 7. Two Battlefields: Ilion and Gallipoli.

1. A lone traveler contemplating the
Cappadocian landscape, 1987.

2. Fairy chimneys in Cappadocia.

3. A young girl and her donkey near Nemrut Daği.

4. Standing lion, temple at Nemrut Daği.

5. The author in 1987 at Nemrut Daği.

6. Lion's head, Nemrut Daǧi.

7. View of Nemrut Daǧi temple from nearby mountaintop.

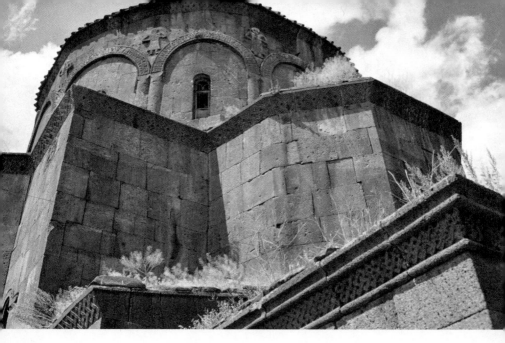

8. Kars Cathedral (abandoned).

9. Ruin on a plain near Kars.

10. Mehmet and relatives at their family farm.

11. Mehmet's extended family.

12. Kars Citadel (above).

13. Ruins of Kars Military Cathedral (inside the citadel).

14. Mount Ararat seen from the cliffs of the "evil place".

15. Ishak Pasha Palace, 1987.

16. View of Ishak Pasha Palace from the forbidden minaret.

17. Ruins of Termessos, 2015.

18. The author at the Temple of Euromos.

19. Tomb of a war criminal.

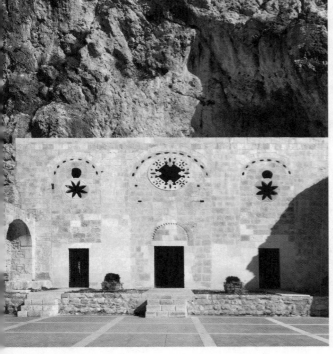

20. Church of St Peter, Antakya, 2016.

21. *Mezarlık* on Musa Dagh, 2016.

22. View west from Musa Dagh.

23. The author at the *Vapur* monument on Musa Dagh.

24. Sumela Monastery (on cliff face) and access road.

25. Vault fresco of the Hagia Sophia Mosque, Trabzon, 2016.

26. Ottoman houses and Pontic tombs, Amasya.

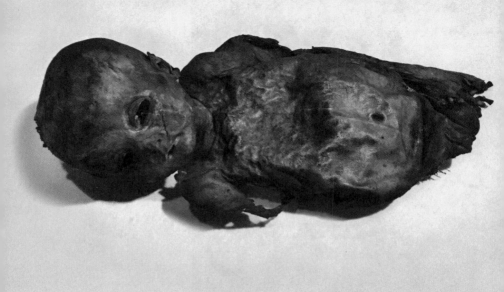

27. Mummified Seljuk baby, Amasya.

28. Theater of Pergamon, 2016.

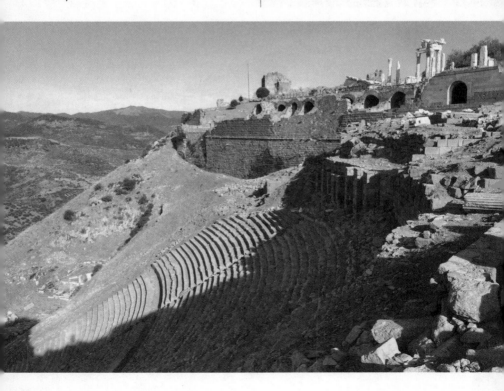